Beasts of Burden

SUNY series, Studies in the Long Nineteenth Century

Pamela K. Gilbert, editor

Beasts of Burden

*Biopolitics, Labor, and Animal Life
in British Romanticism*

Ron Broglio

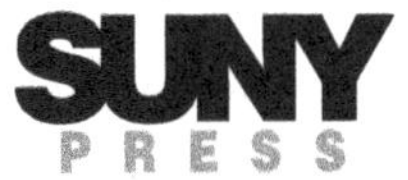

Cover image: Thomas Barker, *Sheep Shearing* 1812, Holburne Museum, Bath

Published by State University of New York Press, Albany

For information, contact State University of New York Press, Albany, NY
www.sunypress.edu

Production, Diane Ganeles
Marketing, Kate R. Seburyamo

Library of Congress Cataloging-in-Publication Data

Names: Broglio, Ron, 1966– author.
Title: Beasts of burden : biopolitics, labor, and animal life in British
  Romanticism / Ron Broglio.
Description: Albany, NY : State University of New York Press, 2017. | Series:
  SUNY series, studies in the long nineteenth century | Includes bibliographical
  references and index.
Identifiers: LCCN 2016031433 (print) | LCCN 2016050700 (ebook) | ISBN
  9781438465678 (hardcover : alk. paper) | ISBN 9781438465685 (pbk. : alk.
  paper | ISBN 9781438465692 (e-book)
Subjects: LCSH: English literature—19th century—History and criticism. |
  Animals in literature. | Human-animal relationships in literature. | Farm
  life in literature. | Animals in art. | Romanticism—Great Britain.
Classification: LCC PR468.A56 B74 2017 (print) | LCC PR468.A56 (ebook) | DDC
  820.9/007—dc23
LC record available at https://lccn.loc.gov/2016031433

10 9 8 7 6 5 4 3 2 1

For the animals and idiots;
the future's future belongs to you.

When power becomes bio-power, resistance becomes the power of life, a vital power that cannot be confined within species, environment or the paths of a particular diagram. Is not the force that comes from outside a certain idea of Life, a certain vitalism, in which Foucault's thought culminates?

—Gilles Deleuze, *Foucault*

Contents

Illustrations

Acknowledgments

"Try again. Fail again. Fail better," as Samuel Beckett says in *Worstward Ho!* This is a book that began in failure. There were academic failures that led me to write the chapter here on vulnerability. And there have been failures in living—the difficulty of comportment in a world that, as Simon Critchley says, requires an ethics that is "infinitely demanding" and always in excess of one's ability to adequately respond. Amid the infinite demands are those of the animals and animality—how does one respond to the cosmopolitical proposition and the idiots who show us ways of thought beyond our representational capacities? This book then is not so much an achievement as a marker in responding with fragility and care to worlds that exceed my capacities. Many have helped me along the way, and I am grateful for the opportunity to thank them here.

I am deeply indebted to Cary Wolfe, whose writing on animal life provides a mode of thought that informs my work throughout and whose thought is evident in many chapters of this book. Cary, your companionship has made all the difference for me. For their critical eye and creative insight in art and animal life, many thanks to my comrades in the animal revolution, Bryndis Snæbjörnsdóttir and Mark Wilson. To Marcel O'Gorman, thank you for your persistent friendship through it all.

I am pleased to thank Arizona State University, which has provided me an immeasurable number of ways to write, think, and produce scholarly work. I am grateful for the Provost's Humanities Fellowship, which afforded me time to complete this manuscript (and thanks to my colleagues and Fellows who read my work, Christopher Hanlon and Catherine O'Donnell). Thanks to Dean George Justice for his continued support of this and many other of my projects. And thanks to the chair of the English Department, friend, and fellow Romanticist Mark Lussier for his continued belief in my work. Thanks too to my ASU colleague Devoney Looser, who made the completion of this manuscript seem viable and who helped see me it through to its end. Thanks to the director of Arts, Media, and Engineering, Sha Xin Wei, and the director of the Laboratory for Critical Technics, Adam Nocek. Xin Wei and Adam, I cannot imagine a cosmopolitical future without you. ASU has provided a significant amount of support for me through the Institute for Humanities Research and the Global Institute of Sustainability. Thanks to both of these institutes and their directors.

The scholarly community in British Romantic literature and culture is rich and diverse. I am grateful to many in this field. Among them, Thora Brylowe and Dave Baulch have been steadfast readers and careful critics of my work for whom I am very thankful. David Collings's *Monstrous Society* was the impetus for writing *Beasts of Burden*; I am indebted to you, David. Thanks too to Katey Castellano and her *Ecology of British Romantic Conservatism*, which has informed my writing. I am grateful for the life and work of David Clark, who has taught me how to think and live critically. Thanks to Jacque Khalip for helping me to think the ruin of things. Thanks to Maureen McLane for her support and careful reading of my work, especially what is now chapter 3 of this book. Thanks to Richard Sha, who has seen me through many dilemmas in my writing and thinking Romanticism. Many thanks to Paul Youngquist and Alastair Hunt for their intellectual camaraderie in Foucault and Romantic subjectivity.

Outside of my university and my Romanticism community, the Society for Literature, Science, and Art (SLSA) has been a home to me, one for which I remain immensely grateful. In particular thanks to Susan Squier, who helped make the early writing on this project possible through an animal conference at Penn State. Thanks to Kari Weil, who has written wisely on animal life and has been a patient reader of far too much of my own work. Thanks to Eugene Thacker for the years of thinking life together and for your continued ventures beyond the realms of the human. Thanks too to Tim Morton for ecological and new materialist work that has helped me along the way. I'm grateful to the Society for Biopolitical Futures—a quasi-gnostic group, you know who you are and what you are about. Thanks as well to Maria Whiteman for her friendship and her astronauts and umwelts. Thanks to two former graduate students, Robert Bisnoff, with whom I thought the corn laws, and Jason Price, with whom I continue to think animality. Many thanks to Dominic Broglio with aid in indexing this work. Thanks to Amiee Swenson whose art, passion for sheep shearing and wrangling pigs, and all around perseverance in the world inspires so much of this work. Thank you to Ty Fishkind and Alma Byrd Jacobson with whom I have explored the wonders of generosity, fragility, and finitude.

I am grateful to the Yale Center for British Art, where I spent a summer on fellowship. Many of the reflections on art in this book come from my time at the YCBA. Pamela Gilbert, thank you for believing in me over many years and for taking on these beasts. Thanks to Amanda Lanne-Camilli and State University of New York Press for bringing this project to print.

Finally and most importantly, I am deeply grateful for my family, which has seen me through the making of this work.

1

Animal Life and Rural Labor

Literary and Material Resistance in Biopolitical Britain

In George Morland's painting *Outside the Alehouse Door*, two men are talking outside a rustic thatch-roofed alehouse. One man sits at a simple outdoor table and holds a beer and a pipe. His companion has his hands on the table and leans toward the seated man as if engaged in earnest conversation. The man seated with his beer is slightly turned away from the viewer, and the brim of his hat covers part of his face. Light focuses the viewer's eyes on the men while a darker atmosphere surrounds them, including a darkened doorway, shadows cast by the roof and a tree, and a sky with mixed weather of dark and light clouds. We are left to wonder what these men could be discussing.

Known for his agricultural paintings of labor and leisure, Morland is one of the most prodigious painters of the Romantic period.[1] His work was well known throughout the nineteenth century, and John Barrell's *The Dark Side of the Landscape* brought Morland to contemporary notice. As Barrell notes, such wondering about the conversation between the men at the alehouse turned to anxiety for at least one of Moreland's Romantic-period biographers. William Collins, in his 1805 *Memoirs of a Painter*, describes the painting as "[a] group of English figures regaling themselves, which, like true sons of liberty, they seem determined on in spite of all opposition."[2] Collins's use of the term "true sons of liberty" carries with it the connotation of populism and radicalism, which coupled with "the word 'English' has a disturbing political implication. He [Collins] recognizes these labourers as 'free-born Enlishmen,' men who are represented as actually resisting—they are 'determined'—the demand that they should accept the status of mild, temperate, industrious, submissive labourers"[3] According to Collins's sensibility, rather

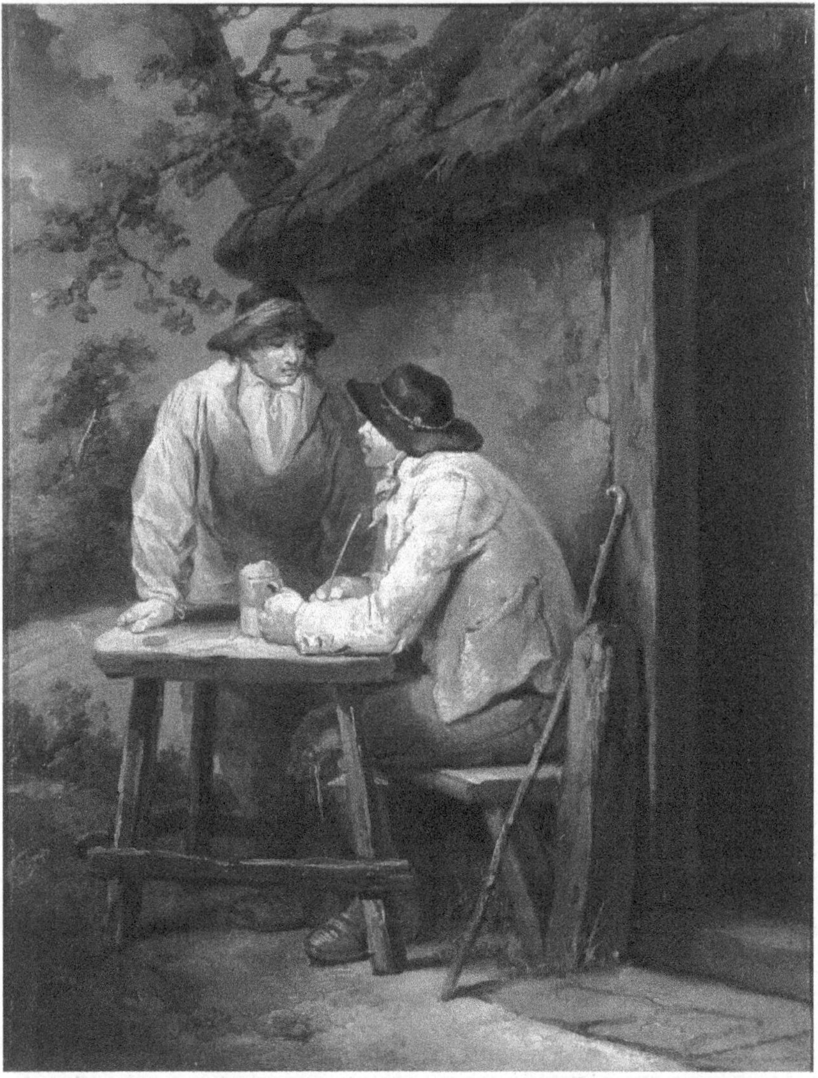

Figure 1.1. George Morland. *Outside the Ale House Door.* 1792. Tate Gallery.

than drinking beer, these men should be figures of industry, and like proper laborers in picturesque paintings, they should be working in the fields.

Barrell explains that with one beer between them and their serious demeanor, the men are not "regaling themselves." Rather, discomfort over the ale comes from "this jug of ale [as] a symbol of their indiscipline and revolt—

[because] it is not diluted by any reassuring passivity of attitudes. . . . their little money would be better spent on the wants of their families than on their own coarse pleasures; and that pint becomes for Moreland's critics a signpost on the road that leads from idleness to insurrection."[4] A turn to biopolitics—or biological life made political—extends Barrell's line of thinking and sees it as more than anxieties over the political capacities of the laboring class. The worker is drinking beer brewed from a grain in the fields in which he has toiled or from other fields nearby. It is a local product of his labors and those of his fellow field hands. On the eve of war with France and with perceived distance between landowners and field hands, the men in *Outside the Alehouse Door* must place the sweat of bodies in the field, their labor, and their liberty in relation to a larger political world of a growing nation.[5] The beer is in contrast to French wines, which became the fashion of landowners and was derided as a political betrayal by William Cobbett and other class-conscious critics of rural life. As Robert Bloomfield laments, the landowners now "violate the feelings of the poor; / To leave them distanc'd in the mad'ning race, / Where'er Refinement shews its hated face."[6] What these men at the alehouse door eat and drink, how the product of their labor is used and to whom it is distributed, where they are allowed to congregate, and how they are allowed to use their "free" time are all matters of biopolitics as the social body peers into the biological life of a people.

Pipe and beer as signs of Englishness appear some years later in Edwin Landseer's painting *Low Life,* where a stocky dog with wide chest and thick jaw sits at the worn wooden doorstep of his master's home, loyally awaiting his return. Beside him rests a mug of beer and a pipe. Through the cultural signification of objects, the animal is interpolated within the same social, economic, and labor world as his master.[7] The political connection between beer, bully breed dog, and England is evident in James Gillray's cartoon *Politeness.*[8] A stout Englishman sits with his pint of beer in his hand and his bulldog at his feet. Behind him hangs a large cut of red meat on a hook. He stares down at a Frenchman seated to his side. In contrast to the beefy Englishman, the thin Frenchman wears refined clothes and a wig. He holds a container of snuff rather than a British beer. At his feet is a mousy dog cowering from the growling British bulldog. Where the Englishman has large slabs of meat behind him, the Frenchman has two small frog legs.

Returning to Morland's painting, to further the contrast between these field hands and the landowners, where "Refinement shews its hated face," a walking stick rests next to the seated man. From its appearance, the stick is likely made from hawthorn or blackthorn—both of which were used as barbed hedgerows to reinforce land enclosure in a fence-like fashion. A walking stick cut from the barriers to liberty of trespass reveals a defiance against laws that restrict the movement of people and forecloses the use of common pathways. A knotted, thorny shrub changes value. It transforms from plant to a fence that reinforces state and local laws.[9] In the hands of a field worker, it becomes an object of defiance of such laws. The walking stick refashions the biopolitical tool from fence to instrument of motility.

One can read bodies, their vitality, and their capacities by creating new assemblages of material objects; dogs, beer, and earnest laborers set in a rural environment create a mosaic of a political life that affects the very biological being of the dog and workers, their food, and their rural ecology. Maurizio Lazzarato summarizes how forces become a power, in this case biopower, and how such power is used by the state as biopolitics. According to Lazzarato, "biopolitics is the strategic coordination of these power relations in order to extract a surplus of power from living beings. . . . Biopower coordinates and targets a power that does not properly belong to it, that comes from the 'outside.' *Biopower is always born of something other than itself.*"[10] Moreland's painting, along with Landseer's and Gillray's, show how the "surplus power from living beings" is called upon for political ends. Collins's uneasiness about the leisure of laborers in *Outside the Alehouse Door* reveals how the life of the worker is circumscribed to toil in the fields. Any surplus time and energy carries with it the social demand that it be spent in moral and industrious pursuits of benefit to the family and society. Ale and beer serve as ambiguous signs: they can represent the well-being of a people who have the ability to expend time in drinking but also the possible careless or riotous mood drink can induce.

The dogs in *Low Life* and *Politeness* are tough-looking, muscular beasts. Their attributes of loyalty and ferocity move from dog to human owner. In this move, the canine is part of a fearsome animality within the Englishman. The politics of muscular bodies, what they eat to build themselves, and how these bodies can be used for ends of power and the state are part of what Lazzarato means when he says that "*biopower is always born of something other than itself.*" Biopower attempts to harness the forces within masses of living bodies toward civil and social ends.

As will be evident throughout this book, bodies insist, resist, and weigh.[11] Biopower causes something new to emerge: populations, labor expenditures, food intake, economic outputs, and so on. But the "something else" from which biopower extracts its ability does not have to abide passively. While biopower is a mode of production by assembly and assimilation of forces not properly its own, resistance to biopower creates yet other modes of production: "Foucault is interested in determining what there is in life that resists, and that, in resisting this power, creates forms of subjectification and forms of life that escape its control."[12] Friction to state machinery and biopolitical schemes creates other modes of living and dwelling. Such resistance is a line of flight from the formation of the modern state and its ability to "make live and let die." Each chapter in this book provides a reading of not only apparatuses that create biopolitical subjects, but also alternative forms of life.

In his essay on public health in the eighteenth century, Foucault sketches a methodology for reading biopolitical apparatuses. He proposes to examine "the whole of a complex material field where not only are natural resources, the products of labor, their circulation and the scope of commerce engaged, but where the management of towns and routes, the conditions of life (habitat, diet, etc.), the number of inhabitants, their life span, their ability and fitness for work also come into play."[13] I apply a similar methodology of investigation where material fields meet representation and apparatus of production (biopolitical and otherwise). Some of the texts, such as Malthus's and Adam Smith's work, are symptomatic of the biopolitical apparatus, while other texts, such as the labor class poetry of Bloomfield and Robert Burns, bear witness the workings of biopolitics "in the field," as it were. Still other texts provide alternative assemblages and ways of dwelling over and against interpolation by the state, as is evident in the James Hogg's rural tales and select work of Edwin Landseer.

By way of illustration, consider another brief example of material life and politics from the Romantic period, this time taken from the twenty-fifth chapter of the Book of Deuteronomy: "Thou shalt not muzzle the ox that treadeth out the corn" (Deuteronomy 25:4). During the Romantic period, this biblical phrase was used by advocates of gleaning to justify this common practice. For centuries, workers and their families have gathered for their own use the sparse remaining stalks of grain from harvested fields. Gleaning functions outside the wage-labor system but within the social economy by which families supplement their provisions and income. Taken literally, the biblical phrase invites working livestock to partake in the fruits of their labors, which otherwise become commodities for humans. The passage expands the community and economy by which humans and nonhumans dwell. By using the passage from Deuteronomy as a rhetorical tool for justifying gleaning, advocates of the practice collapse the human–animal distinction, bringing both together as beasts of burden. Although the physical labor of humans and animals was part of the economic system of agriculture, the beasts of burden are claiming that their physical labor should feed their biological need. The ox eats the corn to sustain further milling, and the farm hands and their families glean grains to keep hunger from their doors. The biblical passage pits biological bodies and their capacities against economies that overlook the needs for sustaining life.

Those who opposed gleaning sought to bring the labor practice under a singular system of accounting. In it, not only the work of gathering grain but its food value, too, would be measured within the quantifiable sums of a monetary economy and capitalist market. Along with gleaning, food riots were a way of rebelling against the market-driven system. Agricultural laborers believed it their social right to be able to buy the bread made from the grains they grew and harvested. These concerns of life, agriculture, and capitalist economy are addressed in chapter 2, but here I would like to develop the utility of biopower as a concept by which to reevaluate less known literary and cultural texts of the Romantic period. *Beasts of Burden* explores how a number of interested parties and systems attempted to manage not only labor practices but more broadly the health and well-being of the humans and animals who worked the fields and how these beasts of burden resisted such systems. The book is a proof of concept for how the extension of social power into biological life has far-reaching implications for the Romantic period and for scholarship on aesthetic and cultural texts of the period.

Michel Foucault's early work on disciplinary societies accounts for the regulation of labor practices as a regulation of bodies. These are "techniques of power that were essentially centered on the body, on the individual body."[14] For agricultural labor during the seventeenth and eighteenth centuries, this means everything from pricing systems for labor to technologies such as new seed drills and plows; it includes soil regeneration by way of crop-rotation systems and the use of manure. Each of these mechanisms, large and small, changed how the laboring body functioned in the fields. However, the disciplinary society does not adequately describe the relationship among commodity markets, governmental practices, and the livelihood of laborers. Gleaning, for example, means not only labor practices but also a regulation of food, life, and livelihood both on and beyond the scale of the individual body.

In the mid-1970s, Foucault began describing a different modality of power that he saw as "the greatest transformation political right[s] underwent in the nineteenth century." According to Foucault, various technologies, apparatuses, and governmental structures cohere in a new power: "the power to make live and let die."[15] Governments have long had the power to kill, including sentencing citizens to execution or sending them to fight in wars. This new power, what Foucault calls "biopower," is the regulation of life en masse. In his lectures published as *Security, Territory, Population*, Foucault defines biopower as "the set of mechanisms through which the basic biological features of the human species became the object of a political strategy, of a general strategy of power."[16] Rather than control over the individual subject and individual bodies, biopower is concerned with populations and systems by which populations can be normalized and controlled. In Foucault's words, this means a power "applied not to man-as-body but to the living man, to man-as-living-being; ultimately, if you like, to man-as-species"; it is a "taking control of life and the biological processes of man-as-species and of ensuring that they are not disciplined, but regularized."[17] Moving politics to the scale of the biological expands the arena of social control and what "counts" as a social text.

Foucault situates this new power historically at the end of the eighteenth and beginning of the nineteenth century—during the Agricultural Revolution. The gains in agricultural production freed labor to leave the fields and fill the cities during the rise of the Industrial Revolution. Shifts in population, food and its distribution, and health became a concern of the nation. They were monitored by new apparatuses such as statistical models, exacting ordinance surveys, censuses, measurements of resources and their distributions, and forecasts.[18] Significantly, Britain's war with France (1793) and Malthus's *An Essay on the Principle of Population* (first published in 1798) heightened the sense of urgency in managing the population and the material assets of the nation. While Thomas Paine's *Rights of Man* (1791) was interested in the individual as a citizen of the nation and how each citizen is counted, Malthus moves the counting from a political concern of representation to a matter of biopolitics.[19] In other words, Paine's citizen is not only a participant in a government; he is also according to Malthus a biological being whose life is enabled and managed by the state.

Foucault's lectures on biopower and his subsequent *History of Sexuality* focuses on sex and population as the matters of biopolitical concern.[20] What he leaves out—but what I take up in this book—is how food and the labor of producing it are also implicated in biopower, and particularly so during the early formation of the biopolitical systems in Britain. Where Foucault marks race as the site of "fragmenting the field of the biological,"[21] I am interested in class as a set of material labors, powers, and practices that leverage the capacities of bodies, both human and animal, within a larger social system. It is not that Foucault is unaware of the capacities of agriculture within his delineation of biopower; he outlines, for example, the role of agriculture in the formation of a nation and the role of the Third Estate in ensuring "the substantive and historical existence of the nation" in eighteenth-century France.[22] However, such interventions by Foucault into food as biopolitical apparatus are rare.

It is only more recently with the work of Cary Wolfe in *Before the Law*, Nicole Shukin in *Animal Capital*, and Mick Smith in *Against Ecological*

Sovereignty that biopower has been explicitly linked to agricultural and animal concerns. Shukin's *Animal Capital* looks at how the title's two terms cyclically feed each other such that animal life and capital finance recursively sustain one another. As Shukin explains: "The tautological ring of this book's title seeks to make audible a related time of real subsumption effected by material and metaphorical technologies pursuing the ontological indifference of capital and animal life."[23] Much of Shukin's work outlines the "material and metaphorical" ways that capital and technology construct and limit animal life. It is in the final chapter and afterword that she begins to trace zoonotic diseases and possibilities of pandemic (from mad cow to H5N1) as a blowback to such an animal-capital system. Shukin and Wolfe in particular provide the system analysis necessary to understand the apparatus as a precursor to thinking after biopolitics. *Before the Law* appears throughout several early chapters to help construct my argument.

Extending Shukin and Wolfe's work, my project considers how the life and liveness of the subject resists and exceeds the frameworks used to render subjects units of operation within the *dispositif* of capital and state. The goal is to find moments early in the formation of biopolitics where other modalities of living and dwelling were at odds with the biopolitical regime that continues to the present. Little work has been done on biopower and the Agricultural Revolution in Romantic-period Britain, and it is to this task that *Beasts of Burden* sets itself. Moreover, this book furthers my earlier work on agriculture, aesthetics, and nationhood in *Technologies of the Picturesque*.

Beasts of Burden explores how laboring classes represented rural life during the rise of biopolitical apparatuses. I have coupled this with representations of working animals such as the horse and sheep dog along with a few wild animals such as lions and polar bears that do social and political work through their wildness.[24] The result is a different Britain than the one depicted by well-known authors of the Romantic period.[25] I try to trace "the emergence of *a multiple and heterogeneous power of resistance and creation that calls every organization that is transcendental, and every regulatory mechanism that is extraneous, to its constitution radically into question*."[26] In other words, the constitutions of economic, political, and state machinery built on the biological forces are defamiliarized. Their reasons for existence and the realities they produce are denaturalized as other ways of dwelling emerge from the multiple and heterogeneous forces.

Several scholarly works have taken up the problem of population in relationship to Romantic-period literature and culture. Most notable among these are Maureen McLane's *Romanticism and the Human Sciences: Poetry, Population, and the Discourse of Species* and, published at almost the same time, Philip Connell's *Romanticism, Economics, and the Question of "Culture."*[27]

Both highlight the well-known population debates characterized best by the work of William Godwin and Malthus as well as literary figures such as Hazlitt and Wordsworth, who opposed Malthus's treatment of the poor. Percy Bysshe Shelley's poetic masses of humanity and Mary Shelley's *Frankenstein* are representative second-generation Romantic texts for these authors. Connell addresses rural life in a brief section on Cobbett, but otherwise his view of population is through primarily well-known and well-read authors, few if any of whom had themselves farmed the land.[28] David Simpson's recent *Wordsworth, Commodification, and Social Concern* provides a similar lens for reading rural populations through well-known Romantic-period authors.[29] The framing of life and how life is used, in short a biopolitical framework, is absent in these historical readings of population and community; this is, at least in part, the contribution *Beasts of Burden* seeks to make.

What Simpson raises and what Katey Castellano brings forward in *The Ecology of British Romantic Conservatism, 1790–1837* is a conservatism within liberal thinking about rural economies and the environment. As Castellano explains, there is a desire to project into the future an idealized image of past relationships between laborers and landowners and between humans and natural resources:

> Romantic conservative critiques of modernity—found in texts as diverse as poetry, novels, political philosophy, natural history, and agricultural periodicals—all manifest conservative-conservationist reactions against the progressive ideology of capitalist modernity. Like the *Reflections* [*on the Revolution in France*], they locate communal futurity in the past by championing localized, customary communities and practices that have been, in Burke's words, "formed by habit."[30]

A biopolitical frame brings to this conversation the shift in scale of British nation building. Forces applied globally to colonial subjects are at work within the boundary lines of the nation as well during the constitution of a modern state and its citizens. Moreover, these forces work at the level of life itself, not simply on bodies or citizen-subjects. Whether it is Adam Smith's *Wealth of Nations* projecting a plan for regional or national production and capital or the conservative view of Burke, the new apparatuses of survey, census, statistics, and record keeping create new ways of managing life, normativity, and productivity for masses of humans and animals.

It is difficult to discuss rural labor without also addressing the place of animals in British life. While the first appearances of animal studies in Romantic scholarship were around 2001, the field has grown considerably since then. Christine Kenyon-Jones catalogues the appearance of animals in works by major Romantic authors in *Kindred Brutes: Animals in Romantic-Period Writing*.[31] David Perkins outlines the beginning of the animal rights movement alongside Paine's *Rights of Man* and Wollstonecraft's *Rights of Women* in his *Romanticism and Animal Rights*. Since these works, there have been a number of collected essays in eighteenth- and nineteenth-century scholarship in animals and culture.[32]

Beasts of Burden does not address animal rights for several reasons. Perkins's book serves as a good overview of this terrain, as does Harriet Ritvo's *Animal Estate*, where she describes the birth of the Society for the Prevention of Cruelty to Animals.[33] More importantly, biopower provides a different way of approaching animal life. As Cary Wolfe explains in *Before the Law*:

> Foucault argues that this shift from sovereignty to biopower involves a new concept of the subject, one that is endowed with fundamental interests that cannot be limited to or contained by the simple *legal* category of the person. But a trade-off is involved here. If the subject addressed by biopolitics comprises a new political resource, it also requires a new sort of political technology if it is to be fully controlled and exploited. The biosubject, you might say, is far more multidimensional and robust than the "thin" subject of laws and rights; that is both its promise and its challenge as a new object of political power.[34]

Rights discourse attempts to address the subject under "a transcendental ethics of communication," of which Jürgen Habermas is the most relevant current proponent.[35] However, as Wolfe notes, such a characterization of the human and animal subject is "thin" in that the more "multidimensional and robust" elements of life are either left out or forced within the frame of a transcendental ethics. Biopower gives us a more comprehensive view of how human and animal life are made political and put to use by the nation and by the demands of capital. The rise of a new sort of subject under biopolitics calls for a different language from the all-too-weak modalities of common sense and rational communication projected by rights discourse.

Tobias Menely's *The Animal Claim* bridges rights debates with a corporality that precedes any possible discussion of rights and social recognition. He is interested in how animals give voice, how their voices are heard culturally, and how they are taken up for advocates for animal rights within the cultural and political systems of eighteenth-century Britain. For Menely, sensibility and affect provide avenues by which animals give prelinguistic signals of liveness, potency, and vulnerability. Tracing the animal question in philosophy and poetry of the period, *The Animal Claim* considers how "[s]ensibility . . . puts pressure on the symbolic order, and thus on a model of community as necessarily human . . . by relentlessly defining its operations with response to the impassioned voice, an unintegrated origin and never fully actualized surplus of meaning that precedes the signifier itself" (4–5). Something is going on in the animal, as evidenced by voice, and it is this something to which the poets bear witness. While Menely is primarily interested in how aesthetics can bear witness or help claim a space for animals, "voice, an unintegrated origin and never fully actualized surplus of meaning" also provide evidence of a friction between human community and an unintegrated (and perhaps unintegratable) animality. Such friction reveal what I believe is a resistance to biopolitical regimes as they develop in the Romantic period.

As Jacques Derrida explains in "The Animal That Therefore I Am (More to Follow)," the word *animal* is all too human and covers too many different creatures and ways of life to be particularly useful as a designation.[36] Instead, Derrida advocates that we examine the various fractured lines in specific human–animal relations. In *Beasts of Burden*, I am interested in how animal life is represented and used within culture and in ways that animals provide friction to the interlocking gears of our social systems. Where they do create friction, animals reveal the often overlooked machinery of subjectification and commodification. And, as is perhaps obvious, because animals live not only within our cultural worlds but also within worlds beyond our comprehension, they point to other ways of dwelling. In the final chapter and the afterword, I project out the implications of animal worlding at the limits of human culture. In doing so, I develop how biological life and animality can be used over and against political apparatuses and how the concept of biopower pushes cultural thought to the limits of what it is capable of understanding or even conceiving.

Before proceeding further, it is worth briefly noting why I am primarily using Foucault's articulation of biopolitics rather than Agamben's use of the term in relation to the state of exception and bare life. Agamben traces his terms back to the Greeks. The emphasis throughout his corpus is "on sovereignty and the abjection of the body [particularly the human body] as 'animal,' which in turn becomes a kind of abstract philosophical *topos*. What we're talking about here instead is a kind of biopolitics that is very, very specifically articulated in relation to different, particular kinds of bodies."[37] Foucault places biopower within very specific historical contexts and apparatuses, while Agamben's matrix remains an abstract frame based on foundational workings of culture dating from the distinction between *bios* or "the good life" and *zoe* or "animal life" (and for humans excluded from bios, there is a bare life). Certainly Agamben's terms can be used in relation to the human and animal spheres I address in this book; however, much of the historical specificity would be lost. The result would be an analysis of human and animal life that could equally describe many other cultural and historical moments.[38]

There is much that this book does not cover. Its scope is rather narrowly on farm life and the depiction of domesticated and wild animals. Notably absent is the role of slavery in the wealth of the nation. West Indian labor helped build the British Empire. Timothy Morton's work on blood sugar in *The Poetics of Spice* is well known. Paul Youngquist and Grégory Pierrot's ongoing work on Caribbean slavery takes up many biopolitical concerns, as does Paul Youngquist's *Race, Romanticism, and the Atlantic*.[39] Also absent is the history of agricultural experimentation and the growth of Britain's beef culture. I have addressed both of these topics in *Technologies of the Picturesque*. Finally, readers interested in labor-class poets of the Romantic period will notice that I have not included John Clare in my discussion. Ranging from John Barrell to Jonathan Bate to James McKusick, Tim Fulford, and Timothy Morton, much has been written on Clare's poetry from a historical, Marxist, and ecocritical perspective.[40] While a biopolitical reading of Clare is certainly useful, I did not feel I could sustain an original discussion of his work in light of so much written about him. Moreover, the larger arc of this book would not have been advanced by including a discussion of his poetry.

It is worth noting that a recent work on Clare, Sara Guyer's *Reading with John Clare: Biopoetics, Sovereignty, Romanticism*, examines how language (and rhetorical or figural language, as she invokes Barbara Johnson and Paul de Man) creates poetics with a power of life—a biopoetics—over and against biopolitics as governmental power to let die and make live. For Guyer, Clare makes life visible in ways different from the political apparatus of the nation, "politics—and biopolitics—can seem to 'hinge' on the structure of a poetic figure . . . to recognize this structure is to see poetry and politics as two forms engaged with questions of viability."[41] Guyer's extensive close readings and invocations of a poetics as politics will be welcomed work within Clare studies and beyond. Her work and mine share a concern over what is made visible, by whom (or by what apparatus) and for whom. Where Guyer is concerned primarily with the Romantic-period formation of the lyrical subject and its power, my work is primarily focused on a more conventional Foucaultian constitution of subjectivity. While I do not address Clare, and Guyer's study is primarily on Clare, we share an interest in how life appears as a political sum and those ways in which life works over and against the biopolitical *dispositif*.

Beasts of Burden builds a narrative of biopolitical Britain by looking first at the constitution of a citizenry from the heterogeneous masses of people and regions. It then turns to labor-class poetry and prose from Bloomfield to Batchelor to Burns to Hogg. The book then looks at animal imagery ranging from domesticated animals to natural history accounts. Finally it moves from hunting scenes in Landseer to his inhuman landscapes and ends with a nonhuman world replete with animality but absent of human culture and its biopolitical scaffolding. By using a range of cultural texts including literature and art, I have attempted to provide a broad view of how thinking with biopower can change how we think about the problem of life in the Romantic period.

The second chapter uses Burke's comment about the "swinish multitude" of British citizens to explain how disparate groups of humans and human–animal assemblages worked against being counted and so interpolated within the nation-state. A number of institutions attempted to use population data to create policies to control and appease the crowd of distressed poor and working-class people, but those in distress resisted institutional apparatuses that they did not understand and that did not provide the immediate remedies they sought. The chapter uses James Gillray's illustrations, Spence's utopics, Sussex pigs, and Cobbett's *Rural Rides* to push against the narrow parameters by which population understands and represents life.

Chapter 3 folds the problem of life into counting death by way of how animal death is represented in picturesque art and literature, including an extended discussion of Robert Bloomfield's and Thomas Batchelor's poetry. Throughout the chapter, the machinery of biopolitics at work on the material, biological, and political body of laborers is revealed through the figure of animal death. Human bare life and animal life are interconnected. The chapter ends with Robert Burns's poem "To a Mouse," which allows us to think of human fragility alongside other species.

The fourth chapter ratchets up the modes of resistance to biopower as evident in the works of James Hogg. Too often his stories of witches and brownies are read as quaint gothic entertainment for the reading public. His shepherds' tales are considered nostalgia written for an urban public that likes to pine for an idealized bucolic past. The fairy and witch stories provide a particular way of seeing. In pairing these "superstitions" with the life of shepherds, this chapter links a variety of Hogg's rural tales as ways of dwelling counter to the "light" and "civilization" and English conquest of Scotland, which brought the region into modernity, a new capitalist economy, and the purview of the rising nation-state.

Whereas the early chapters focus primarily, though not exclusively, on literary texts, the next two chapters look at artists well known for their representation of domestic and wild animals. Chapter 5 examines the role of natural history in the machinery of classification and biopolitical utility during the age of global exploration. Yet, as much as natural history serves utility and human understanding, it discounts much of animal life. The artistic works of Thomas Bewick and George Stubbs move between the scientific ends of natural history and an artistry that works not as a handmaid to science but rather as a way of creating wonder at nonhuman life. Chapter 6 conjectures a radical revaluation of the Edwin Landseer's work as something other than sentimental animal portraiture and Victorian hunting scenes. Working backward from the later painting *Man Proposes, God Disposes* to his Romantic-period works of the 1820s and 1830s, I pursue the collapse of animal–human worlds and hierarchies precariously built within a number of his famous Highland and hunting paintings and portraits of loyal dogs. In the end, Landseer is haunted by an animality that disposes of culture.

The devastating vision of life without humans portrayed in some of Landseer's paintings provides a path for chapter 7 as a brief afterword in which I examine well-known Romantic literature that experiments with limits of human life and culture. These works point to extreme environments as a leveling force that disrupts and will eventually overcome human worlding. In such works, we meet not simply the limits of the biopolitical but the limits of human worlding altogether. These works, written during the rise of biopolitical apparatuses, use the limits of human life as a political weapon against culture.

By proclaiming that man is dead, Foucault famously extended Nietzsche's comment that God is dead and man killed him.[42] The death of "man" exposes the fictional quality of the privileged interiority of the human subject so valued by Romanticism and its expressive theory of poetry.[43] Behind this privileged interiority lurks a biopolitical apparatus that structures the very discourse of citizen, subject, and the poets as "unacknowledged legislators." As will become evident throughout this work, man or the citizen-subject is a convenient mask that allows other apparatuses of power to work behind the scenes without notice. Across its chapters, *Beasts of Burden* calls into question basic concepts of Romantic scholarship from the individual and the citizen to the limits of history and historical scholarship and finally to the limits of reason. The chapters are meant as experiments in thinking Romanticism otherwise—deploying commonly used tools of criticism but then exceeding their limits to reveal other material worlds, other ways of thinking and dwelling, and other lives during the Romantic period.

2

Docile Numbers and Stubborn Bodies

Population and the Problem of Multitude

"Along with its natural protectors and guardians, learning will be cast into the mire, and trodden down under the hoofs of a swinish multitude."[1] Edmund Burke's brief mention in *Reflections on the Revolution in France* about the "swinish multitude" trampling on learning unleashed a swarm of cultural responses. In his swinish multitude comment, he makes clear the distinction implicit elsewhere in *Reflections*. Burke attempts to keep separate "the deferential subjects, instinctively loyal, and the [learned] argumentative citizens," the latter being the "tiny political nation needed to—could be permitted to—shoulder the daunting demands of citizenship."[2] However, his comments created an uproar from the underclass. This chapter is concerned with the problem of figuring the multitude and how the multitude functions in politics during the Romantic period. In particular, it notes how in the age of political economy swine and populous masses are subsumed within, yet resist, biopolitical ends.

Perhaps most striking among the cultural responses to Burke are James Gillray's 1795 illustrations: the apocalyptic pigs and the starving swine. In the apocalyptic pigs image *Presages of the Millennium*, William Pitt rides a white Hanoverian horse and wields famine and destruction on a herd of pigs and politicians, the "souls of Multitude." The textual commentary at the foot of the image is adapted from the Book of Revelations:

And e'er the Last days began, I looked & beheld a White Horse, & his name was Death, & Hell followed after him . . . And I saw under him the Souls of the Multitude, those who were destroy'd for maintaining the word of Truth, & for the Testimony.

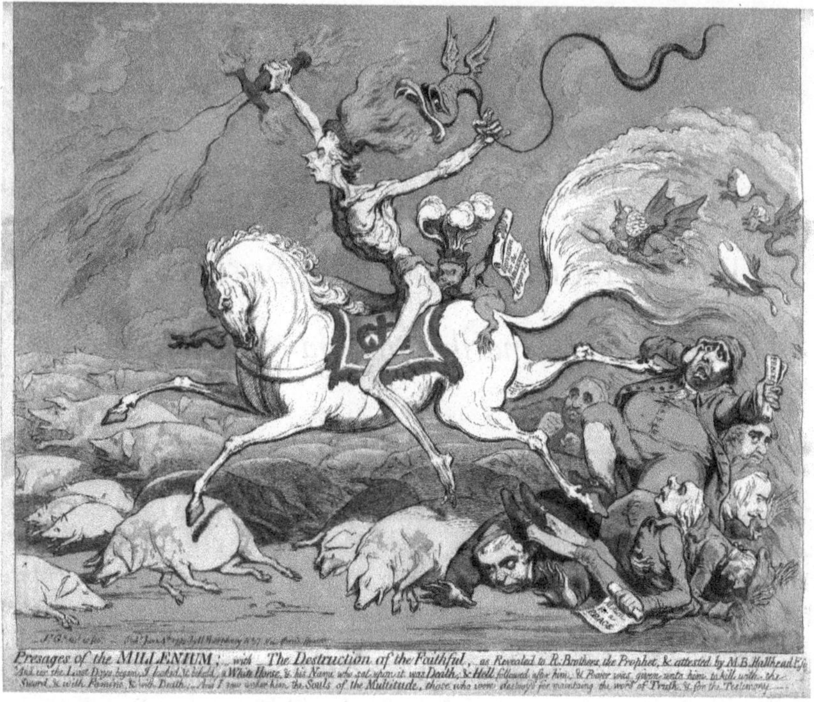

Figure 2.1. James Gillray. *Presages of the Millennium*. 1795. British Museum.

Kissing Pitt's backside is George, Prince of Wales, while emerging from the horse's tail are horned and winged figures, Edmund Burke and Henry Dundas, the first secretary of state for War. Whig leader Charles Henry Fox, who holds a plea for peace with France, is trampled along with various parliamentary allies and a sea of swine.[3]

Later in the same year, Gillray illustrates the *Substitutes for Bread*, which calls attention to the poor harvests of 1794 and 1795 and the famine that followed. The laboring poor amass in the streets and outside the window of a landowner's house. They hold signs including "Petitions from Starving Swine" and seem poised to rush upon the wealthy inside, who in luxurious attire consume roast beef, poultry, and gold coins in the shape of fish as their opulent "substitutes" for bread. On the wall of the gentleman's house hangs a notice, "Proclamation for a General Fast, in order to avert the impending Famine," beside which hangs a separate note of acceptable substitutes for bread, including "venison," "roast beef," "champaign," and so forth. So, during this grain crisis, the elite turn to a range of food that signifies their

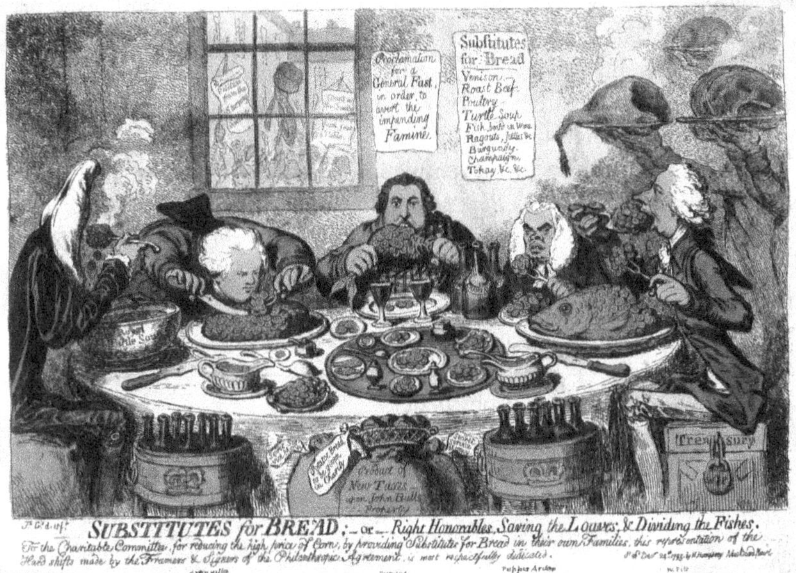

Figure 2.2. James Gillray. *Substitutes for Bread; – or – Right Honorables Saving the Loaves and Dividing the Fishes*. 1795. British Museum.

place apart from the crowd. Pork is not on the list of items to be eaten, but the swinish masses clearly feel eaten into as they call out to be noticed. In Gillray's illustrations, the swinish multitude works as a figure for masses that cannot be contained or controlled by institutional authority.

Gillray joins together the human masses as a "swinish multitude" with a noted characteristic of swine: stubbornness. As the traditional Sussex folk verse of the period says:

> And you can pook
> And you can shove
> But a Sussex pig
> He won't be druv.

This final line appears on Sussex Rye pig mugs of the 1800s. The head of the clay pig comes off, and the mug is stood on its tail to hold liquid. The decanter is traditionally filled with beer. Around the neck of the clay pig is often embossed "He won't be druv."[4] So accumulates the signification of the masses: a swinish, beer drinking, intoxicated, stubborn multitude. The immovable nature of pigs is used in a number of political forums, even prior to Burke. As Dr. Johnson notes (in Boswell's *The Life of Samuel Johnson*): "The peers have but to *oppose* a candidate, to ensure him success. It is said, the only way to make a pig go forward is to pull him back by the tail. These people must be treated like pigs."[5]

One might add to the accumulation several 1790s tracts: the socialist utopics of Edmund Spence's *Pig's Meat* and Daniel Issac Eaton's *Politics for the People; or A Salmagundy for Swine*.[6] Likewise, Eaton's *Hog's Wash* is populated with swinish contributors such as Brother Grunter, Porkulus, A Liberty Pig, and The Learned Pig, among others.[7] Robert Southey's political pig of 1799 ("The Pig: a Colloquial Poem") is another example:

> Is he [the pig] obstinate?
> We must not, Jacob, be deceived by words,
> By sophist sounds. A democratic beast
> He knows that his unmerciful drivers seek
> Their profit and not his.[8]

And if Gillray can invoke the Book of Revelations for his apocalyptic pigs, then the other pig of the New Testament worth noting is the herd of swine into which Christ cast the demons that had possessed a man. From the point of view of the wealthy who dine on lavish "Substitutes for Bread," the swinish multitude of mankind indeed seemed possessed with a demonic force beyond their comprehension. These cultural and intertextual references for the swinish multitude seem to multiply, much like the innumerable voices, bodies, and demands they are meant to represent.

Gillray's *Substitutes for Bread* is occasioned by the food crisis of 1794 and 1795. In the wake of the crisis, a number of agricultural, governmental, and charity institutions developed a new discourse of population for describing the disaffected masses. The gambit for these institutions was that, by understanding population—numbers of people, their distribution, their ages, and their occupations—they could create policies to control and appease the crowd of distressed poor and working-class people. Furthering the discussion from chapter 1, this chapter examines biopolitics as the political constitution of population that creates a narrow space for containing the multitude of life. The political forces manipulating the biological power of life (biopower), forces Foucault terms "biopolitics," did not spring fully formed into being. The early years of creating a population from the masses saw many complex problems of how to manage human and animal bodies. While population provides an ordering of life, the "swinish multitude" serves as a figure for life in excess of population. The goal of this chapter is to sketch some of the lines of biopolitical construction and resistance early in the Romantic period by beginning with Foucault's 1976 lecture on biopower and then placing it in relation to a mosaic of period texts.

As mentioned in the introductory chapter, Foucault's March 17, 1976, lecture published in *Society Must Be Defended: Lectures at the Collège de France 1975–1976* provides the touchstone for understanding biopower. Biopower is the biological that becomes tended and controlled by the State.[9] The political rationale and the legal and rhetorical justification for such control are termed biopolitics. Foucault explains, "Biopolitics deals with the population, with the population as political problem, as a problem that is at once scientific and political, as a biological problem and as power's problem."[10] While regulating the citizens as a mass is a general concern of governments throughout the ages, Foucault claims that the eighteenth century saw a rise in technologies for regulating the life of citizens. Such regulation was not the age-old negative modality of regulating death: the right of a State to take the life of a citizen who violates its laws and the right of the State to send citizens to war. This new power included

> mechanisms with a certain number of functions that are very different from the functions of disciplinary mechanisms. The mechanisms introduced by biopolitics include forecasts, statistical estimates, and overall measures. . . . [They] intervene at the level at which these general phenomena are determined, to intervene at the level of their generality.[11]

At the turn of the nineteenth century, a number of mechanical, information, and economic technologies align to "maintain an average, establish a sort of homeostasis" for the population of bodies.[12] The State co-opts and fosters these technologies toward a greater control of the population. It is not that the State has control of these technologies. Rather, a critical number of bio-political technologies emerge, such as cartography, surveys, and statistics.[13] Under the banner of rising nationalism and under fear of the French—from the French Revolution to Napoleon—the State corrals and co-opts these techniques, technologies, rhetorics, and ultimately powers.

The poor harvest and lack of grain in 1795 figure as an event and a rupture that reveals the way biopower began to get hold of bodies in the British Isles. Rather than a singular narrative, I provide instances within this event. These instances form a mosaic of power relations within Britain and a figure of resistance, what Foucault calls "homo oeconomicus." As Cary Wolfe explains,

> In opposition to what Foucault calls *homo juridicus* (or *homo legalis*)—the subject of law, rights, and sovereignty—we find in this new subject, *homo oeconomicus*, "an essentially and unconditionally irreducible element against any possible government," a "zone that is definitively inaccessible to any government action," "an atom of freedom in the face of all the conditions, undertakings, legislation, and prohibitions of a possible government." "The subject of interest," Foucault writes, thus "constantly overflows the subject of right. He is therefore irreducible to the subject of right. He is not absorbed by him. He overflows him, surrounds him, and is the permanent condition of him functioning." *Homo oeconomicus* thus founds a new domain of "irrational rationality" that is of a fundamentally different order from sovereignty and the juridical subject. "Economic rationality," Foucault writes, "is not only surrounded by, but founded on the unknowability of, the totality of the process" and *homo oeconomicus* thus says to the sovereign "you cannot because you do not know, and you do not know because you cannot know." But such a creature, of course—and for that very reason—poses a threat to power. And this threat is what will in time give rise to the regime of governmentality and its exercise of biopower.[14]

I briefly trace this *homo oeconomicus* as a mass or stubborn bodies against the docility of manipulating numbers. In other words, modes of quantification—counting bodies and counting them as citizens of the State subject to its control—become the means of rhetorical and material control of peoples. In contrast, *homo oeconomicus* uses qualitative differences between people as a way of evading quantification and counting. *Homo oeconomicus* leverages a biopower—the biological capacities and resistances of bodies—as that which has yet to be co-opted by the biopolitical.

Scarcity in 1795 set in motion a number of biopolitical debates as to whether and how the government should intervene in the problem of hunger. King George's October 1795 speech on the high price of goods motivated the November 3 parliamentary debate on the laws regarding the Assize of Bread and Ale and other governmental means of conserving grain and curbing costs. Pitt and with him Fox were cautious of any intervention in markets;

however, they did advocate for the laboring poor, who had been brought to a degraded state. Samuel Whitbread advanced a bill to set minimum wages for the poor, but despite repeated attempts the bill failed. Edmund Burke replied to Whitbread, first in Parliament, then in *Thoughts and Details on Scarcity*, published posthumously in 1800. The publication is a mixture of political conservatism and agrarian observations; the political elements are mainly at the outset of the book and read like a political treatise, while the agricultural details are in fragments at the end of the work and read like something akin to a report to the Board of Agriculture.

Contrary to Whitbread, Burke does not believe in setting a minimum wage but rather believes that the market of supply and demand should set the labor prices. More astonishingly and contrary to Adam Smith, Burke believes "in the case of the farmer and the labourer, their interests are always the same, and it is absolutely impossible that their free contracts can be onerous to either party."[15] Burke doubts that workers are worse off in 1795 than in the past, and his remedy for any low costs of labor and high prices for food is charity rather than government intervention. As David Collings explains, "The duties of public office and of private charity that Burke tries to separate had long since been blended in the tradition, which regarded the church or the state as the agent of collective charity and which therefore build an element of communitas into its public institutions. By attempting to strip away this element [the poor laws], Burke violates his cardinal principle, the maintenance of long usages."[16] Burke as advocate of custom becomes Burke, advocate of the free market.

Yet, oddly, agrarian parts of Burke's *Thoughts and Details Written on Scarcity* are not always on the side of the market. He delineates for pages the poor quantity of the year's wheat, oats, barley, beans, clover, rye, hay, and grasses. He then extrapolates from this to the costs and quality of meat, noting, "When the food of the animal is scarce, his flesh must be dear,"[17] This is in contrast to his political claim early in the book that it is in the best interest of farmer and worker that "the labourer is well fed, and otherwise found with such necessaries of animal life, according to its habitudes, as may keep the body in full force, and the mind gay and cheerful."[18] One might combine Burke's two observations: when the food of the human animal is scarce, his flesh must be dear. It is to this very dearness of their flesh that the multitude gives voice in pressing against hunger. Burke praises the laboring man as an "instrumentum vocale" or full-throated voice but then seems deaf to the cries.[19]

The dearness of human life in times of scarcity was a long-running debate in the eighteenth century as free market economists such as Adam

Smith weighted the ability of the markets to correct (often only after devastating human loss) against government intervention, which could prolong the scarcity as it maintained a population in excess of the food available. Smith outlines his strong free trade position in the "Digression Concerning the Corn Trade and Corn Laws" chapter from book 4 of *Wealth of Nations*. As scholars have noted, for the most part he avoids the issue of emergency and starvation. He is unwilling to play out the consequences of his insistence on a free market of grain without government interference. In their very well-crafted *The Other Adam Smith*, Mike Hill and Warren Montag explore the extended history of the grain debates (particularly in France) that informed Smith's work and subsequent British policies, including the necropolitics of starvation. The two positions precede Smith's writing and continue to inform the Romantic-period conversation about the price of bread and the corn laws. As Louis Paul Abeille advocated, the state must allow the maintenance of private property (including grain hoarding to sell at high prices); otherwise, property is not private but only provisionally so until needed by other groups within society. Alternatively, as Abbe Galiani rebutted, the state must intervene because it is the government's duty to safeguard the well-being of its citizens (and no person would enter a social contract that would license his or her death).[20] Malthus read with particular interest Smith's discussion of scarcity and government policy in China (with its thin veil pointing to European famine). For Malthus, "there appeared in the description of China precisely a theory of the market as a mechanism that, far from expanding without limit if allowed to operate according to its own rationality without external political interference [as Smith advocated], would infallibly adjust the proportion of laborers to the fund available for wages by withholding food from the social ranks whose numbers exceed their ability to obtain subsistence."[21] Where Smith sees a structural problem with the market and an optimism for its possible correction, Malthus reads the larger biopolitical problem of how a State is to manage what he believes is inevitable and natural scarcity.

Not long after Burke's 1795 speech on scarcity, his health began to fail. Nevertheless, Sir John Sinclair, president of the Board of Agriculture and author of *Statistical Account of Scotland*, leaned on Burke to write a chapter on wages and food for the report to the Board. Sinclair was rapidly compiling agricultural statistics and reports. In his July address to the Board of Agriculture, Sinclair announced that every county of Britain had an agricultural survey in print or soon to be in print. From these, "the public would see to what a pitch of perfection agricultural knowledge was likely to be brought, by the accumulation of so many valuable materials."[22] From surveys, the Board hoped that methods in "improved" agriculture would spread;

indeed, "there is no duty more incumbent on a board of agriculture than that of recommending such measures as are most likely to provide a sufficient quantity of food for the people."[23]

To press Sinclair's case, the notable agricultural improver Arthur Young, then secretary of the Board, visited the ailing Burke in May 1796. Young reported back to the Board that Burke would be unable to fulfill the requested chapter on wages and food: "His conversation was remarkably desultory, a broken mixture of agricultural observation, French madness, price of provisions, the death of his son, the absurdity of regulating labour, the mischief of our Poor-laws, and the difficulty of cottagers keeping cows."[24] Indeed, much of *Thoughts and Details Written on Scarcity* carries this same "broken mixture." Yet the mixture is revealing. Agriculture does not stand on its own but is part of a larger political and labor ecology. How and what people eat depends on a mixture of agricultural observation, "French madness," prices of provisions, labor regulations, poor laws, and a cottager's cows. Burke's only fault here is not keeping these various categories from spilling out one into another and so too-haphazardly showing the effects of one upon the other.

Burke's unwritten chapter, partly visible in *Thoughts and Details Written on Scarcity*, shows how administrative tools were deployed toward developing a biopolitics of Britain. Sinclair's other administrative works serve as good examples. In accord with a number of agricultural treatises and surveys of the period, Sinclair created and managed the ambitious twenty-one–volume *Statistical Account of Scotland* (1791–1799). His use of the word *statistical* was rather novel at the time and called for his explanation:

> Many people were at first surprised at my using the words "statistical" and "statistics," as it was supposed that some in our own language might have expressed the same meaning. But in the course of a very extensive tour through the northern parts of Europe, which I happened to take in 1786, I found that in Germany they were engaged in a species of political enquiry to which they had given the name "statistics," and though I apply a different meaning to that word—for by "statistical" is meant in Germany an inquiry for the purposes of ascertaining the political strength of a country or questions respecting matters of state—whereas the idea I annex to the term is an inquiry into the state of a country, for the purpose of ascertaining the quantum of happiness enjoyed by its inhabitants, and the means of its future improvement; but as I thought that a new word might attract more public attention, I resolved on adopting it, and I hope it is now completely naturalised and incorporated with our language.[25]

Sinclair relied on roughly 900 local parish ministers to conduct the survey with some help from hired agents. The survey included 160 questions covering geography, population, agriculture, and industry. While ostensibly seeking "the quantum of happiness enjoyed by its inhabitants," the survey actually recorded normative behavior of the population and laid the groundwork by which Sinclair and others would argue for improvements. Furthermore, it made significant inroads in representing Scotland to the rest of Great Britain and through quantification categorized and normalized Scottish life.

While conducting the survey, in 1793 Sinclair was instrumental in establishing the Board of Agriculture (officially chartered as the Board or Society for the Encouragement of Agriculture and Internal Improvement). With a number of individuals and local societies advocating improvement of agriculture and livestock, it was simply a matter of time before farming was centralized and nationalized in a Board of Agriculture. According to the biography of Sinclair by his son, Reverend John Sinclair, the idea of forming a national board first occurred through Sinclair's discussion of the Corn Bill in 1791, titled "An Address to the Landed Interest on the Corn Bill." Sinclair had "been deeply impressed by the fact, that while we were alleged to be dependent on foreign countries for food, there existed in England alone twelve millions of acres almost in a state of nature; and that many statesmen were looking helplessly for subsistence to other countries, while they overlooked the abundant capabilities of their own."[26] According to the biography, Prime Minister Pitt was impressed with this information, which would prove "important to the safety and independence of the kingdom."[27]

From the Society for the Improvement of British Wool to the *Statistical Account* to the Board of Agriculture, Sinclair is fundamentally interested in what Michel Foucault would call biopolitics and biopower. The basic parameters of these terms are outlined in Foucault's March 17, 1976, lecture published in *Society Must Be Defended: Lectures at the Collège de France 1975–1976*. Biopower is the event of the biological tended by State control.[28] The political rationale and the legal and rhetorical justification for such control are termed biopolitics. Foucault explains, "Biopolitics deals with the population, with the population as political problem, as a problem that is at once scientific and political, as a biological problem and as power's problem."[29] Although regulating the citizens as a mass is a general concern of government throughout the ages, Foucault claims that the eighteenth century saw a rise in technologies for regulating the life of citizens. Such regulation was not the age-old negative modality of regulating death: the right of a State to take the life of a citizen who violates its laws and the right of the

State to send citizens to war. This new power included "mechanisms with a certain number of functions that are very different from the functions of disciplinary mechanisms. The mechanisms introduced by biopolitics include forecasts, statistical estimates, and overall measures. . . . [They] intervene at the level at which these general phenomena are determined, to intervene at the level of their generality."[30] At the turn of the nineteenth century, a number of mechanical and information and economic technologies align to "maintain an average, establish a sort of homeostasis" for the population.[31] The State co-opts and fosters these technologies toward a greater control of the population. We see the concern for measuring, forecasting, and regulating population played out in the debate between Godwin and Malthus, then in Southey's review of Malthus in the *Annual Review* 1803 (published in 1804).[32] The issue is central to Goldsmith's *Deserted Village* and George Crabbe's *The Village* and *Tales in Verse*. By claiming that Sinclair's labors can be understood under the modality of biopower, I am also making a larger claim about the link between humans and animals.

Sinclair's concern for yields of wool and meat, his development of statistical reports and agricultural habits, and his development of a Board that promoted norms and improvements in agriculture, including livestock, all link the health of British citizens with the cultivation of their animals. In his lecture, Foucault considers the regulation of sexuality to be a pivotal example of biopower: "It is, I think, the privileged position it [sexuality] occupies between organism and population, between the body and general phenomena, that explains the extreme emphasis placed upon sexuality in the nineteenth century."[33] I would simply add that food, too, functions as a mode of regulation between "the body and general phenomena" of the masses. This is not "simply" the problem of feeding a people and preventing famine. It is also an issue of the sort of food, its cost, and its distribution.[34]

One could add the cartographic survey of the nation and the census to the list of biopolitical machinery. Both were under way at the turn of the century, and over the coming decades these inscriptions became refined instruments for representing a population. It is from such work that later John Snow would be able to create his famous epidemiological map of the cholera epidemic and trace a particular outbreak to the Broad Street water pump. For agriculture, maps of low-lying swamps and bogs reveal places that would, over the course of the century, see drainage and "improvement" toward greater enclosure as well as expanded tillage. Additionally, Sinclair's study can be placed in the lineage of what the seventeenth-century author William Petty termed "political arithmetick." Petty is the "progenitor of quantitative study of 'power'" who considered quantitative data as a means to reveal new sets of relationships at the national level. Even with the incomplete quantitative studies of his period, he attempted to estimate the wealth potential of territory and compare English wealth potential against that of other nations.[35] Closer to Sinclair's own time and region, Andrew Wight published *Present State of Husbandry in Scotland* in 1778, and James Anderson published his *Account of the Present State of the Hebrides* in 1785.[36] More ambitious was the Scotsman George Chalmers's *Estimate of the Comparative Strength of Great Britain, during the Present and Four Preceding Reigns*, which was "the first work successfully to pull together a picture of national wealth and power using chiefly central sources."[37] All of these were efforts post 1745 to accord the productivity of Scotland with that of Great Britain as a whole and to reveal Scotland as a significant contributor to the wealth of the nation.

In cartography and the census, everyone counts, which is to say everyone is folded into quantity indifferent to difference in kind. Every *one* is interpellated as citizen within the nation and within a common system of evaluation. As Althusser lays out in "Ideology and Ideological State Apparatuses," "*all ideology hails or interpellates concrete individuals as concrete subjects*."[38] Ideology happens concretely, and we are subsumed within it by concrete circumstances, by the accepted practices and rituals of a culture: "you and I are *always already* subjects, and as such constantly practice the rituals of ideological recognition, which guarantee for us that we are indeed concrete, individual, distinguishable and (naturally) irreplaceable subjects."[39] Finding oneself on a map or being counted as part of a population of a locale means being a subject given over to the representation of the map, survey, or census. As Steven Daniels explains, "Maps were not merely illustrations of the changing economic and political landscape of Britain; they were instruments of its planning, production, and regulation. They helped to coordinate Britain, in people's minds as well as on the ground, as a national network of localities and regions."[40]

The power of the census and cartography is evident in the Settlement Act and subsequent settlement laws. These serve as an example of biopolitics at work. The laws prevent moving from one parish to another without gainful employment. The settlement laws were passed to prevent vagrants from drawing charity from parishes of which they are not native; however, they also had an effect on field workers and day laborers. When workers were in demand, authorities overlooked the law so as to bring in more hands to tend to the fields; and with more workers, lower wages followed. Only when there was little work did the authorities prevent movement into their parishes. By binding the laboring poor to a particular locale, by preventing freedom of movement, the law prevented the laborer from selling on the free market his one commodity, himself as labor. In *Wealth of Nations*, Adam Smith takes to task this prohibition:

> The obstruction which corporation laws give to the free circula-
> tion of labour is common, I believe, to every part of Europe. That
> which is given to it by the poor law is, so far as I know, peculiar
> to England. It consists in the difficulty which a poor man finds
> in obtaining a settlement, or even in being allowed to exercise his
> industry in any parish but that which he belongs. . . . The difficulty
> of obtaining settlements obstructs even that of common labour.[41]

Parish boundaries, citizenship, and economic pricing of labor are *accepted practices and rituals in culture. These biopolitical apparatus* move from textual inscriptions on paper to interpellation of bodies in which the laborers are *"always already* subjects."

Thomas Malthus's sheer quantification of bodies in his *Essay on the Principle of Population* provides an exemplary instance of counting flesh. Malthus's fundamental formula raises great anxiety: human population grows exponentially, while agriculture grows arithmetically. Such a quantification of bodies in dire circumstances serves as a justification for the expansion of bio-politics in a range of areas including but not limited to enclosure, agriculture, animal husbandry, and the clearances in Scotland.[42] Anxiety regarding popu-lation exceeding agricultural production legitimates the gathering of data and the quantification of life. In terms of bodies made *"always already* subjects," throughout *Principle of Population*, Malthus makes individuals responsible for their place in society. It is only by their industry that they contribute to the body politic. In a particularly shocking passage, the orphan without parents to care for him and unable to provide for himself "is, comparably speaking, of no value to society, as others will immediately supply its place."[43] Note here the use of the words "comparably" and "others." Every person is placed in quantitative relation to the next and is comparable to the next. Each person counts equally and must supply his or her relational "value" to society.

In *Monstrous Society*, David Collings points to a curious moment in the 1803 edition of Malthus's essay that does not appear in subsequent editions. Here Malthus employs the figure of the harvest table, but with an inversion of the figure's normal use. Traditionally, the harvest table—both in custom and in texts about the event—is a moment when the cornucopia of earth's bounty is on display. The landowner sits with his laborers to share a feast from the harvest. The harvest table is employed in a number of labor-class poems and is perhaps best known in Robert Bloomfield's *Farmer's Boy*:

> Yet Plenty reigns, and from her boundless hoard,
> Though not one jelly trembles on the board,
> Supplies the feast with all that sense can crave;
> With all that made our great forefathers brave.[44]

Bloomfield goes on to lament the loss of this custom as landowners sit at a separate table and eat "refined" rather than the wholesome foods of their forefathers.

Malthus employs the table differently:

> A man who is born into a world already possessed, if he cannot get subsistence from his parents on whom he has a just demand, has no claim of *right* to the smallest portion of food, and in fact, has no business to be where he is. At nature's mighty feast there is no vacant cover for him. She tells him to be gone, and will quickly execute her own orders, if he do not work upon the compassion of some of her guests. If these guests get up and make room for him, other intruders immediately appear demanding the same favor.[45]

Malthus continues by explaining that "harmony" of the feast is placed off balance and scarcity ensues. Eventually, "the guests learn too late their error, in counteracting those strict orders to all intruders, issued by the great mistress of the feast, who, wishing that all her guests should have plenty, and knowing that she could not provide for unlimited numbers, humanely refused to admit fresh comers when her table was already full."[46] For Malthus, no longer is the landowner and community responsible for who attends the feast; instead, "the great mistress" Nature dictates the limit in numbers. Indeed, the table becomes a problem of counting rather than surplus, excess, bounty, and a joyous mass of humanity. In short, Malthus inverts the festival of the feast. Now each individual must bring something to the table to gain admission. Taken alongside other texts laid out above, Malthus constructs a biopolitical individual who is responsible to the state but to whom the state bears no responsibility should the individual not meet requisite productivity.

A pause here is in order to consider the implications of these diverse biopolitical inscriptions. As already noted, these works are not always a coordinated effort. They may draw one from another—for example, as Malthus, in each of his progressively copious editions of *Principle of Population*, adds more and more data taken from surveys and census reports—but the works are not centralized. Nor is the government the sole or even main force initiating the quantification. Over the nineteenth century, the government will increasingly take control of methods for gathering data as well as providing government imprimatur for published reports.

The general drift of these works is to place all citizens within a restricted economy. The general, or unrestricted, economy of heterogeneous place, personhood, and food is narrowed. In a restricted economy, all bodies within the cartographic borders of the state fall under the rubrics of citizenship and the census. All bodies count quantitatively. Later, there is room for some qualitative and quantitative differentiation—comparing populations from different regions or by livelihood, gender, wealth, ethnicity, and so on. However, any differentiation is subordinated to or falls "below" the categories determined by the matrix of quantification. Quantified sets of information determine in advance the status of the bodies, so one is or is not a citizen. From there, one is from a region, of a particular gender, a particular trade, a particular race and religion, and so forth. There is no room for qualitative differentiation, no space by which the matrix allows at the outset for a heterogeneity or general economy in which, for example, one is a field worker by day, a weaver in the evenings, and a maker of homemade cheese to be sold at market. In other words, identity fits within a matrix of information.

Food is a way in which biopower of the masses, the swinish multitude, resists quantification. In food fights, the masses demand a heterogeneity of eating habits that does not fit within a prescribed homogeneity of citizenship and ideal distributions of food. This resistance and demand can be illustrated through the debates over a substitute for bread, of which Gillray's illustration discussed earlier is one example. Potatoes and potato bread are perhaps the most famous substitutes advocated by agriculturalists. Catherine Gallagher has provided an exemplary overview of the potato-versus-wheat debates in England.[47] As for potato bread, this too is a complex subject. The ratio and contents of bread had undergone a variety of regulation for some time, as in the 1763 Act for the Making of Bread, in which the size, weight, and cost of white and wheat breads were regulated as well as labeled. Introducing potato bread complicated the bread category. The wetness of potatoes varied, as did the texture and cooking rate.

Shifting to potato bread was not a simple task. "Whimsical Expenses of Economy" in *Gentlemen's Magazine* of 1795 parodies the situation. The speaker tells a Mr. Urban that he has decided to abide by "the number of substitutes for flour which have been suggested by the ingenious Sir John Sinclair, president of the board of agriculture."[48] He then relates a long story of purchasing potatoes, ordering a home oven, and purchasing fuel for the fire, followed by his wife's various trial recipes for potato bread, with some very soggy, some burnt, others half done until "we had reduced 20lbs of potatoes to 2, and had made excellent starch of it, though we could not make bread. We had consumed half the stock of potatoes that was to serve us all winter, without getting a single loaf that was eatable."[49] The narrator tells Mr. Urban, "Never did a poor man pay so dear in order to save money and it is all owing to the cry that you and others have set up about scarcity, that I am fairly driven out of my own house, and am the laughing-stock of all my neighbours."[50] While potato bread makes sense economically as a mode of distributing food, it meets resistance in practical application—where the materiality of the food items meets preparation, tastes, and digestibility.

Even amid scarcity and a 50 percent increase in wheat prices during the blights of the 1795 and 1800 harvests, laborers demanded fine wheaten bread. As E. P. Thompson explains, "laborers accustomed to wheaten bread actually could not work—suffered from weakness, indigestion, or nausea—if forced to change to rougher mixtures."[51] Thompson uses this among other food-riot examples to explain the "delicate tissue of social norms which regulate life," which he characterizes as the moral economy of the crowd.[52] In an excellent study of shifts from fine wheat bread to coarser cereal grains, Roger Wells details resistance from working-class consumers and even the millers who knew such shifts in foodstuffs would not be palatable and would go undersold—indeed at times even risking riots.[53] In brief, the swinish multitude could demand fine wheaten bread over more coarse and indigestible substitutes because it was perceived as a right or a custom that linked the citizens within the community.

Other food resistances reveal how the restricted economy of a homogeneous diet for the nation runs afoul of the heterogeneity of stomachs and kitchens. Consider oats. They are an acceptable food in Scotland, and a number of writers correlate the hardiness of the Scots to their eating oats. More said, negatively, that oats were for animals but were digestible to Scots because of their more animal constitution. J. L. and Barbara Hammond give a more comprehensive overview of the ecology and economy of eating oats. They explain that with a diet of bread and tea, laborers in Southern England had "too delicate a digestion to assimilate the coarser cereals, and that there was, apart from climate and tradition, a very important difference between the labourer in the north and the labourer in the south."[54] There is a heterogeneity in climate, geography, and tradition and, as the Hammonds note, there is also the problem of access to milk: "Now oatmeal eaten with milk is a very different food from oatmeal taken alone, and it is clear from a study of the budgets that if oatmeal was to be acclimatized in the south, it was essential to increase the consumption of milk. But the great difference in consumption represented not a difference of demand, but of supply."[55] In brief, enclosure had fenced in (or fenced out) commons by which the laborer would be able to keep a cow. Large dairies in the south sent much of their milk supply to Bath and London. There are even complaints that the hogs had more access to milk for fattening than did the workers. So, just as eating potato breads is not a satisfactory equivalent to wheaten breads, eating oats is not equal for all laborers. People repeatedly present qualitative differences in that which is digestible. Theirs is a protest of culture and of the stomach—a resistance even at the most biological levels.

But eat one must. Just as the worker's power to sell his labor is restricted by the Settlement Act, enclosure restricted food production. Loss of common pasture lands meant forfeiting a cow, which would provide milk, cheese, and butter without a need to purchase these goods at market. The Hammonds explain:

> The loss of his cow and his produce and his common and traditional rights was rendered particularly serious to the labourer by the general growth of prices. For enclosure, which had produced the agrarian proletariat, had raised the cost of living for him. The accepted opinion that under enclosure England became immensely more productive tends to obscure the truth that the agricultural labourer suffered in his character of consumer, as well as in his character of producer, when the small farms and the commons disappeared.[56]

In short, the laborer must buy items. He does not possess the work of his brow nor the capacities for sustenance that a garden and cow supply. He cannot buy wholesale from a local farmer, as the increasingly large farms sell only to middlemen. The laborer is forced onto a particular capitalist market configured through a series of restrictions. Roger Wells summarizes the dynamics of the "improved agriculture":

> [H]eavy capital investment underpinned marked rises in agricultural productivity while increased market orientation of profit-maximising farmers came to dominate most rural communities economically. . . . Farmers' demand for labour therefore became paramount and the main source of agrarian labour's exposure to free-market forces. Workers' dependency on the market for employment was paralleled by their dependency on it as consumers, for food, fuel, clothing and housing.[57]

Such an economy restricts what constitutes economic activity, as opposed to a general economy by which the laborer with cow and commons supplements his livelihood.

In *Annals of Agriculture*, Arthur Young sympathizes with laborers who have been stripped of the commons: "The poor in these parishes may say, and with truth, all I know is that I had a cow and the Act of Parliament has taken it from me."[58] And as with cows, so too with a number of cottage industries that promoted a self-reliance outside the restricted economy of labor exchanged for wages. In place of work at home, the laborer had to work for another and make wages that in themselves were not eatable but were exchanged for goods at market. In sum, the laborer was forced into a national monetary economy. Writing in England during the ongoing movement of bodies into a wage economy, Karl Marx characterized this shift as the making of a proletariat. As Michael Hardt and Antonio Negri summarize Marx, "proletarianization was accomplished first by the enclosures of the common lands and the clearing of peasants from the estates, and then by the brutal punishment of vagabondage and vagrancy. The English peasant was thus 'free' from all previous means of subsistence . . . and made ready for the wage relation and the discipline of capitalist production."[59]

This shift from a general economy to a restricted economy is illustrated by George Willis's report printed in Young's *Annals of Agriculture*:

> The cottager who commands milk, has within himself, a daily supply of a nutrition's aliment for the purpose of his family, while another who has not these advantages out of his poor pittance, purchases at the village shop, *this black compound* of trash and inequity [tea], at the same time he empties his purse, he brings home to his miserable wife and family, a gradual and corrosive poison.[60]

The role of cows as companion species to humans has a long history even to the present. Willis's report illustrates the cow as a biopolitical animal claimed by the laborer on one side and the Act of Parliament on the other. At work here is a question of who can make claim to the animal's productivity and how such productivity is to be channeled within a cultural (and eventually a monetary) economy.

With some brevity I mark out two more examples of production and labor shifting from a general economy to a restricted economy: beer and gleaning. As seen in the introductory chapter, John Barrell has commented on the political role of the alehouse as depicted in the paintings of George

Moreland. William Cobbett's occasional hobbyhorse of beer is also worth noting. Cobbett decorates his entries of *Rural Rides* with a report of the size, quantity, and quality of beer he tastes while working up a thirst traveling across the countryside and giving speeches. He gives reports of the joyous company he meets in alehouses. Cobbett notes that with the rise in taxes for the wheat and barley and beer itself, beer making is no longer a common cottage industry. The tax money for military barracks, he comments, "came out of the people's labour; and when you hear Mr. Ellman tell the Committee of 1821, that forty-five years ago every man in his parish brewed his own beer, and that now not one man in that same parish does it . . . [you] might be able to estimate the effects of what has produced the barrack."[61] For Cobbett, taxes redistributed productivity to nonworking thieves, knaves, and nobles, but, more to the point here, beer was no longer a local, inexpensive home skill. This tradition and way of life was lost. Beer was now a commodity bought on the market.

For Cobbett, beer became synonymous with a lost abundance that in days past was shared between workers and landowners. One example is the case of Charington. While in Surrey he comes upon the workers of Squire Charington, whom he believes to be far worse off than in generations past. He begins by lamenting that laborers are paid solely on a monetary system rather than, in part, through lodging and food, as was the custom. The new system is a detriment to the workers and "gives them a living *cheaper* to him [the landlord]." Then, much like Bloomfield and contra Malthus, Cobbett uses the figure of the harvest table as a way of judging past solidarity and prosperity among workers and the landowner. Within the harvest table trope, beer over and against wine becomes a sign of past English prosperity and present French-influenced degeneracy. So similar is Cobbett's complaint and use of the harvest table to that of Bloomfield that it is worth quoting in full.

> The land produces, on average, what it always produced; but, there is a new distribution of the produce. This 'Squire Charington's father used, I dare say, to sit at the head of the oak-table along with his men, say grace to them, and cut up the meat and the pudding. He might take a cup of *strong beer* to himself, when they had none; but that was pretty nearly all the difference in their manner of living. So that *all* lived well. But, the 'Squire had many *wine-decanters* and *wine-glasses* and "a *dinner set*," and a "*breakfast set*," and "*desert knives*"; and these evidently imply carryings on and a consumption that must of necessity have greatly robbed the long oak table if it had remained fully tenanted. That long table

could not share in the work of the decanters and the dinner set. Therefore, it became almost untenanted; the labourers retreated to hovels, called cottages; and, instead of board and lodging, they got money; so little of it as to enable the employer to drink wine.[62]

In his newspaper style, he gives the feel of reportage happening spontaneously and immediately by his own encounters and stories heard. Anecdotes and hearsay are an important part of *Rural Rides* and Cobbett's rhetoric for mounting his argument. He uses incidents and reports to build a case for the livelihood of field hands, which he links to the prosperity of agriculture and the nation.

Cobbett also laments the loss of gleaning, where workers—often women and children—gathered or gleaned wheat that was not bundled in the harvest and so claimed by the landowner. Cobbett comments: "I saw several wheat stubbles from 40 rods to 10 rods. I asked one man how much wheat he had from about 10 rods. He said more than two bushels. Here is bread for three weeks or more, perhaps; and a winter's straw for the pig besides."[63] Capel Lofft—known for his patronage of Robert Bloomfield—also advocated gleaning as a tradition and common right. Yet as the price of grain rose during years of scarcity, the landowners pushed harder against the tradition and prosecuted gleaners for the wheat they labored to gather.[64] With wheat, as with milk and beer, all labor and objects become commodities within a restricted economy. The prohibition against laborers and their families gleaning from their labors was seen to work against the biblical adage "Thou shalt not muzzle the ox that treadeth out the corn" (Deuteronomy 25:4). As Thompson summarizes the dilemma, "The breakthrough of the new political economy of the free market was also the breakdown of the old moral economy of provision."[65]

As I hope these pieces of a mosaic illustrate, bodies resist quantification where biopower of the body cannot be subsumed by population, statistics, and homogenization of the biopolitical apparatus of capture. Either workers are given wheaten bread, or they and their stomachs will not work. Either a family has a cow and milk, or they will not eat oats. Either beer is accessible to laborers, or the alehouse will become a meeting ground for political discontent. Either the workers are granted the right to glean wheat, or their families will be hard-pressed to survive the winter. The heterogeneous demands of bodies weigh not only by quantification but also by a massification—a mass in excess of capture, a mass that pushes, resists, and weighs.[66] Like the possessed demon swine of the New Testament, the swinish multitude resist control.

3

On Vulnerability

Studies from Life That Ought Not to Be Copied

In his 1806 encyclopedia of images *Microcosm,* William Henry Pyne illustrates daily tasks of rural peasant life. Workers draw water from a well, they bail hay, shoe horses, tend cattle, and watch over sheep. As A. E. Santaniello's introduction explains, "The men and women depicted in *Microcosm,* those masses of English workers, led hard lives; what was hardest was that they were also silent and to most of their more fortunate compatriots, invisible. *Microcosm* was one of the first books to do for the common man the great and lasting service of making him visible."[1] The images are set out according to typical picturesque groupings and so provide professional and amateur artists with "studies from life" from which to take inspiration. Within the two-volume work, one page stands out as a unique set of images: "Slaughter-Houses" (image 3.1).[2] Although illustrating the slaughter of cattle by poleax, the artist has cleverly hidden the deadly head of the ax in each illustration. We never see the blunt mallet head of the instrument.[3] Such a lacuna haunts the moment of death. The textual commentary by Pyne's companion Gray informs the reader that these images of slaughter "ought not to be copied" by the reader using *Microcosm* to learn how to make picturesque sketches, and so Gray furthers the lacunae where the instrument of death should be. Gray insists the animals should not be copied despite the observation that "slaughtering cattle is a necessary evil."[4]

I am not interested here in the obvious animal-rights claim that empire builds itself on the flesh of animals. True as this may be, there is a more complex series of connections between the working class and the evasive depiction of animal death. This dynamic of the nonrepresentable event housed within the bucolic can be clarified through an examination of the pastoral

35

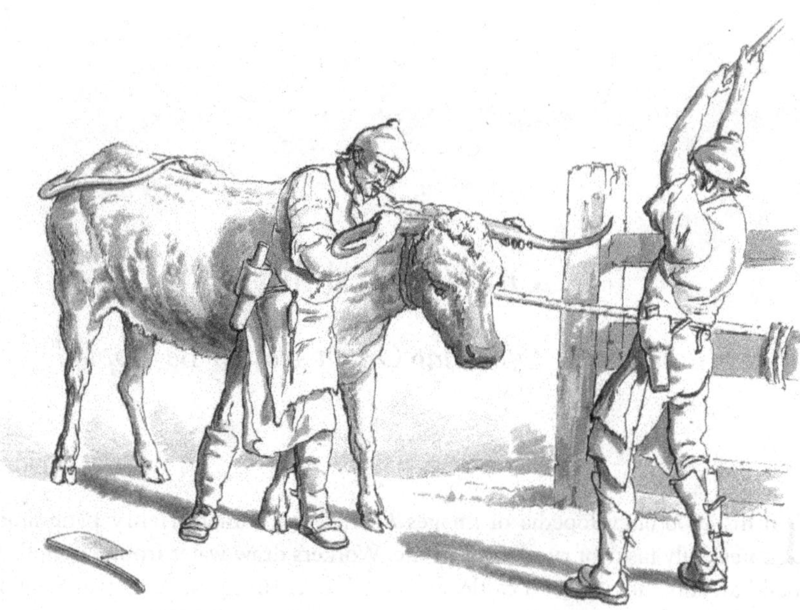

Figure 3.1. William Henry Pyne. Slaughter-Houses. *Microcosm, or, A Picturesque Delineation of the Arts, Agriculture, and Manufactures of Great Britain.* 1806. Yale Center for British Art.

mechanisms, which increase national productivity of the workers while circumscribing laborers as political subjects. The machinery of biopower at work on the material, biological, and political body of the agricultural laborer can be read through the figure of animal death. More potently, in the Agricultural Revolution, human life and labor function in the same manner as the life and labor of livestock. Human bare life and animal life are interconnected.

This chapter pursues the representation of the slaughter and death of livestock in labor-class agricultural poetry and the picturesque. During the eighteenth and early nineteenth centuries in Britain, landscape poetry and painting that self-consciously depicted the countryside often obfuscated the end result of farmhands' labors. My conjecture is that the oddities and omissions surrounding representations of livestock death are due to a discomfort over the mutual vulnerability felt between humans and animals. This is what Cary Wolfe describes as "the physical exposure to vulnerability and mortality that we suffer because we, like animals, are embodied beings."[5] It is a vulnerability particularly felt by farm laborers. Indeed, the embodiment of these "embodied beings" entails the friction of contact between human and animals in ways not common to upper classes. Animal death would remind the worker of his or her own expendability. The body of the laborer and that of the animal are often given value not in and for themselves but rather as means toward serving national prosperity. Their embodied being and daily tasks lead not to their own benefit but to their work, whose value will be appropriated by others. The death of domesticated animals is of interest because, like these animals, laborers lived within a social structure that they served but that rarely looked out for their welfare.

Before proceeding, I would like to give a word of caution. Equating laborers with animals is too facile an analogy. It is true that given their low social standing, rural laborers may well have felt their lives to be close to that of domesticated animals. Indeed, the comparison was often made, as in Timothy Nourse's *Campania Foelix, or a Discourse of the Benefits and Improvements of Husbandry* (1700), where "as with the men, *so are the Cattle*."[6] Historical specifics of the Agricultural Revolution and the technologies and techniques devised in this period provide a clearer understanding of the animal–laborer dynamic. Of interest here are the specific forces within the eighteenth and early nineteenth centuries that made vulnerability viscerally potent for laborers. This chapter begins with a series of examples of representation of livestock death and the discomfort such death invoked. It then proceeds to examine how animals and humans fit within what was termed "improved agriculture." With the rise of statistics and surveys of land, and with the enclosure movement shifting the rhetoric of land toward a wealth of the nation, the State began to govern life and to do so in a way that flattened distinctions between rural laborers and domesticated animals or at times valuing livestock over the working poor as a greater benefit to the nation.

Before detailing the relationship between animals and laborers, let us return to the opening example of Payne's image and Gray's textual commentary. Gray insists that the deaths are unsightly and asks the reader to avert his gaze:

> But let us turn from a scene which the artist has given us too lively a copy of, not to inspire us with horror, and which can only set the mind of sensibility a thinking of the hourly, indeed, the unintermitting scenes of misery, and we fear, too often of cruelty, caused by our enjoyments at table of harmless animals. Necessary they may in part be; but the less we see and think of them, the better.[7]

Despite such insistence, Gray provides a table with weights of animal carcasses sold at London's Smithfield market from 1710 to 1804 (image 3.2). The average weight of beeves of beef rose from 370 to 800 pounds, sheep from

	Cattle.	Sheep.
1731 to 1740, yearly average	83,906	564,650
1741 to 1749	74,194	559,891
1750 to 1758	75,351	623,091
1759 to 1767	83,432	615,328
1768 to 1776	89,362	627,805
1777 to 1785	99,285	687,588
1786 to 1794	101,075	707,456

Figure 3.2. William Henry Pyne. Smithfield Statistics of Slaughter. *Microcosm, or, A Picturesque Delineation of the Arts, Agriculture, and Manufactures of Great Britain.* 1806. Yale Center for British Art.

28 to 80, and lambs from 18 to 50. Gray goes on to list the number of cattle and sheep sold at Smithfield every decade from 1730 to the 1790s. Here, too, numbers increase, starting with a yearly average of 83,906 cattle and 564,650 sheep in 1730 and ending with 101,075 cattle and 707,456 sheep in 1794. At the level of statistical averages, Gray has no problem drawing dead animals. While he instructs us to "turn" from the image of "cruelty, caused by our enjoyments at table," he provides just such a table in his table of statistics of animals slaughtered. In Gray's case, his tables are numerical and so sufficiently abstract from the slaughter of the flesh on dinner tables. Indeed, as is evident in a later discussion of John Sinclair and the Board of Agriculture, statistics drove the demand for more meat.[8]

Gray is not the only one to avert his eyes from slaughter. In the very popular *The Farmer's Boy* (1800), the peasant poet Robert Bloomfield paints a bucolic picture of rustic labor throughout the seasons but creates a figuratively and rhetorically troubled picture when it comes to animal slaughter. Before proceeding to animal death, first consider how Bloomfield sets a scene of rural fecundity. Amid praise for the labor and liberty of English life, Bloomfield intertwines the life of animals, both domestic and wild. In putting his plowhorses to bed, he "pats the jolly sides of those he loves."[9] He milks the "full-charg'd udders" of the cows and "tugs o'er his pail, and chants with equal glee."[10] There is a picturesque or bucolic pleasure to his labors. Of course, Romantic-period readers would also notice the sexualized double meanings in these lines. Ploughmen and milkmaids represented wholesomeness and naturalness but also sexual abundance. As Robin Ganev explains, "The use of ploughing for bawdy purposes was elaborate and sophisticated [in poetry and ballads]. One song advises girls that ploughmen could not be trusted because 'they used so much to ploughing their seed for to sow, / That under your apron its sure for to grow.'"[11] Likewise, "milking the cow was often a metaphor for masturbation."[12] So Bloomfield's language of ploughing and milking carries with it a sexual excess or opulence:

> The full-charg'd udder yields its willing streams,
> While *Mary* sings some lover's amorous dreams;
> And crouching *Giles* beneath a neighbouring tree
> Tugs o'er his pail, and chants with equal glee

Giles is not particularly a sexualized character in the poem. However, the sexual figuration of milkmaids during the period creates a bawdy double meaning for both Mary and Giles. Cows and milkmaids seem to invoke this aspect in him, or rather he comes to occupy a particular figural position within a rural landscape.

From William Hogarth's *The Milkmaid* and Thomas Gainsborough's *Landscape with Woodcutter and Milkmaid* through to in Thomas Rowlandson's *Doctor Syntax with the Dairy Maid*, and from novels such as John Cleland's *Fanny Hill* to Thomas Hardy's *Tess of the d'Urbervilles*, milkmaids' contact with nature carries signification of wholesomeness but also sexual potency. These maids' labors involve tugging the teats of cows that have given birth. The udder as stand-in for human breast and milk as connected to human lactation bring with them both a sense of maternal care and a sexual opulence. Elizabeth Hands's "Written, Originally extempore, on seeing a Mad Heifer run through the Village where the Author lives" connects the cow as out of its proper place, or "mad," to the author, who as a female, rustic, laboring class poet is both out of place and exactly in the proper place for her poetry. In doing so, Hand plays against the rhetoric of cows and maids as sexualized figures in the landscape.[13] Moralists and reformers turned the period figuration of the potent field laborer versus the impudent urban aristocrat in a new light of promiscuity and population crisis.[14] Malthus (with moral and class prejudices) would deride the rural poor as the very cause of overpopulation. The farmhands Giles and Mary are in close proximity to animals and with them labor to make the land productive. For the likes of Malthus, this productivity, of course, would have its dark side in overpopulation that exceeded the pace of agricultural productivity. As such, death was figured within the very seeds of vegetative, animal, and human life.

Productive opulence and death are nowhere more closely brought together than in the spring scene of lambs in the field. Giles's close proximity and contact with animal life make the spring slaughter of young lambs difficult:

> Ah, fallen rose! sad emblem of their doom;
> Frail as thyself, they perish while they bloom!
> Though unoffending innocence may plead,
> Though frantic ewes may mourn the savage deed,
> Their shepherd comes, a messenger of blood,
> And drives them bleating from their sports and food.
> Care loads his brow, and pity wrings his heart,
> For lo, the murd'ring BUTCHER with his cart
> Demands the firstlings of his flock to die,
> And makes a sport of life and liberty![15]

The shepherd, who identifies his labors with English liberty and metonymically with the joy of the young lambs, has briefly revealed a darker side to the English pastoral landscape. Pointing to this passage, Donna Landry claims that "the georgic ethos rewrites the pastoral as fantasy, and itself as pragmatic reality, but it cannot exist without feeding on the very pastoral it repudiates."[16] Giles's liberty comes at the expense of other life. This realization is too much for the poet, who ends the section with patriotic phrases designed to cover the omitted scene of the animals' death:

> Down, indignation! hence, ideas foul!
> Away the shocking image from my soul!
> Let kindlier visitants attend my way,
> Beneath approaching *Summer*'s fervid ray;
> Nor thankless glooms obtrude, nor cares annoy,
> Whilst the sweet theme is *universal joy.*[17]

Once the butcher's deed is done, the poet celebrates the land's bounty epitomized in the landowner's feast with his workers. Old and young, day laborers, yeomen, and artisans join the feast, where "Plenty reigns, and from her boundless hoard" and every food is to be had that "made our great forefathers brave." But what of the lamb or the pigs and chickens featured earlier in the poem? What of the cattle? Again, the animal's death is omitted because it is an unpastoral but "necessary evil" inscribed within the feast of all that is good in England's green and pleasant land. In the feast, the mutual vulnerability Giles felt with the lambs—whose death "makes a sport of life and liberty!"—becomes a thankful celebration for having survived where others were killed. The farmhand's work is hard, but at least he has not died for it.

After stanzas of praise for the harvest table, Bloomfield changes the table arrangements. These feasts, where "The master, servant, and the merry guest, / Are equal all," have changed.[18] Those *were* the days:

> When Pride gave place to mirth without a sting;
> Ere tyrant customs strength sufficient bore
> To violate the feelings of the poor;
> To leave them distanc'd in the mad'ning race,
> Where'er Refinement shews its hated face:
> Nor causeless hated; . . . 'tis the peasant's curse,
> That hourly makes his wretched station worse;
> Destroys life's intercourse; the social plan
> That rank to rank cements, as man to man:
> Wealth flows around him, fashion lordly reigns;
> Yet poverty is his, and mental pains.[19]

Labor is not for shared benefit; rather, it is divided with a "separate table and the costly bowl."[20] It seems that it is not only the butcher who "makes a sport of life and liberty," but also the landowner who has separated himself from those who produce the bounty of his fields.[21] Bloomfield ends the scene and this section of the poem with the lines "Let labour have its due; . . . then peace is mine, / And never, never shall my heart repine."[22] One wonders what happens if labor is not given its due. Certainly the peace of the peasant would be disturbed, but would the master's peace be threatened as well? Latent in these lines is the possibility of more spilt blood, not of animals but of humans.

As a boy, Bloomfield had worked as a day laborer on his uncle's farm in the village of Honington, Suffolk. He was too small and frail to work in the fields, so he did other, more menial tasks. Eventually he left farmwork for London to apprentice under his brother as a shoemaker. It was in the city that he crafted his poetry about country life. *A Farmer's Boy* sold some 26,000 copies in three years, and with it Bloomfield became a celebrated peasant poet and the standard by which other working-class poets were measured.[23] One such poet, writing at the same time as Bloomfield, was Thomas Batchelor (also spelled Bachelor), who is compared with the more popular Bloomfield in the 1805 *Eclectic Review*. Unlike Bloomfield, who left rural life, Batchelor was a tenant farmer under the Duke of Bedford at Lidlington, Bedfordshire, about forty miles north of London.[24] Francis Russell, fifth Duke of Bedford, was a member of the Board of Agriculture, which set about surveying the nation's farms county by county to record normative and best practices and through dissemination of knowledge increase farm yields. Russell built and developed a model farm on his estate at Woburn. The annual Woburn sheepshearing, made famous by George Garrard's engraving, was a prominent regional fair for the promotion of new methods of breeding animals and improved modes of farming. The Duke was also the first president of the Smithfield Club, founded at Smithfield market and designed to improve breeds for market. An examination of Batchelor's work takes us deeply into the complex technological, economic, political, and moral forces at work in modernizing agriculture in the eighteenth and nineteenth centuries. As author of *General View of the Agriculture of the County of Bedford* for the Board of Agriculture, Batchelor was keenly aware of the role of the survey and the movement toward improvement. He generally agreed with the new agricultural methods, yet, as an examination of Batchelor's *The Progress of Agriculture; or Rural Survey* will make evident, peasants and animals alike were caught up in a modernization that did not look out for their best interests.

Much of Batchelor's poem explains how the wild and rude land has been tamed so that "around my natal soil I see / The bless'd effects of peaceful industry."[25] Patriotic "fair Freedom" gives a "generous hand" and "guards, improves, and dignifies the land."[26] The irregular ground is smoothed: "There oft the plough has turn'd the glowing sand, / The spade, the pickaxe, smooth'd the rugged land."[27] Even the "industrious peasant" has a plot "[r]ichly supplying all domestic wants" and so the laborers give thanks "to gen'rous *Russel's* name."[28] As the poem proceeds extolling the virtues of the Duke of Bedford and the Board of Agriculture's methods of improvement, it comes as little surprise that Russell's favorite livestock, the sheep, holds a pride of place. After listing the treasures of other lands, such as India's spices, Gaul's wines, and East India's sugar cane, Batchelor extols the British Isles:

> Yet thy own wealth attracts the richest stores
> With power magnetic to thy favour'd shores.
> And chief thy flocks, that crown each mountain's brow,
> And deck each vale, from these thy riches flow;
> These meet my view, innumerous grazing wide,
> Their unshorn lambs yet sporting by their side.
> Some destin'd soon, by unrelenting fate,
> To smoke on tables of the rich and great;
> but those of fine shape, and noblest size,
> Again must view the vernal year arise,
> Spread thy young progeny around the land,
> And yield their fleeces to the shearer's hand.[29]

Interesting here is that the wealth of nations does not reside foremost in the labor of its people but in the value of the country's animals: "chief thy flocks." As with Bloomfield, Batchelor provides a pastoral line about the "sporting" spring lambs. Also like Bloomfield, the lambs are slaughtered and in this case "to smoke on tables of the rich and great." It is surprising that the poet who praises Russell and the Board of Agriculture clearly marks class differences. Animals and laborers are joined in two ways in this passage. First, both create a material wealth that does not serve themselves but rather serves the rich. Second, the sheep replace humans as the "richest stores" of the nation.

Despite his praise for agricultural improvements, Batchelor realizes that the laborer's work is not his own but is used to benefit the landed:

> Still glow thy fields in summer's fruitful ray,
> Thy harvests flourish, all thy meads are gay;
> But not for me fair Nature spreads her store,
> Life's smiling prospects must be mine no more!
>
> . . .
>
> Monopoly has rear'd her gorgon head
> To strike the source of rural comforts dead![30]

The lambs give their life for the tables of the rich, and the laborers give their toil to the same end. Batchelor's *General View of the Agriculture of the County of Bedford* provides an assessment of farms and labor that ultimately will solidify the power of those who hold a monopoly on the land. His poem as a "Rural Survey" is yet another mode of counting the landed's wealth and mapping the trajectory of prosperity from raw materials and labor to seats of power.

Greatest among the raw materials that build the wealth of the nation are its livestock, who become more valuable than the laborers. Batchelor is not simply using a rhetorical flourish or pastoral trope in calling sheep the "chief" treasure of the nation. From the mid-eighteenth century well into the nineteenth, tenant farmers, day laborers, and commoners were moved off of arable land, which was then used to pasture livestock, most commonly sheep. Despite the Duke of Bedford's investment in sheep, Batchelor laments the practice of clearing the land of its people and replacing them with animals:

> Green pastures spread where harvests wont to smile,
> who change for herds, the life-supporting grain,
> With *woolly tribes* displace the reaper train,
> Who build a *palace* for the wealthier few,
> But drive to squallid [sic] huts the *ruin'd* crew;[31]

Through a poetic syntactic chiasmus, Batchelor shows how sheep replace humans and grazing replaces harvesting. The *"woolly tribes"* of animals are put in place of the human tribes of laborers. Rather than driving sheep across the land, the landed "drive to squallid huts" the rural poor. These sheep are so valued that they are depicted by Batchelor as the means by which the British raised themselves from barbarism:

> Yet sure yon patient, woolly tribes demand
> The generous care of man's providing hand;
> Unless for them his shivering limbs must bare
> Th' enfeebling rigours of th' inclement year.
> Or, wrapt in skins, the human form debase,
> To a vile semblance of the savage race;[32]

In this poetic chiasmus, humans provide for the sheep, but it is the sheep that through their wool lift humans from "form debase" of wearing animal skins. In light of sheep replacing people on the landscape, the poet's description that "the woolly tribes *demand* the generous care" of humans increasingly sounds like a demand made by the landed and imposed on the laborer through the medium of the sheep. The Scottish Shetland, along with the rise of the Spanish Merino in Britain, increased the value of the British wool industry and made sheep on the land more valuable and easier to manage than tenanted farmers.

Of course, sheep in themselves are demanding in that domesticated livestock require care. As the grazier and author William Youatt observed for the Society for the Diffusion of Useful Knowledge:

> Cattle are like most other animals, the creatures of education and circumstances. We educate them to give us milk, and to acquire flesh and fat . . . when he has lost the wild freedom of the forest, and become the slave of man, without acquiring the privilege of being his friend, or receiving instruction from him, instinct languishes, without being replaced by the semblance of reason. But when we press him into our immediate service . . . he rapidly improves upon us; he is, in fact, altogether a different animal; when he receives a kind of culture at our hands, he seems to be enlightened with a ray of human reason, and warmed with a degree of human affection.[33]

The domesticated animal requires care precisely because humans have domesticated it; the animals have "lost the wild freedom of the forest" in exchange for "a kind of culture at our hands." Humans have created the labor that the woolly tribe demands. The exact nature of these demands depends not simply on the animal but also on the humans, whose selective breeding changes the nature of the animal and its needs. For example, when King George III began the rearing and experimental breeding of Spanish Merino sheep on his model farm at Windsor, he signaled a change in how the animal would be used.[34] He shifted slightly what sort of commodities would be gleaned from the animal. While many British breeds yield medium-grade wool along with some respectable meat, the Merino (and to lesser degree the Shetland) dominated the discourse on agriculture from the late eighteenth century onward. In summary, breeding practices promoted by the gentry fashioned the sort of demands the animals made upon the laboring class, including replacing farmers with sheep even on arable lands, tending and feeding livestock (including diverting land for human food to land for animal foods), and increasing the British wool industry.

In Scotland, the replacement of humans with sheep was called "the clearances." As Batchelor mentions, such clearance occurred throughout Britain; however, its effects were particularly devastating in Scotland, which had seen changes in land management throughout the century after the Act of Union. In 1822, Major-General David Stewart recorded the effects of the clearances on the land, animals, and people of Scotland in *Sketches of the Character, Manners, and Present State of the Highlanders of Scotland*. His descriptions arose from a request by his commanding officer in Scotland to provide a history of the people and terrain. Stewart supplemented his own recollections with those of other officers, including some who served in Scotland as early as the 1760s. Throughout the eighteenth century, Scotland was an experiment in military occupation that included building roads, bridges, and forts to bring the wayward Scots into the fold of the British nation.

Although the pastureland could be used for cultivation, farming required more capital and manpower than did the tending of livestock: "That the pasture was more easily managed; that with ten men and twenty dogs, they would take care of all the sheep and cattle in the glen, which, under cultivation, supported 643 persons."[35] Stewart gives numerous examples of the working poor run off tenant land. Occasionally they have enough time to pull up the boards of their cottages and move to the coast. At other times the houses are burned and the families are left homeless and forced off the land. As with much of the English control over the Highlands, a new, "enlightened" system was imposed to increase productivity and to break the Scots of their independence and traditions. Stewart recounts:

> After the new system of managing lands and laying out farms had commenced in the Highlands, the ancient occupiers and cultivators were often overlooked by those who undertook to new-model

gentlemen's estates. *Their* future happiness or misery formed no part of the new plans, and seemed as much disregarded as the fate of the ancient breed of horses and sheep. The old Highlanders were considered unfit for the new improvements.[36]

Humans and animals that have developed alongside one another on the land have been replaced with "new improvements" in farming and breeding. The disregard for Scottish breeds is part of a larger rewriting of agriculture. Breeding of animals indicates a way of life on the land. The number of animals and their uses are determined by a way of thinking about agriculture that has unfolded over time. Usually sheep grazed on land with soil too poor or rocky or inaccessible for farming. This delimited the number of animals. Likewise, the type of livestock (cattle, sheep, or hogs) and their size depended on the ecology of the landscape, the amount and types of food available for humans and animals, and the needs of people for milk or meat or wool. Just as Scottish animals were disregarded as part of an inefficient ancient system, so too the Highland farmer was considered unproductive. The humans and animals together materially signify a way of life. As the "enlightened" live-stock edged out "the ancient breed," so too a way of life, a human–animal ecology, transformed.

The Scottish politician and agricultural writer Sir John Sinclair played an important role in changing Highland agriculture. Sinclair's background proves representative of the shifts from an older mode of government and farming to an "improved" plan. He was the son of George Sinclair of the Earls of Caithness in the very northern mainland of Scotland. John Sinclair studied at the University of Edinburgh and then at Glasgow, where he was a pupil of Adam Smith. The management of national productivity evident in Smith's *Wealth of Nations* (1776) is manifest in Sinclair's own work. Because of Caithness's rocky terrain, he focused on sheep production on his property, first trying five hundred Cheviot on his land and then increasing the number to six thousand. Then he set out to improve the wool of the native Shetland to be competitive with the Cheviot. In 1791, he established a sheep-shearing festival at Queensferry and at the same time formed the Society for the Improvement of British Wool.[37] His material, political, and rhetorical investment in sheep helped further the clearances. As recorded in the *Biographical Dictionary of Eminent Scotsmen*, Sinclair claimed: "Of all the means . . . of bringing a mountainous district to a profitable state, none is so peculiarly well calculated for that purpose as the rearing of a valuable breed of sheep. A small proportion alone . . . of such a description of country can be fit for grain; and in regard to cattle, for every pound of beef that can be produced in a hilly district, three pounds of mutton can be obtained, and there is the wool into the bargain."[38] Eventually, sheep occupied not only the hilly districts but the arable land as well, and brought landowners greater prosperity and agricultural prominence than would be obtained by leasing land to tenant farmers.

While Sinclair and his fellow agriculturalists, such as Arthur Young and Francis Russell (the Duke of Bedford), consider variables of agriculture and their effects in a general sense, the working-class laborer feels the material events of such regulation. It is rather standard fare for agricultural improvers to deride farmers for their backward practices and for not adopting innovation. The resistance to innovation can more properly be understood as a problem of vulnerability. If crops fail or livestock do not fatten on a model farm, the wealthy landowner loses little. By contrast, the tenant farmer trusts a tradition that has been tried on his particular locale and soil amid varying weather over decades rather than gamble his crops and livestock on innovation. Agricultural innovators can think in terms of "forecasts, statistical estimates, and overall measures," while tenant farmers—particularly the less wealthy sort—and day laborers are tied to their particular patch of earth.[39] These laborers are more concerned with immanent vulnerability than with the abstract value of agriculture as promoting the "safety and independence of the kingdom."[40]

It is not that gentlemen agriculturalists and innovators are unaware of the specificity of their crops and livestock. Indeed, some, such as Bakewell and Townsend, pay close attention to the details of their sheep and turnips, respectively. However, these details are understood and fashioned through the technologies of biopower. By contrast, the members of the laboring class, who tend to crops and livestock, have a visceral connection to the animals through their bodily labor and daily contact. Their connection to the animal is through physicality and vulnerability. Anxieties over animal death manifest in the picturesque and in select labor-class poetry reflect this mutual vulnerability between the workers and the livestock. They share "the physical exposure to vulnerability and mortality that we suffer because we, like animals, are embodied beings."[41] The argument of a shared animality is based not on the animal's capabilities or on that of humans but on a mutual fragility. This same nonpower provokes Jeremy Bentham's question, "Can they suffer?," which establishes a moral relationship between humans and animals not based on ability or productivity but on an incapacity to act.[42]

The capacity to suffer is a potent element of Robert Burns's poetry. Much can be made of how the poet links the fate of the Scottish people to the death and resurrection of rye in "John Barleycorn." Ploughed down, cudgeled, crushed by stones, his blood becomes the liquid that pours through the Scotsman until "a man forget his woe" and John Barleycorn's "great posterity / Ne'er fail in old Scotland!"[43] Burns connects the people not only to the crops but also to a variety of animals. Best known, perhaps, is "To a Mouse, On turning her up in her nest with the plough" (1785). As winter comes and the fields are barren, the mouse finds a home in the stubble of the field. The narrator's plough upturns the nest, "proving foresight may be ain; / The best-laid schemes of mice an men / Gang aft agley."[44] The speaker addresses the mouse and explains that if it feels pain, consider the worse fate of the laborer:

> Still thou art blest, compar'd wi me
> The present only toucheth thee:
> But, Och! I backward cast my e'e.
> On prospects drear!
> An' forward, tho' I canna see,
> I guess an' fear![45]

The forward and backward glances of the laborer reflect the uncertainty of his fate and the fate of his crops. The temporal glance is doubled by a physical look backward and forward as he aligns his plow to create evenly spaced and equally deep furrows in the soil. The physical act of his plowing coincides with his anxiety over future crops and his ability to feed himself and his family.[46] The mouse and human are aligned in their vulnerability, but because of his capacity for forethought, the human feels the anxiety more intensely.

The odd singularity of details in Burns's encounter with a field mouse reveals a particular intensity and affect in the lives of the working poor. From lacunae in representing death to anxious moments of maintaining a livelihood, representations of farm animals (or, with Burns's mouse, animals on the farm) reveal a larger set of forces at work on beasts and citizens alike. Laborers were often incapable of directly challenging the construction of biopower during the rise and reach of British nationalism; however, they could deflect or adversely reflect these powers through representing the state of affairs for themselves and the animals that were their responsibility and their livelihood.

4

Wonder as Resistance

Sheep, Fairies, and James Hogg the Ettrick Shepherd

Goin' home, late last night
Suddenly I got a fright
Yeah I looked through a window and surprised what I saw
A fairy with boots and dancin' with a dwarf,
All right now!
Yeah, fairies wear boots and you gotta believe me
Yeah I saw it, I saw it, I tell you no lies
Yeah, fairies wear boots and you gotta believe me
I saw it, I saw it with my own two eyes.

—Black Sabbath, "Fairies Wear Boots"

The *Black Sabbath* song "Fairies Wear Boots" is a countercultural marker of resistance.[1] As Ozzy Osborne, who sees the fairies, repeatedly pleads, "you got to believe me." Knowing the singer's antics, why do we have to believe him? He wants our belief, because to believe him is to cross over to the other side, another world where there are fairies, and these things and much more are possible. And you have to believe him because—having seen the doctor—the narrator worries he is losing his mind. If no one else sees or believes in these fairies, then he is stuck in his own hallucinatory, psychedelic mind world. If others believe, then we are all in this magical world together.

Of course, this is where James Hogg the Ettrick Shepherd comes in. His tales of gothic witches and fairies are not quaint entertainment for the reading public. Rather, they are a particular Scotland that is not the Scotland of the English, not the Scotland of reason—and not of its companion the rational, economic man. It is the other Scotland, which has been fading under the "light" and "civilization" and English conquest and British colonization. It is no mistake that Jane Bennett picks up on this in *Enchantment of Modern Life*, where she delineates modernists' belief in moments of wonder as a curative to modern life and its encroachments, not only technological encroachments but also more sinister psychological intrusions.[2] One buys into civilization by believing it, and only then do its technologies make sense. Conversely, if one buys into fairies wearing boots, then one has established a realm to which the modern world does not have access. As chapter 2 on docile numbers and stubborn bodies points out, there are communities or "multitudes" that do not want to be subsumed under a modern Enlightenment notion of community. This chapter on Hogg, shepherds, and fairies furthers this contrast.

James Hogg fashions a particular line of resistance using tales of fairies and witches and stories about the lives of shepherds far from the cultural center of Edinburgh. The fairy and witch stories provide a particular way of seeing. In pairing these "superstitions" with the life of shepherds, this chapter links a variety of Hogg's rural tales as biopolitical resistance against modes of co-opting human and animal bodies into productivity for the rising nation-state. Hogg finds ways of resisting the homeostasis that benefits the nation but is detrimental to traditions in Scottish rural life. Wonder produced in Hogg's tales signals a way of dwelling that is incompatible with national "progress." The stories refuse the fashioning of an isomorphic national space and instead place locales across Scotland as heterotopic communities not to be subsumed under the homeostasis and homogeny of a unified Britannia.[3]

Hogg's maternal grandfather was said to be the last man in the Borders to speak with fairies.[4] Indeed, Hogg knew the world of fairies, if not directly then from his immediate family. Hogg claimed to be born into a family whose ancestors were witches, the most famous of whom was Lucy Hogg, whose contest with a warlock ended her life.[5] His mother, Margaret Laidlaw, knew a number of ballads and tales, some of which they shared with Walter Scott for his *Minstrelsy of the Scottish Border* (1802–3).

Scott's success with *Minstrelsy of the Scottish Border* provides an audience and impetus for Hogg's retelling of tales and fashioning new of ones. But Hogg's style is markedly different. Hogg criticized Scott for making the Scottish Border ballads too English—which is to say, he made them less oral (with transgressions and organic evolution of versions of the tales over generations) and more digestible for a reading audience.[6] Scott toned down dialect to make the stories readable to an English audience, and he avoided the more politically overt stories. Hogg's mother, Margaret Laidlaw, famously told Scott, "There was never ane o' my sangs prentit till ye prentit them your-sell, an' ye hae spoilt them a'thegither. They war made for singing, and no' for reading; and they're nouther right spelled nor right setten down."[7] Indeed, one of the distinctive differences between Scott and Hogg is that the former sees ballads as a past to be preserved in print, while Hogg considers the oral tradition as living and ongoing alongside written culture.

Scott frames the Scottish past as an antiquarian and places social and political differences with England safely to rest in decades past. Meanwhile, Hogg's tales remain vibrant possibilities for a uniquely Scottish identity over and against assimilation into Britain. Critic Murray Pittock is particularly eloquent in pointing out these differences, and most poignantly in *The Invention of Scotland*, where he explains:

> Scott is himself a seductive historian. By rendering the clash of [Scottish] nationalist against Unionist . . . as one of emotion versus reason, id against ego, he creates an idea of history as intellectual or personal development. As Scott's characters become more rational, they leave behind emotional responses to things. One of the premises of this development is that Scottish patriotism is emotive and therefore primitive, overtaken by the "rational" decision to make Britain one nation. This idea has provided many damaging allegations about the backward-looking nature of Scottish patriotism.
>
> Scott's view of Scotland emphasizes the beneficial necessity of change. In doing so, it promotes two ideas: the inadequacy of Scottish patriotism in coping with historical change, and the incompetence of Scots in ruling themselves (due to their historic divisions).[8]

Hogg's works are more than nostalgic stories about a past Scotland still lingering at the outskirts of the progressive cities. They are modes of seeing, living, thinking, and dwelling heterogeneous to Scott's ides of Unionist progress.

Given that the prolific Hogg wrote a great number of ballads, tales, verse, and prose stories, a small, illustrative sample will have to suffice. A less well-known short work, but one exemplary of my point, is "The Dreadful Story of Macpherson" in *Winter Evening Tales* (1820). Major Macpherson and his associates set out on a hunting expedition in the Grampian hills (a large swath of forest south of Inverness in the Highlands). The setting is described as follows:

> Many are the scenes of wild grandeur and rugged deformity which amaze the wanderer in the Grampian deserts; but none of them surpasses this [the mountains between Athol and Bedenoch] in

wildness and still solemnity. No sound salutes the listening ear, but the rushing torrent, or the broken eldritch bleat of the mountain goat. The glens are deep and narrow, and the hills steep and somber, and so high, that their grizly [sic] summits appear to be wrapped in the blue veil that canopies the air. But it is seldom that their tops can be seen; for dark clouds of mist often rest upon them for several weeks together in summer . . . and during the winter they are abandoned entirely to the storm. Then the flooded torrents, and rushing wreaths of accumulated snows, spend their fury without doing harm to any living creature; and the howling tempest raves uncontrolled and unregarded.

Into the midst of this sublime solitude did our jovial party wander in search of their game.[9]

What follows is a sort of horror story where the gleeful party is out of its depth and is confronted by bad omens and the wrath of a powerful supernatural force.

Things begin well enough for the Major and his group: "They were highly successful [in their hunt]. The heath cock was interrupted in the middle of his exulting whirr, and dropped lifeless on his native waste; the meek ptarmigan fell fluttering among her gray crusted stones, and the wild-roe foundered in the correi [cirque]. The noise of the guns, and the cheering cries of the sportsmen, awakened those echoes that had so long slept silent." The party wielding death and joy in the hunt appears incongruous with the sublime surroundings, where even the wild torrents of water cascading from the mountains "spend their fury without doing harm to any living creature." The story makes clear that the animals are native to the land and emblems of the terrain. The killing of the native animals by these "invaders" in the woods and the sounds of guns awaken "echoes that had so long slept silent." The meaning of these awakened "echoes" is unclear but seems ominous. Only then does the narrator tell us that Major Macpherson was despised by the common people of the land for his "extreme cruelty and injustice in raising recruits in that country" (presumably to fight in the Napoleonic wars, although the tale has few historic markers). He was otherwise considered a socially well-connected and "respectable character"—at least among the gentlemen class with whom he shared the hunt.[10]

To add to the omens foreboding ill, a young man of "mysterious appearance" arrives suddenly and talks harshly to the major, at which point Macpherson's mood changes from mirth to trepidation. Nevertheless, he gathers his hunting party again, and despite ill weather he insists on hunting in the forest of Glenmore. The hunters never return. A search party finds their dead bodies mangled and scattered: "It was a scene of wo [sic], lamentation, and awful astonishment, none being able to account for what had happened; but it was visible that it had not been effected by any human agency. The bothy [rustic shelter] was torn from its foundations, and scarcely a vestige of it left—its very stones were all scattered . . . there was one huge corner stone in particular, which twelve men could scarcely have raised, that was tossed to a considerable distance." As ominous as this story is, the ending is even more haunting. "In every mountainous district in Scotland, to this day, a belief in supernatural agency prevails, in a greater or less degree. Such an awful dispensation as the above was likely to rekindle every lingering spark of it."[11] Such a conclusion makes Hogg's world of spirits and superstition insistently alive rather than part of Scott's antiquarian past.

The Macpherson story is an interesting contrast to the encounter with a fisherman in the third chapter of "The Shepherd's Calendar" in *Winter Evening Tales*. Unlike Macpherson, the fisherman is a caretaker of the land who minds laws and customs that allow salmon to spawn and regenerate their schools (as long as poachers do not get to them first). The narrator describes this fisherman as simple and honest yet with a particular wisdom that goes undervalued: "I soon found, that though this hind had something in his manner and address the most uncultivated I had ever seen, yet his conceptions of such matters as came within the sphere of his knowledge were pertinent and just. He sung old songs, told us strange stories of witches and apparitions, and related many anecdotes of the pastoral life, which I think extremely curious, and wholly unknown to the literary part of the community. . . . He loved to talk of sheep, of dogs, and of *the lasses*, as he called them; and conversed with his dogs in the same manner as he did with any of the other guests."[12] These two stories contrast modes of comportment in the landscape: one with an attitude of conquest and one of respect for the place and its traditions.

Much like the supernatural spirit in the Grampian Mountains, fairies and brownies and witches in Hogg's tales function often, although not always, as unpredictable correctives to authorities. These beings are licensed by their very nature to play by rules that differ from civil law and reason. In "The Brownie of the Black Haggs" from *Shepherd's Calendar* (1829, first published in Blackwood's *Edinburgh Magazine* 1818), the lady of a manor house acts as a particularly cruel and "inexorable tyrant" who "quarreled with her servants, often cursing them, striking them, and turning them away; especially if they were religious."[13] One day the lord of the house hires a small and lithe servant who proceeds to pester, prod, and confound the mistress. Every ill deed she schemes for him rebounds upon her and her family. People begin to speculate: "Some thought he was a mule, between a Jew and an ape; some a wizard, some a kelpie, or a fairy, but most of all, that he was really and truly a Brownie." Eventually he leaves the manor, but the lady is so bent on revenge that, "in spite of locks and keys, and watching and waking, the Lady of Wheelhope soon made her escape and eloped after him. The attendants, indeed, would have made oath that she was carried away by some invisible hand, for that it was impossible she could have escaped on foot."[14] The brownie appears to an elderly peasant couple. He carries in tow the Lady of Wheelhope, who is manifestly haggard and abused. The supernatural creature explains:

> I came to do you a service. Here, take this cursed, wretched woman, whom you style your lady, and deliver her up to the lawful authorities, to be restored to her husband and her place in society. She is come upon one that hates her, and never said one kind word to her in his life, and though I have beat her like a dog, still she clings to me, and will not depart, so enchanted is she with the laudable purpose of cutting my throat. . . . Take her. Claim the reward [from the lord] in full, and your fortune is made.[15]

Through the brownie, the servants of Wheelhope have their revenge upon the abusive Lady, and an elderly couple is made rich by claiming the reward money for her return. As she is "restored to her husband and her place in society," the wretchedness of society is exposed through "this cursed, wretched woman," who serves as a metonymic part for the whole.

Like the Macpherson tale and "The Brownie," Hogg's poem "The Witch of Fife" has a political punch line. When an old man asks his wife why she looks so worn down, a fast-paced and spirited story ensues in which the wife tells her husband that she is a witch who has been up at nights dancing with fairies and animals in the woods and traveling vast distances by magical transport. One night the old man watches his wife and learns her spells and uses them to follow her. Unfortunately for him, he is found the next morning by "five rough Englishmen" as he is passed out on a hillside. Apprehended for pillaging the bishop's vault and drinking the bishop's wine, the old man is sentenced to be burned. When the fire is lit, his wife flies to him in the form of a bird and aids him in a spell of escape. He takes to the air and

> He lukit back to the Carlisle men,
> As he borit the norlan sky;
> He noddit his heide, and gae ane grin
> But he nevir said gude-bye.
>
> They vanisht far i' the liftis blue wale,
> Nae maire the English saw,
> But the auld manis lauche [laugh] cam on the gale,
> With a lang and loud gaffa.[16]

The superstitious powers of the old Scottish couple allow them to overcome the rough English and even plunder the bishop's vault and drink wine. Church and class and nationhood are set topsy-turvy in this tale.

While it may be unclear if fairies do wear boots, we "got to believe" Hogg if we are to access a world that is counter to the narrative of progress put forward under Unionism. Recall that the Lady of Wheelhope "was carried away by some invisible hand." And Macpherson's hunting party encounters an equally devastating invisible and inhuman hand. These incidents are set directly against Adam Smith's "invisible hand" of capitalism and an Enlightenment civilization where the Lady of Wheelhope has her "place in society," and Macpherson exerts "extreme cruelty and injustice in raising recruits" for Britain, and the bishop of Carlisle drinks his stores of wine.

While Britain uses the Enlightenment tropes of reason, civilization, and progress to banish the traditional life-world of the Scots, these tales of superstition expose the barbarity of authority. Or, as Walter Benjamin says in "Thesis VII on the Philosophy of History": "There is no document of civilization which is not at the same time a document of barbarism."[17] From the point of view of those who told such tales and felt political forces brought to bear on their agrarian laborers, reason proves unreasonable and civilization is barbaric. So while from the perspective of the civil world the tales of fairies and brownies seem irrational, from the perspective of the world in which there are fairies, not to believe in them would be nonsensical. While the force of reason pushes out of bounds and to the margins all that is unreasonable according to its own terms, what Enlightenment reason does not count on is a counterblow from seemingly irrational folktales. Rural communities use these tales as a force over and against the island of reason (and its urban centers); the rational community becomes overwhelmed by the greater dominion of a-rational, superstitious folk who follow a different logic and line of thinking.[18] This struggle over a way of life and modes of dwelling can be placed in contemporary theoretical terminology as a resistance to what

Hardt and Negri (following Marx) call formal and real subsumption. While formal subsumption brings workers and their labor into the folds of capital, real subsumption invests "not only the economic or only the cultural dimension of society but rather the social *bios* itself."[19] The struggles in Hogg's tales are between ways of life and living well (as *bios*).

To understand the ways in which the invisible hand of superstition works over and against the invisible hand of the market and to further the implications of a fairy world, it is worth turning to another theme in Hogg's work—sheep, shepherds, and dogs. The shift from fairies to sheep may seem abrupt, but for a rural Scotsman they were part of the same modes of dwelling in the period. In Hogg's shepherds' tales, he makes visible both sorts of invisible hands (superstition and capitalist) on the landscape through the farmer's folk wisdom and the political forces attempting to shape agricultural land under the rubric of improvement. Hogg was born in Ettrick and worked as a farmhand and then as a shepherd from an early age and through much of his adult life, particularly in the Yarrow Valley. It was not until 1810, at the age of forty, that he moved to Edinburgh, having started a career publishing ballads and original tales, and then helped William Blackwood launch his *Blackwood's Edinburgh Monthly Magazine*, in which Hogg published a range of rural stories. John Wilson based his character Ettrick Shepherd on Hogg for his *Blackwood* series *Noctes Ambrosianae* (a satiric set of conversations about urban and rural Scottish life and politics).

Before launching into the complexity of the biopolitics of agricultural improvement, it is useful to understand Hogg's perspective from the point of view of his shepherd characters. "Storms," the gripping opening story in *The Shepherd's Calendar*, sets a tone and frames the rest of the work in the collection. The narrator, who is a stand-in for Hogg himself, gives a factual account from personal recollections of a severe snowstorm on January 24, 1794. The narrator develops a thick description of the atmospherics. In a long paragraph, he makes careful note of the light, snow, cloud, and wind conditions of the day preceding the storm and the folk wisdom of his uncle, who helps him read the clouds and predict the weather. He describes what he can see from the heights of particular hills and how the storm unfolds over time. When the storm finally does hit with fury, he and his fellow shepherds venture into the landscape to find and retrieve their sheep, which his master had pastured the day before.

The snow falls with such intensity that the men can barely see each other as they walk in a single file toward the fields. After a few false starts, the narrator as lead shepherd successfully finds the sheep, and the party moves them to better grounds. Throughout, he navigates the terrain despite the blinding conditions: "I was not the least afraid of losing my way for I knew all the declivities of the hills so well that I could have come home with my eyes bound up and indeed long ere I got home they were of no use to me." The shepherd is briefly caught in "utter amazement" and "enchantment," as if the storm were a judgment and a curse. Only with great effort does he "escape from the fairy vision."[20] The next day, with the help of his faithful sheepdog, Sparkie, he recovers the rest of the sheep, which are buried in the snow. Most are found because of the dog's keener sense of smell; "the greater part of these [sheep] would have been lost had it not been for the voluntary exertions of Sparkie."[21] The narrator then describes with some detail how Sparkie finds the sheep and digs into the snow to mark their location for the shepherds to pull them out. All told, this was no average snowstorm, and by the narrator's count seventeen shepherds died in the region, thirty were found insensible, and farmers lost on average sixty to eighty sheep each.

But why this long account of rescuing sheep in a storm? It is more than a tale of rural adventures for urban readers and more than nostalgia for an imagined pastoral life.[22] Using detailed and thick description, Hogg attempts to make viscerally available to the reader the invisible forces in the remote hills, pastures, and forests of Scotland. Storms, and particularly this snowstorm, are an unseen power unfolding over time. The signs of its coming appear for those who know how to read the weather. Either one believes these signs (told like fairy tales from generation to generation) and can divine them, or one does not believe and cannot predict the coming storm. The imperative to see these unseen forces has real consequences: "You got to believe me." Interestingly, the narrator is on his way to a book club meeting when, upon reading the ill omens of the sky, he turns back. The narrator finds himself between worlds: that of books and civil culture and the world of sheep, pastures, and ill weather. Despite his inclination to go to the book meeting and despite "bringing reason" to aid his desire, he judges wisely and turns back to his fields to tend the animals. Rather than listening to "reason" or rationalization, he abides by the world in which invisible forces leave signs in the sky as warnings of impending destruction. In making this decision, the narrator is akin to the salmon fisher discussed earlier and in contrast with Macpherson, who does not heed the signs in the landscape.

The second half of the story, retelling finding sheep the day after the storm, also has invisible signs manifest to the sheepdog. Sheep scents are there in the snow but unseen and undetectable by humans. They are as invisible as fairy worlds. Yet, aided by Sparkie, the shepherds find their livestock. The dog is a trusted companion species and a furry technological prosthetic for the shepherds.[23] It is not just their skills of smelling that make these dogs valuable. Notably, a well-trained dog is an excellent herder. As Hogg explains in his essay "Dogs" for *The Shepherd's Calendar*, Scotland and sheep are possible only because of sheepdogs:

> A single shepherd and his dog will accomplish more in gathering a stock of sheep from a Highland farm, than twenty shepherds could do without dogs; and it is a fact, that, without this docile animal, the pastoral life would be a mere blank. Without the shepherd's dog, the whole of the mountainous land in Scotland would not be worth a sixpence. It would require more hands to manage a stock of sheep, gather them from the hills, force them into houses and folds, and drive them to markets, than the profits of the whole stock would be capable of maintaining.[24]

Think for a moment about this claim. Later I explain the biopolitical implications of Hogg's statement, but for now it is enough to note that the Scotland of the 1820s is only possible because of dogs. Without them, the costs in human labor would make sheep husbandry unsupportable, and Scotland would subsist on a mode of farming prevalent a century earlier, before agricultural improvement and the introduction of new breeds of sheep. It is also notable that the chapter on dogs appears before the chapter on women, or, as Hogg says with both humor and seriousness, "utility should always take precedence of pleasure. A shepherd may be a very able, trusty, and good shepherd, without a sweetheart—better, perhaps, than with one. But what is he without a dog? A mere post, sir—a non-entity as a shepherd—no better than one of the grey stones upon the side of his hill."[25] Hogg is pointing out a set of visible and invisible ties in a community and the politics and the biology that make these relationships work. He admits that "it may appear a singular perversion of the order of nature to put the dogs before the lasses."[26] In doing so, he makes visible a community that sets up its labor and relations such that dogs become valued over women and their domestic and agricultural labor. The stability of productive livestock and their utility precedes human companionship and reproductivity.

It is briefly worth noting that even the sheep bring with them sets of relations that are not readily visible except to those who live within rural communities. Hogg discusses these traits in a brief essay called "Sheep" in *Tales and Sketches of the Ettrick Shepherd* (1837). He explains that sheep have "a strong attachment to the place of their nativity," have a "natural affection . . . the instances that might be mentioned are without number," and "that the more inhospitable the land is of which they feed, the greater their kindness and attention to their young."[27] He provides incredible stories to illustrate each of these points, such as a sheep who traveled from Glenn-Lyon to Harehope (well over a hundred miles) to return to his native land. Do we "Got to believe"? This rather unexceptional essay by Hogg brings the reader into a life-world that includes characteristics of animals that exceed human capacity and how agricultural communities abide with such nonhuman worldings.

Given the economic and agricultural structure of Scotland in the early and mid-1800s, the region relied on its shepherds. With such dependence on shepherds, they had potential—usually never exercised—as a formidable political group. Their skill was in such demand that Lowland shepherds were well paid to work pastures and train men in the Highlands and shepherds from northern England traveled to Scotland for better job prospects. In the story "Rob Dodds" in *The Shepherd's Calendar*, a landowner jests with his wise old shepherd: "There is no class of men in this kingdom so independent as you shepherds. You have your sheep, your cow, your meal and potatoes; a regular income of sixteen to thirty pounds yearly, without a farthing of expenditure, except for shoes; for your clothes are all made at home. If you would even wish to spend it, you cannot get an opportunity, and every one of you is rich."[28] While being "rich" is surely a jest and potatoes held no value compared with bread, the landowner has a veiled point in his satire. Shepherds have the basic staples of sustenance and can live "off the grid" of civil, cultural, and economic commerce. Yet Scotland, and indeed Britain, needs the Scottish shepherd (and his dog). During the early 1800s, under the rubric of improvement and national productivity, agricultural production shifts from each area of the nation, growing and maintaining all its needs (and so being independent) to regional specialization, whereby each area produces select agricultural goods intensively for the rest of the country. Scotland becomes a primary site for sheep, which supply raw materials for the wool industry in northern England.

Scotland and particularly the Highlands is the last region of Britain to experience the shift from traditional farming to regional production for the whole of the country. The scale of the shift and the rapidity of the change were devastating to whole towns, which disappeared as their way of life dramatically changed. This was the time of the Clearances. Prior to this shift, traditional farming was generally mixed use, along with some cattle rearing and droving for markets in northern England. Landowners leased out plots to peasant farmers. During a population growth in the eighteenth century, the increasing subdivision of land across generations created an anxiety that the soil could not produce enough to provide for the people living on it, much less sustain the increasing urban populations. After 1745 and the battle of Culloden, Scotland was increasingly folded into the Union. With the union came the forces of what was known as agricultural improvement, and thus came the sheep.

The sheep began occupying niches of Scotland as various landowners experimented with livestock. Then, over a span of forty years, sheep spread across Scotland like an inevitable and relentless force. W. J. Carlyle has carefully mapped the migration over time in his essay "The Changing Distribution of Breeds of Sheep in Scotland, 1795–1965."[29] Scotland has a native sheep, the Dunface, but it produces short wool and does so sparingly. In the mid- and late eighteenth century, two breeds were brought in from England, the Cheviot and the Blackface, also commonly called the Linton or Forest breed. Both Cheviot and Blackface are long-wool breeds whose wool was in demand. Most importantly, they can weather harsh climates and rough terrain. Unlike the native breed, which shepherds were accustomed to housing nightly, the Cheviot and Blackface can be left in pastures during much of the winter (as in the story "Storms"), and they did well in the abundant mountains, with the Blackface particularly adept in rocky terrain. The Marino sheep, a breed favored by King George, was only briefly introduced to the area but could not abide in the climate. The Cheviot was championed by Sir John Sinclair of Caithness, author of the twenty-one-volume *Statistical Account of Scotland* and a well-recognized agricultural improver.[30] The Blackface had no notable advocate but was well known to be fitted to the region.

The demand for wool made sheep a viable commodity. Initially because of the war with France, wool rates increased throughout the early 1800s in both the Lowlands and the Highlands. A landowner could get from four to ten times as much money in rents by leasing to shepherds than he could from tenant farmers. But with sheep came the displacement of people. Sheep need land for grazing, and to do so on a sizable scale meant removing farmers from arable plots. The high prices for wool and to a lesser extent meat meant the "growth of a pastoralism more attuned to the market."[31]

Sinclair provides an interesting example of the problem throughout Scotland and particularly the Highlands. As is evident from *Statistical Accounts* and his work in establishing the Board of Agriculture as well as various sheep clubs, Sinclair was earnestly involved in measuring and assessing the value of agriculture in Scotland. Initially, he had hoped to provide improved methods of farming to maintain and even *grow* the population in the Highlands. Eventually he came to realize the problems of overpopulation. By introducing Cheviots, Sinclair hoped to increase productivity while still maintaining traditional mixed-use agriculture. As Eric Richards explains in his sweeping two-volume account of the Clearances, "Sinclair—certainly one of the best motivated of landlords—was unable to reconcile the introduction of sheep farming with the preservation of the best parts of the older system. He too removed the old peasantry and converted them into crofters and day labourers."[32]

In many respects, Hogg's position was similar to that of Sinclair. As a shepherd, he knew the productivity of sheep on the landscape. In 1802–3, Hogg traveled the Highlands in part to find productive terrain for sheep farming, where he "was aware that the glens were being cleared of people but much of the time he was able to gloss over the human consequences."[33] He bought a sizable plot of land on Harris, an island in the Outer Hebrides, to transform the terrain from arable land to pastures. But because the renter was not allowed to legally sublet the land and because Hogg never pursued the case further with the landowner, he never moved there. Hogg published his Highland tour in installments for *Scots Magazine* and, hoping to better the lot of agriculture, wrote "Essay on Sheep Farming in the Highlands" for the Highland Society. While he was aware of the productive potential of the land and advocated Blackface sheep, Hogg, much like Sinclair, was sympathetic to local life and custom, which he feared would be disrupted. H. B. de Groot summarized the predicament: "Hogg was committed to a major expansion of sheep-farming in the Highlands, while at the same time advocating the granting of secure tenancies to those already on the land. The two were simply not compatible."[34]

Hogg's primary concern was the distribution of human and nonhuman animals across the Highlands. There were a few irreconcilable tensions that reflected the general concerns of the period: how many people should live on the land versus how many sheep? Then Hogg added, how many cattle in relation to people and sheep? And to a lesser extent he asked how much land is lost to foxes. All of this was a concern of rations and relations. Hogg concluded, "stock your mountains with sheep, and your valleys with men and cattle." He went on to say, "with men who are capable of manufacturing the wool of these sheep into cloth . . . with men ready and able to avail themselves of the inestimable sources of wealth, conveyed yearly to their shores in immense shoals of fishes;—with men who will defend their native mountains, though the world combine in arms against them. It is thus, and thus only, that the real value of the Highlands of Scotland shall ever be thoroughly known, when, like a well finished machine, one wheel always sets another in motion."[35]

Hogg's ambition for the Highlands mapped what was being tried throughout the area and relied on sheep for its success. By the end of the war with Napoleon, wool prices began a steep and steady decline that exacerbated the redistribution of people and livestock. Kelp farming on the coast for soap production saw a similar decline, and so those displaced from farms to the coast suffered yet another loss. The agrarian transformation of the Highlands created profound economic blight for the laboring classes throughout the first half of the nineteenth century.

The rationale for the Clearances follows Edinburgh economist Adam Smith's logic in *The Wealth of Nations* whereby the "invisible hand" of free and open markets would properly price land and labor and yield the highest productivity for the nation as a whole. Richardson explains, "Smith employed the Highlands as the standard model of a backward society poverty-bound because the division of labour had been narrowly restricted. Specialization of production in the Highlands had made virtually no progress, so that 'every farmer must be a butcher, baker and brewer to his own family.' "[36] Smith believed that after the Scottish rebellion of 1745, the national investment in roads, canals, and infrastructure that connected the Highlands with the rest of the country created open markets. Agriculture could develop regional specialization alongside trade with the rest of the country, and so the region could move from a feudal system to capitalism. While Smith's sentiments reigned, some, like Stewart of Garth, believed in government intervention to alleviate hardships for the region in transition. He refused to see moving vast populations off of land as productive; how, he asked, could "the welfare of the state be promoted by the diminution of the population, which must be the necessary consequence of a want of employment."[37]

Sheep, it would seem, facilitated capitalist economic change. But, as I have been arguing and conclude below, sheep and fairies become a mode of life in opposition to capitalist and nationalist narratives of progress. This resistance can be understood best through the lens of biopower and biopolitics. I have laid out elsewhere the basic concept of biopolitics in Foucault—that is, the regulation of life through technological apparatus, or *dispostif*, such as statistics, census, and forecasts that become regularized through governmental and cultural enforcement.[38] Cary Wolfe's *Before the Law: Humans and Animals in a Biopolitical Frame* condenses and lays bare many of the stakes of biopolitical control. In terms of Cheviot and Blackface sheep, it would be wrong to read them only as objects and mechanisms of agricultural progress foisted onto the populace by economic and political regimes. As Wolfe explains,

> Rather than remain within the subject/agency vs. object/abjection opposition, the brilliance of Foucault's analysis is to demonstrate just how unstable and mobile the lines are between political subject and political object—indeed, to demonstrate how that

entire vocabulary must give way to a new, more nuanced recon-
ceptualizaton of political effectivity. And equally important is that
Foucault's introduction of "life into history," of the body in the
broadest sense, into the political equation, does not lead directly
and always already to an abjection.[39]

Hogg's stories of sheep and shepherds and sheepdogs such as "Storms" illustrate a series of affective relationships and invisible ties. Shepherds die for
their sheep; dogs labor beyond human sensibilities; and sheep are mobile
variables in the landscape for which one cannot give a full account. Sheep,
shepherds, and dogs are not just political objects of a region's economy;
they are also a networked way of life, a culture that stands over and against
Edinburgh with its civil and urbane culture. Hogg's sheep stories sound as
if they are of another place and time because they are; which is to say, they
are another world and a different temporality from that of Edinburgh and
even by extension the larger national interests.

While the state might call upon the citizen-subject to yield productivity
for the wealth of the nation—in what Giorgio Agamben refers to as a state
of exception—the shepherds remain a dangerous class because they can live
"off the grid" or defiant of the state. Recall the landowner's chiding of the old
shepherd in "Rob Dodds": "no class of men in this kingdom so independent
as you shepherds. You have your sheep, your cow, your meal and potatoes."

At question is how the state apparatus frames and enframes its citizens.
Wolfe writes:

> [T]he frame is not simply a logical or epistemological problem,
> but a social and material one, with consequences. Framing decides
> what we recognize and what we don't, what counts and what
> doesn't; and it also determines the consequences of falling outside
> the frame (in the case at hand in this book, outside the frame as
> "animal," as "*zoe*," as "bare life").[40]

Biological life—the ability of life to exert itself—does not always follow biopolitics, or the attempt of the political machinery to harness biological forces.
Or, as Maurizio Lazzarato argues, "Biopower coordinates and targets a power
that does not properly belong to it, that comes from the 'outside.' *Biopower
is always born of something other than itself*."[41] It is this "something else" that
shows up time and again in Hogg's work. He reminds the reader of forces
that will not be co-opted, be they sheep, shepherds, dogs, witches, brownies,
or fairies.

Unlike Scott, whose work betrays a nostalgia for a past that is safely in the past, Hogg offers a vitality in rural life that is in excess of what can be co-opted by Britain with its narrative of union and progress. Wolfe's comments on contemporary factory farming fit with the objectification of sheep and shepherds and transformation of rural life in Scotland:

> the deadening and diminishing of "animality" itself in all its energy, vitality, and multiplicity, which would in turn forestall our own ability to discover the multiplicity in ourselves via animality as a creative force for our own evolution. In the docility and torpor of the factory farm, where the ratio of purpose bred harvestable flesh to resistance is calculated to be as high as possible, Nietzsche and Sloterdijk would suggest that we humans catch a glimpse of our own biopolitical future, the "herd" toward which the masses of humanity are tending.[42]

Hogg's message throughout is that the shepherd and his sheep will not be herded. If they seem stubborn or backward or out of touch, it is because they have an "energy, vitality, and multiplicity" that will not be forestalled.

Hogg's rural tales are stories of wonder and as such are stories unhinged from our modern sensibilities. Philosopher Jane Bennett asks "whether the very characterization of the world as disenchantment ignores and then discourages affective attachment to that world. The question is important because the mood of enchantment may be valuable for ethical life."[43] The affective relationships in Hogg's world work over and against the rational actor and his self-interest in the economic enlightenment of Adam Smith. Hogg sees Smith's world of open markets and trade as an unfolding disenchantment of a world where his uncle would be the last man in the Borders to speak to fairies. To work against disenchantment and the open access of Scotland to the rest of the Union, Hogg presents heterotopic zones, zones of difference where the world seems to function differently than according to the rules of civil society.

Caroline McCracken-Flesher deftly summarizes the perception of Hogg through the voice of two London Scotsmen:

> Allan Cunningham declared: "James Hogg [. . .] is acknowledged on all hands to be the living and visible head of this national school of song; his genius seems the natural offspring of the pastoral hills and dales of the Border." Thomas Carlyle was dubious: "Is the

charm of this poor man chiefly [. . .] that he is a real product of nature, and able to speak naturally [. . .]? An 'unconscious talent'; though of the smallest, emphatically naive."[44]

Contemporaries were unsure how to position Hogg because he was working between the narrative forms of rural, oral culture and Edinburgh's print culture and between affective relations among humans and animals displaying an "energy, vitality, and multiplicity" that was not sensible to Carlyle as a London Scotsman. As Ian Bogost notes, commenting on the loss of wonder, "wonder has been all but eviscerated in modern thought, left behind as a naive delusion."[45] Carlyle reads Hogg as "emphatically naive," as Hogg's world was being eviscerated from modern thought.

Returning to my opening gambit, why does one have to believe in fairies? It is not because they provide a nostalgic recollection of a lost past, as Sir Walter Scott and much later the Kailyard School believed, nor because they are precursors to imaginative, modern, virtual digital life, as Michael Saler argues in *As If: Modern Enchantment and the Literary Prehistory of Virtual Reality*.[46] Rather, the wonder of Hogg's rural world is a life lived in excess—the possibility that life dwells in ways beyond our ability to harvest it for all-too-humanist ends.

5

Animal Dwelling in Natural History

Thomas Bewick, George Stubbs, and Corporality

In short, the being of sensation is not the flesh but the compound of non-human forces of the cosmos, of man's non-human becomings, and the ambiguous house that exchanges and adjusts them, makes them whirl around like winds.

—Gilles Deleuze and Félix Guattari, *What Is Philosophy?*

Thomas Bewick and George Stubbs have created encyclopedic works on animals. Bewick is known for *A General History of Quadrupeds* (1790) and *A History of British Birds* in two volumes, *Land Birds* (1797) and *Water Birds* (1804). Stubbs first came to notoriety with *The Anatomy of the Horse* (1766), which comprised his illustrations of horses carefully dissected and drawn to reveal the muscle and bone structure. At the end of his life, Stubbs returned to anatomical illustration with his unfinished work *A Comparative Anatomical Exposition of the Structure of the Human Body with That of a Tiger and a Common Fowl* (1804–6), parts of which saw publication before his death. Although the two artists worked in different media, Bewick as an engraver and Stubbs as a painter, each was masterful in his craft and each explored the relationship between humans and animals in a way that (as encyclopedias do) is serviceable to culture.

What does it mean to hold a book of animals—classified, bound, and circulated? It is a moment where the liveness of nature is captured to present to culture. And as this liveness is filtered through human interests and concerns, the animals become tools within the social machine.

As we have seen throughout *Beasts of Burden*, biopolitics functions as an abstract machine for capturing and rendering life serviceable to the state. Also evident throughout is the intertwining of human and animal lives. While granting the knotted complexity of living with other animals, much of the first half of this book has emphasized human community. It is with this chapter and subsequent chapters that *Beasts of Burden* turns more decidedly to the problems and possibilities offered by animality. The goal of this chapter is to explore more explicitly the subsumption of animal lives by studying how the exemplary works of well-known animal artists Bewick and Stubbs function within the machinery of biopolitics. In other words, in drawing the lives of animals, do these artists also render these lives for the service of human mastery? At first glance, it would seem so. Bewick authors encyclopedic volumes on quadrupeds and birds. Stubbs is known for his anatomical illustration of horses, for his pictures of horses for wealthy owners, and for capturing exotic animals on canvas. Yet, if this is all that is happening, then the art itself fails to be more than a representational sum. The hope held out in this chapter is that these artists have exceeded or evaded creating merely calculable artifacts for the service of culture. There resides in these works something in excess of lives rendered for human mastery. These masterful artists draw life without mastery over life.

By way of background, it is worth noting at the outset that Bewick and Stubbs were very well respected in their fields, but neither achieved the fame granted to history painters of the period such as Reynolds and portrait painters such as Gainsborough; or the eventual fame accorded landscape painters such as Constable. Because Stubbs primarily painted animal subjects and some agricultural scenes, he was never ranked among the top artists by his contemporaries. His craft was well respected, but in an age of history painting, animals and peasants did not make a name for a painter. As for Bewick, because he worked as an engraver, he was thought of as a tradesman, and his art was considered of lesser value than oil painting.[1] Both artists were praised for lively renderings of their subjects. But overall, during their lives, their work was considered more representational than creative and imaginative. Representation was skill work or craft, whereas imaginative painting was the task of genius.[2] Yet from today's vantage, one can see how Bewick and Stubbs leveraged the limits of their fields in clearly imaginative ways.

Bewick's first major work grew from his dissatisfaction with children's books about animals. As he explains in his memoirs, from an early age, he found the illustrations of the then-popular *Three Hundred Animals* by Thomas Boreman to be poorly drawn (figure 5.1). So, as his first large woodblock endeavor, in 1785 he set out to create a book that would provide "amusement and pleasure for youth."[3] Bewick provided the images, and Ralph Beilby, to

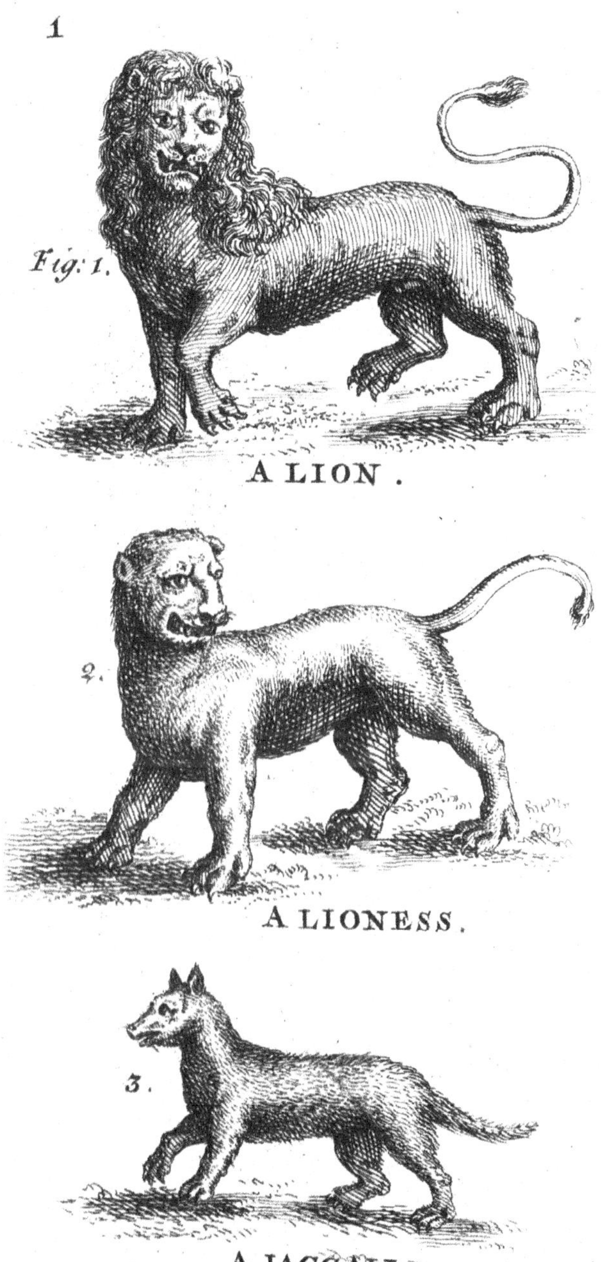

Figure 5.1. Thomas Boreman. Lion, Lioness, Jaccall. *Three Hundred Animals*. 1730. British Library.

whom Bewick had apprenticed, was to provide the text descriptions. In actuality, much of the text became a joint labor between the two men. While initially conceived as a children's book, *A General History of Quadrupeds* became popular among adults and a primer in natural history for people of all ages.

Bewick and Beilby decided not to follow any of the then-existent systems of classifying animals within natural history. They explain their "disregard for systems" in the Advertisement that opens the book:

> [I]t was not so much the object of our plan to lay down a methodical arrangement of the various tribes of four-footed animals, as to give a clear and concise account of the nature, habits, and disposition of each, accompanied with more accurate representations than have hitherto appeared in any work of the kind.[4]

While the authors attempt accuracy, even at the outset they admit to an asymmetry in how they describe various animals. Some animals seem morphologically awkward, with "characters so dubious" that naturalists argue over their "proper place." Examples include "the Elephant, the Hippopotamus, the Rhinoceros, the Cameleopard, the Beaver, the Hedge-hog, the Sloth, the Jerboa, &c." Others, mainly livestock and pets, are so well known that not only is the type recognized, but various breeds are also listed and their unique characteristics described. For example, in illustrating dogs, they explain that there is a large number of entries, yet "to have noticed all the variations and shades of difference observable in the canine race, would have swelled our account, already large, to an immoderate length, and have left us too little room for others of equal importance, in a comprehensive view of this part of the animal creation."[5] Throughout *Quadrupeds*, the amount and type of information given is heavily dependent on the accessibility of the animals for the authors.

So, for example, *Quadrupeds* lists a range of sheep breeds and even specific sheep, such as the Tees-water Old or Unimproved breed and then the Tees-Water Improved breed and even "A Wedder of Mr. Culley's Breed." Because Bewick was from Newcastle, he was well positioned to know sheep. Northern England was the seat of sheep improvement, and as Scotland substituted arable lands for sheep and pastures, the whole region was aware of how sheep "so materially contribute to the strength, the wealth, and the happiness of every nation."[6] Descriptions of sheep include types of hair, mutton yield, fodder, general habits, and care, along with anecdotal incidents. Bewick and Beilby take issue with Buffon's description of sheep as "stupid inanimate creature . . . devoid of every necessary art of self preservation without courage."

They cite the bravery of mountain sheep and even whole flocks, in which "an armed front is presented to all quarters, and cannot easily be attacked without danger or destruction to the assailant."[7]

By contrast, animals far from the sphere of the authors' experience—and, indeed, far from the experience of most British citizens—receive much less detail. For example, *Quadrupeds* ends with an appended creature, the platypus, which is labeled "An Amphibious Animal" and described in a brief paragraph:

> Found in fresh water lakes, which is about the size of a small Cat; it chiefly frequents the banks of the lakes; its bill is very similar to that of a Duck, and it probably feeds in muddy places in the same way.[8]

The entry ends by explaining that the native people (with no location given) "sometimes see them of a very large size." This is followed by a tailpiece that illustrates a family crossing a stream where, one suspects, a platypus might reside. Worth noting is how various tailpieces show possibilities of human engagement with the animal world.

Human engagement with animal worlds as illustrated in tailpieces is part of a strategy of play and interplay between humans and animals. Katey Castellano sees the tailpieces as part of Bewick's moral economy, in which

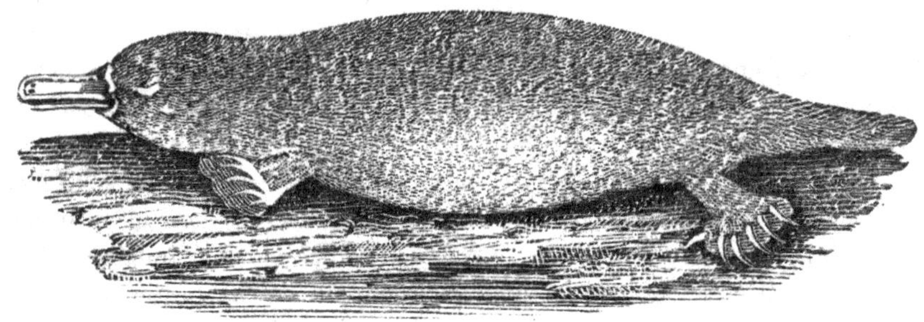

Figure 5.2. Thomas Bewick. An Amphibious Animal [Platypus]. *A General History of Quadrupeds*. 1790. British Library.

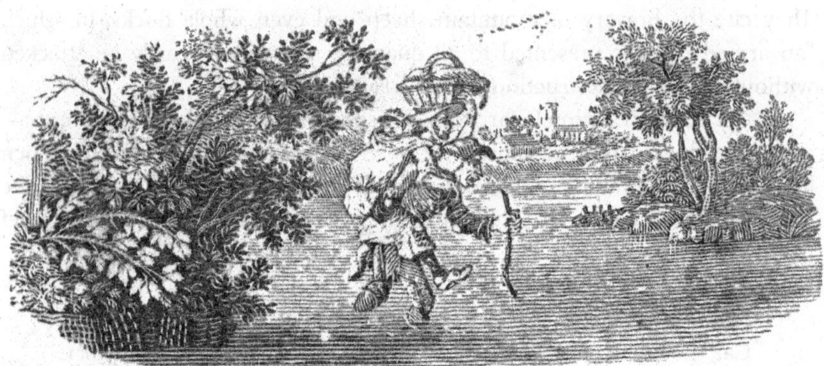

Figure 5.3. Thomas Bewick. Tailpiece to An Amphibious Animal [Platypus]. *A General History of Quadrupeds*. 1790. British Library.

"reciprocity between all living things originates in an understanding of all life as subject to vulnerability. Many engravings show humans and animals alike subject to snow, rain, and wind."[9] Some of the more playful scenes are commentaries on the animality of man, where, as Castellano points out, Bewick creates "engravings of humans in many animal-like, vulgar activities— drunkenness, sleeping, urinating, defecating, and vomiting . . . which call the reader back from abstractions and distances to the known world, not only from the global to the local but also at the same time from the mind to the animal body." In other tailpieces, animality comments on human civilization, such as when a dog defecates amid the ruins of a former human habitat. Other images show a resonance between humans and animals, as in *British Birds* where anglers and a heron are both in a stream fishing. The illustration quotes (in Latin) Virgil's phrase "may I love the woods and streams."[10] The "I" could be the reader or the angler or even, more playfully, the heron.

The tailpieces offer unresolved narratives that undermine any sense that the encyclopedia is comprehensive. Instead, seen through the register of the tailpieces, the encyclopedia is an open-ended compendium of human understanding and interaction with nonhuman animals. Bewick bestowed on the tailpieces a storybook quality reminiscent of period children's books such as *Tommy Trip's* and recalling the spelling books and fables that Bewick illustrated earlier in his career.[11] Bewick was very fond of creating these vignettes and preferred them over the often more prosaic, nonnarrative illustration of the animals that head the encyclopedia entries. As his biographer Dovaston explains, "He does the Birds as a *Task* but is relieved by his working the scenery and background; and after each figure, he flies to cut an ornamental tail-piece with avidity, for in the inventive faculty his imagination revels."[12] Rather than seeing Bewick's animal books as comprehensive, it is useful to see them through the lens of their storybook wonder.

Like many eighteenth-century authors, Bewick saw the natural world as imbued with moral stories that fit into a larger religious truth. As he says in the opening of *History of British Birds*, "when I first undertook my labours in Natural History, my strongest motive was to lead the minds of youth to the study of that delightful pursuit, the surest foundation on which Religion and Morality can efficiently be implanted in the heart, as being the unerring and unalterable book of the Deity."[13] He explains in this preface that the various human systems of categorization are all "like skeletons injudiciously put together, they give but an imperfect idea of that order and symmetry to which they are intended to be subservient."[14] Bewick constantly reminds his reader to be observant of nature, to train one's eyes and hone skills of observation so as to piece together lessons from nature. No human system seems to properly capture the wonders in nature, but the imaginative eye and mind can find within the natural world and within Bewick's natural history glimpses of something greater. It is in the *inability* to capture the larger picture—the inability to judiciously put together the skeletal fragments of nature—that opens a space for the art and imagination.

The ludic elements in *Quadrupeds* are licensed by initially conceiving the work as a children's book. To create "amusement and pleasure for youth," Bewick instills a sense of wonder about the animals and their worlds. So while natural history connotes mastery, playfulness creates a space of incomplete knowledge, curiosity, and possibilities yet untold. Stephen Loo and Undine Sellbach explain how a children's book can leverage the conflict between curiosity for the unknown and knowledge as mastery. By way of example, they discuss Jakob von Uexküll's essay on animal worlds (and biosemiotics) advertised as a "picture book": "In fact, the Picture Book, in its requisite attentiveness, exploits the dissonance between celebrating the incompleteness or the gap between knowledge at hand and objects that are yet-to-come; and over-determining the ideal of whole object based on familiar forms and knowledge."[15]

It is the ways in which Bewick's *Quadrupeds* differs from natural history that make it important. Yes, certainly the encyclopedic work borrows much from the form of natural history, including its name, the lists of animals as entries, illustrations, and some of the descriptive qualities of natural history. Indeed, so convincing is the camouflage that most readers consider the work to be a popularized version of natural history. The difference lies in how natural history constructs a matrix structure and how *Quadrupeds* subtly unworks the genre.

Natural history creates a science of life, or if it does not create it then at least gives it greater scope and precision. Foucault's *The Order of Things* delineates the methodology of natural history. His interest—and mine here— is how natural history creates the preconditions for how things show up as life: how critters become animals and how these animals become objects and placeholders in a larger epistemological matrix. This is a science prior to the formation of biology, in a period when "life itself did not exist. All that existed was living beings, which were viewed through a grid of knowledge constituted by *natural history*."[16]

Through natural history, life is made visible.[17] Natural history becomes an important machinery of classification during the age of global exploration, where Western nations traverse the earth and try to make sense of the diversity of life they encounter. What becomes visible, what shows up, is not the whole of animal life nor all of animal life as perceived by humans. Natural history discounts much of living, or as Foucault summarizes, "Natural history did not become possible because men looked harder and more closely . . . the Classical age used its ingenuity . . . to restrict deliberately the area of its experience. Observation, from the seventeenth century onward, is a perceptible knowledge furnished with a series of systematically negative conditions."[18] Excluded from natural history is hearsay and secondhand knowledge but also a whole realm of sensory experience: taste, touch, and smell. Sight becomes the primary mode of knowing. Indeed, to say that natural history "makes life visible" implies sight, whereby seeing becomes the figure for understanding. Even sight gets restricted: color is secondary to form, and the ecological context of seeing (what surrounds the animal-as-object) is erased.

The ordered system of natural history establishes a mode of comparing animals as objects quantitatively and qualitatively across a field of representation: "Before [i.e., in front of] this language of language, it is the thing itself that appears, in its own characters, but within the reality that has been patterned from the very outset by the name."[19] Here Foucault is making the distinction between pre–natural history when words and things were aligned—the semiotics resided in the beast as with the bestiary—and natural history, where there is no longer a semiotics in the thing but rather in the naming. The often unspoken aspect of natural history is the very space of representation itself: what counts and how it is to be counted. In other words, how is the animal to become object and figure for inscription? The debates between natural historians as to systems of classification are along these lines:

> The natural history rooms and the garden, as created in the
> Classical period, replace the circular procession of the "how" with

the arrangement of things in a "table." . . . Thus arranged and understood, natural history has as a condition of its possibility the common affinity of things and language with representation; but it exists as a task only in so far as things and language happen to be separate. It must therefore reduce this distance between them so as to bring language as close as possible to words. Natural history is nothing more than the nomination of the visible.[20]

This spatial global structure is exemplified in Linnaeus's *Systema naturae* (1735), his first printed systematic classification. One admirer describes it so:

> [With Linnaeus's] Tables we can refer any fish, plant, or mineral, to its genus, and, subsequently, to its species, though none of us had seen it before. I think these Tables so eminently useful, that every body ought to have them hanging in his study, like a map.[21]

Linnaeus himself saw his schema as a "geography of nature."[22] Through the table and the map, natural history creates a spatial grid for life to show up.

This science of life becomes a precursor to biopolitics, wherein life is assembled and arranged for governmental ends. Lisbet Koerner has outlined how Linnaeus envisioned the tables of natural history as a mode toward economic acquisition:

> He spoke of his science as serving the state's economic needs. Also, his voyages and collecting were undertaken in part for economic reasons. As he put it in 1746: "Nature has arranged itself in such a way, that each country produces something especially useful; the task of economics is to collect [plants] from other places and cultivate such things that don't want to grow [at home] but can grow [there]."[23]

Linnaeus sought "such prizes as tea-seeds, herbal medicines, and techniques of porcelain manufacture . . . ; and thus, Linnaeus held, these voyages' ultimate aim, namely to abolish the conditions that now made them necessary, might be fulfilled. The Linnaean ideal voyager, then, was an industrial spy in the busy cities of high civilizations, not a lone wanderer in a pristine natural world."[24] Examples of colonial appropriation of materials are rampant. Cook's voyages are a leading example, with Joseph Banks figuring as a center of calculation and acquisition, and accompanying Banks is Linnaeus's pupil Solander, and on Cook's second voyage Anders Sparrman and Johann Reinhold Forster.

If we are to think of Bewick's and Stubbs's work as other than a "geography of nature" to be used for economic and nationalist ends, then it is necessary to see how they intervene in the spatial matrix that codifies life. Following Foucault, if natural history is a spatial pattern predetermined by the representational function of language, then one can eschew the matrix, maps, and tables by undermining language and its signifying function. In other words, where life is in excess of representation, it can break the matrix of meaning. Seeing the work of Bewick and Stubbs in this fashion opens their work to new possibilities. The gambit here is that while natural history looks to unify life under a rational regime of understanding, life itself stands over and against the flattened, isomorphic representational modes.

Foucault introduces heterotopias as one way of putting the geography of nature off balance: "*Heterotopias* are disturbing, probably because they secretly undermine language, because they make it impossible to name this *and* that, because they shatter or tangle common names, because they destroy 'syntax' in advance, and not only the syntax with which we construct sentences but also that less apparent syntax which causes words and things . . . to hold together."[25] There are a number of ways *Quadrupeds* achieves an energetic dissonance between the gap in tables of knowledge and the tables' ideal whole animal-object connected within a system of other animals turned objects of knowledge. To create these heterotopias, *Quadrupeds* opens to that which is outside the parameters of natural history, creating lines of flight and lines of connection unauthorized by a Linnaean system.

Influenced by theology and by structures in astronomy, mechanics, and optics, Linnaeus looks to fit all life within an immobile taxonomy, most succinctly in his binomial nomenclature introduced in *Philosophia botanica* (1751). He believes there is a universal system under God's plan that reveals the structures of nature. Only late in his life did he haltingly concede that his system was artificial but that he always hoped it would reach a closer approximation to the divine schema. By contrast, Buffon contended that life is too varied and rich for taxonomic classification. As Phillip R. Sloan explains, "Arguing that all man's knowledge is knowledge of and through relations and not of real essences or essential causes, Buffon reasons that the most 'natural' order that could be followed for arranging the animals in the *Histoire naturelle* is in terms of their degree of relation to man."[26] He goes on to quote Buffon:

One judges the objects of Natural History in terms of the relations they have with him. Those which are the most necessary and

> useful to him will take the first rank. For example, he will give
> preference in the order of animals to the horse, the dog and the
> cow. . . . Then he will concern himself with those which, while
> not so familiar to him, [still] inhabit the same locales and the
> same climates, like the deer, rabbit and all the wild animals. . . . It
> will be same for the fishes, the birds, the insects, the testaceans
> and all the other productions of Nature; [man] will study them
> in proportion to the use that he can make of them.[27]

Buffon favored a thick textual description to the binomial system. As Foucault points out, Buffon still remains within a linguistic system of representation; however, he moves further outside a singular grid system. Instead, knowledge of animals is admittedly our knowledge, our contextual understanding based on habits of dwelling. What we know and how we know it is based not only on the privileged scientific apparatus of sight but also on engagement with the world. Moreover, given that our engagement, our way of dwelling, is admittedly limited—there are a multitude of other ways to dwell—then our knowledge admittedly has gaps.

Bewick's quirky classification of animals in his *Natural History of Quadrupeds* follows precisely this line of thought. The asymmetry of knowledge about different animals aligns with how the British dwell—with more entries on horses, cows, sheep, and dogs and fewer on marsupials or other exotics. Moreover, Bewick's alluring woodcuts create several playful quandaries: the scale of the animal is in question because all woodcuts are the same size, the animal image is often articulated without a delineated outline, and the tailpieces provide a humorous commentary of human–animal interactions.

Ultimately, the playful dissonance prevents the predominance of a singular authoritative view. Instead, the storybook modality functions as an open-ended heterotopic system. Following Loo, it "celebrat[es] the incompleteness or the gap between knowledge at hand and objects that are yet-to-come."[28] This opens the knowledge economy onto a nonknowable world. Foucault's critique of natural history is that it tries to align objects and language in a way that makes language a proposition that plays itself out on the grid of natural history. Objects function within natural history as an articulation of a proposition.[29] The storybook and Bewick's approach interrupt the linguistic proposition, indisputably unfolding into a natural-history articulation.

Foucault sees the end of natural history in Cuvier, who moves from the visual external form of animals to an examination of their insides. In Cuvier's comparative anatomy, the assemblages of bodily functions and the dynamism of life take precedent over codification. The organism becomes more important than the Linnaean grid: "One day, towards the end of the eighteenth century, Cuvier was to topple the glass jars of the Museum, smash them open and dissect all the forms of animal visibility that the Classical age had preserved in them."[30] This overturns natural history by directing knowledge into a new way of thinking, and "it was also to be the beginning of what, by substituting anatomy for classification, organism for structure, internal subordination for visible character, the series for tabulation, was to make possible the precipitation into the old flat world of animals and plants, engraved in black on white, a whole profound mass of time to which men were to give the renewed name *history*."[31] Foucault sees in Cuvier a gesture to something outside the mathesis in natural history.

This is where George Stubbs's work becomes more than representational paintings and drawings. Although Stubbs is known for his horse portraits, he started and ended his career with anatomical drawings, which, like Cuvier's work, topple the glass jars of the Museum and structures of natural history. In 1744 and for the next ten years, Stubbs studied anatomy at the newly opened York County Hospital. During this time, Stubbs studied under Charles Atkinson, the house surgeon. His first anatomical drawings for publication were of embryos that presented difficulties in delivery. The publication, *An Essay towards a Complete New System of Midwifery*, was for Dr. John Burton and allowed Burton to advertise his newly invented forceps to aid in birth. By the mid-1750s, Stubbs conceived the idea of illustrating an anatomy of a horse. Initially Stubbs thought of publishing this with this mentor, Atkinson; however, the doctor's duties were the likely cause of his not participating in the project.

Stubbs began his work on a horse anatomy in 1756. Carlo Ruini's 1598 work *Dell' Anatomia et dell' Infirmita del Cavallo* [Anatomy and Infirmity of the Horse] is considered the first work devoted to a single animal other than man and served as the standard of horse illustration for two centuries.[32] Stubbs looked to update Ruini's work. He used many of the same postures but created much more finely detailed and nuanced drawings and then prints for his *Anatomy of the Horse* (1766). For the project, Stubbs rented a room for himself in Horkstow, Lincolnshire, and a separate space where he could draw. His biographer, Ozias Humphry, takes careful note of Stubbs's methodical procedure. He bought live horses destined for the slaughterhouse and bled each to death by slitting the throat. Then he injected the arteries and veins with wax or tallow, as was the fashion for human anatomical corpses, which he likely learned at York County Hospital. In the eighteen months of his study, Stubbs dissected between ten and twelve horses—with each lasting on average six to seven weeks until the decay and stench of the rotting flesh made the corpus unusable. To properly illustrate the dynamic workings of a horse, he devised a harness system that allowed him to keep the horse upright and to suspend the legs and hooves at their proper angel as if in a trot. Following Ruini, he illustrated the animal from the front, back, and side. Stubbs completed a number of studies of horse parts and eventually finished eighteen drawings from which he engraved eighteen plates for publication. As some commentators have noted, one can imagine the smell of rotting flesh, the buzz of flies, the pooling blood, and the difficulty of handling bloody corpses. And yet, in looking at Stubb's prints, the more abject, visceral elements of the work are elided for the clarity of the anatomical design and grace of form. Competing in these works is a raw, physical animality—the flesh of the animal—and the technicity of the artist as craftsman carefully positioning the corpse and with exacting eye illustrating its finer points. Looking at the completed study, the viewer sees skin, then layers of flesh, flayed from the animal, revealing the complex system of muscles, tendons, arteries, veins, and bones.

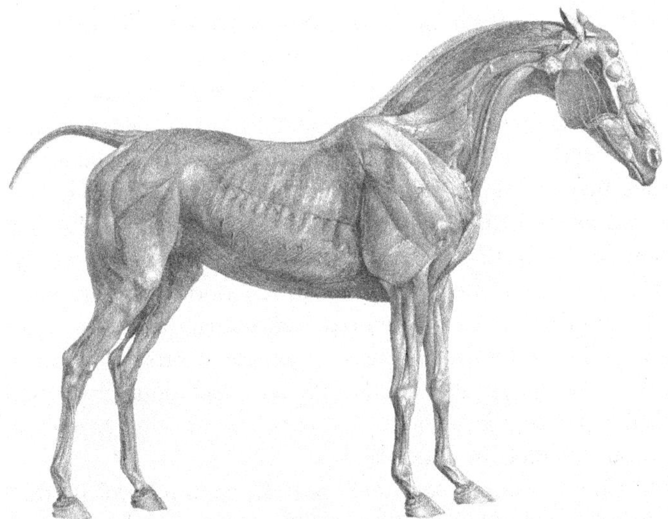

Figure 5.4. George Stubbs. Finished study for the second anatomical table: connective tissue overlying the muscles removed so that the form of the surface muscles is clear. *The Anatomy of the Horse*. RA 3/ D5. Yale Center for British Art.

The images illustrate both the delicacy of flesh and the raw power of the horse's body. Stubbs's precision in illustration coupled with the dynamic postures provides these conflicting characteristics at the same time. Unlike a Linnaean anatomy, we get in these works a more robust sense of the animal; Stubbs offers not only its visible surfaces but also what lies beneath and the complex dynamics of the animal rather than the more facile linguistic definitions of species according to exterior form. Following Foucault's comments about Cuvier, *The Anatomy of the Horse* provides anatomy over classification, organism over structure, and internal relationships over visible character.

Although *The Anatomy of the Horse* was not published until 1766, its prints had circulated among nobility, and from this Stubbs received a number of commissions to paint the elite horses of noblemen. His ability to capture the details of horse anatomy, posture, and movement made him the pre-eminent horse painter of the period. British horse portraiture is a large and wide-ranging field, beyond the scope of this present work.[33] Such painting easily fits within a biopolitical frame by which the horse (including its breed, age, gender, etc.) is figured as a commodity for labor and leisure according to established cultural constructions. Stubbs's *Anatomy* can easily be seen to work within this system. He created the prints to help artists illustrate horses and then secondarily to help veterinarians care for the animals. But to stop here is to fail the animal itself. It is to allow the illustration to cover over the process of its production. If *Anatomy* is to succeed, it is where the work is in excess of the representational, where illustration is not simply another representational language. Instead, if there is a "punctum" or piercing detail to the work that elides representation, it is in the animality, the sheer corporality, that bleeds through the finely printed illustrations. For Roland Barthes in *Camera Lucida*, the punctum is a detail that speaks to the individual observer-as-participant in the work.[34] In Stubbs's *Anatomy*, given the complex, dynamic, and raw physicality in the work, there are any number of possible entry points for this nonrepresentational quality—be it a vein, an elongated tendon, a formidable mass of muscle, a protruding anus, or the bulging eyes. Such physicality disrupts the representational appropriation for biopolitical ends and calls before us the animal as an-other, as a beast foreign to us and our attempts to understand it.

While horse painting and some portrait painting provide the bulk of Stubbs's livelihood, he illustrated a number of exotic animals, including several monkeys and lemurs, the first zebra seen in England (and presented to Queen Charlotte), a kangaroo drawn from its taxidermied form, a live moose brought from Canada for the third Duke of Richmond, and famously *Portrait of a Hunting Tyger* (first exhibition title), later retitled *Cheetah with*

Two Indian Attendants and a Stag, drawn from a live cheetah. Each of these exotic animals and its depiction on canvas carries with it a story of empire, not unlike the Linnaean desire to create a mapped "geography of nature" to obtain international advantages in a global market.

By way of example, consider the moose painting *The Duke of Richmond's First Bull Moose* (1770). The animal was a gift to the duke from General Guy Carleton, governor of Quebec. William Hunter became interested in the moose—the first male moose he had seen—because he wanted to test his theory of extinction. He suspected that the "Irish elk" was extinct because the only evidence of the animal was by excavation of its bones and its notably large horns. He wanted to make sure the Canadian moose did not have similar antlers. Unfortunately for Hunter, it was a young bull moose and so had only very small antlers. The animal did not comply with the schematics Hunter needed. The general did give the duke a pair of large, mature moose horns, and so Hunter commissioned Stubbs to paint the moose and beside it the large horns from a mature moose. In 1773, the general sent the Duke of Richmond a second bull moose—this one mature with a formidable rack of horns. Hunter examined the animal and had Stubbs create a sketch of it. What we can glean from the moose example is the way Stubbs's work on exotic animals often served the ends of empire and natural history.

The story behind *Portrait of a Hunting Tyger: Cheetah with Two Indian Attendants and a Stag* is also revealing. In 1764, a staged encounter or hunt took place in an enclosed area at Windsor Great Park between the Duke of Cumberland's tiger (a term used for any large cat) and a stag. The crowds that gathered were disappointed. The "tiger" was uninterested in attacking the stag. Instead, when released, the animal ran into the woods and there killed a deer far from the sight of the crowd. Lord Pigot commissioned Stubbs to paint the event with the stipulation that it was to be situated not in the Royal Park but rather in India. Stubbs likely used Indian men as models and used a live cheetah as a model as well (possibly one from Pigot's menagerie). The noncompliance of the large cat is a moment of humor. The Duke had set up a situation of savage sport, expecting the animal to comply. Its refusal and then actual killing away from human sight is a moment that reveals something about cultural expectations of the exotic beast and its ability to defy our expectations. While the animal serves as an indexical marker of a wild, ferocious hunter, it also refuses to be such a marker and instead runs off and becomes a wily animal outside human purview.

The last work of George Stubbs's life was *A Comparative Anatomical Exposition of the Structure of the Human Body with that of a Tiger and a Common Fowl*. From this work, Stubbs printed fifteen engravings from 1804 to 1806 and projected another fifteen. It is likely that just after publishing *The Anatomy of the Horse*, he considered creating a comparative anatomy. As Egerton mentions, "Eighteenth-century studies in comparative anatomy, often with seemingly bizarre titles, were not uncommon, testifying to the urge to explore and correlate knowledge which was characteristic of the Enlightenment."[35] He acquired the human body (probably of an executed criminal) from a physician licensed to teach anatomy at St. Thomas Hospital, London. It is speculated that the tiger was obtained through John Hunter, who dissected all of the animals that died in the Tower menagerie. And, of course, the common fowl was easily obtained at any street market. Egerton explains the disciplined seeing required to properly render the different anatomical forms of each species: "Stubbs's *Comparative Exposition* was a continuing exercise in self-education, achieved through unremitting observation of unvarnished nature. He neither attempted nor reached pioneering conclusions in comparative anatomy."[36]

As mentioned earlier, it was Cuvier who was considered the leading figure in comparative anatomy. He moved from static form to dynamic function, not only of external but also of internal characteristics of animals. While the Linnaean system worked reasonably well for plants, where key structures were generally visible, Cuvier opened up the body in a way that allowed for more complete description of animals.

While likely not an intended effect, where Stubbs's comparative anatomy takes a leap into new directions is in his modeling of his subjects. In staging the human, tiger, and fowl for comparison, the bodies are shown as expected: standing and depicted from the front and back. But it is the pictures of the subjects in motion that are more striking and curious. The drawing of the human skeleton with its right arm extended and hand resting looks oddly like an attempted wing when positioned next to the fowl. The human skeleton viewed from a lateral position and crawling and then in another drawing crouching looks as if he is attempting the position of the tiger. Stubbs has a rough drawing of a tiger standing and extending its forepaws as if in a human posture, or, as Terence Doherty notes, it is "Stubbs's most explicit attempt to draw a parallel between the tiger and the human body."[37] Among the anatomical drawings are two of a partially plucked owl with wings folded behind it. Doherty observes that the owl is "shown standing upright, and thus comparable to the standing tiger and the standing human figure."[38] The effect of these comparative structures is what Alex Potts properly calls "both ludicrous and serious at the same time."[39]

The ludicrous nature of the work come from upsetting the established order of things. Readers will recall that (following Foucault's *Order of Things*) the challenge to breaking outside natural history has been to find some way of moving outside linguistic representation and the table, which is a performance of linguistic representation on a large scale. As Potts explains, "We could look at his plates in the comfortable assumption that the human body was self evidently the highest form of living being. But the visual juxtaposition he sets up might easily incline the viewer to entertain thoughts that were subversive of such an assumption."[40] The subversion and what Potts calls "freak" illustrations come from establishing equivalencies between species and a seemingly fluid glide between their forms of life. Stubb's artistic venture in comparative anatomy creates a new set of relations.[41] Perhaps not intended by Potts but latent in his comment on the freak nature of the images are the ways these images perform labor and spectacle in working against codes of normalization (a concern taken up by Paul Youngquist in *Monstrosities* and Robin Blyn in *Freak-garde*).[42]

Postmodern philosophers Deleuze and Guattari critique natural history for its limits in how it schematizes life:

> One of the main problems of natural history was to conceptualize the relationships between animals. It is very different in this respect from after evolutionism, which defined itself in terms of genealogy, kinship, descent, and filiation. As we know, evolutionism would arrive at the idea of an evolution that does not necessarily operate by filiation. But it was unavoidable that it begin with the genealogical motif. . . . Precisely because natural history is concerned primarily with the sum and value of differences, it can conceive of progressions and regressions, continuities and major breaks, but not an evolution in the strict sense, in other words, the possibility of a descent the *degrees* of modification of which depend on external conditions. Natural history can think only in terms of relationships (between A and B), not in terms of production (from A to *x*).[43]

In other words, for natural history, difference is always a difference between two fixed forms, two established species, "between A and B." A comparative anatomy is between fixed form A and form B. There is not space outside these fixed terms and the fixed species. There is no becoming or evolution.

Even Cuvier, who "topple[d] the glass jars of the Museum," believed in the fixity of species and that environmental influences could make only slight changes within limits. By contrast, Jean-Baptiste Lamarck believed in transformationism—the animal's needs causing an adaption of form to fit the environment.[44] Cuvier conceded the possibility of some minimal changes of exterior form but could not believe the complex internal working of the animal could modify to fit the environment. His principle of "prerequisites of existence" maintained that the structure of the organs essential for life could not change because they were too complexly linked to too many variables related to the animal's needs. So, for example, if a bird had to change its type of food, it was not enough that its bill change, but its jaw, digestive track, intestines, sight, and hearing also would need to transform. All of these are linked, and such a transformation seemed to Cuvier to be impossible. Lamarck had to concede the difficulties of change in internal organization systems but maintained that both external and internal systems could change.[45]

Cuvier and Lamarck are working through the problem of an outside, a difference that is not between two fixed species but the possibility of "terms of production (from A to *x*)," as Deleuze and Guattari describe this movement. In natural history, beings are fixed in relation to other beings (two fixed species). Introducing the environment as a factor breaks the table of difference between species and instead creates new terms of production "from A to *x*." If Cuvier's break was to move from external form to internal dynamics, the larger variable is how these dynamics respond to variations in the surrounding environment. How does the organism become itself only by being part of a larger ecosystem? This is what Deleuze and Guattari mean when they introduce the term "haecceity":

> There is a mode of individuation very different from a person, subject, thing, or substance. We reserve the name *haecceity* for it. A season, a winter, a summer, an hour, a date have a perfect individuation lacking nothing, even though this individuality is different from that of a thing or a subject. They are haecceities in the sense that they consist entirely of relations of movement and rest between molecules or particles, capacities to affect and be affected.[46]

At issue here is how can something, some species, become something other than it already is. What variables introduce novelty into the system or, as Deleuze and Guattari ask, how can one move from being to becoming?

This is where Stubbs's *Comparative Anatomy* becomes most interesting, "ludicrous and serious" and "freak" (to recall Alex Potts's insight into Stubbs). Certainly the work can be read—and historically most properly should be read—in relation to comparative anatomy somewhere between Linnaean form and Cuvier's comparative anatomy of organs. However, there are also possibilities for an improper reading, one that sees in the work novelty introduced into the system. If we read the human, the tiger, and the fowl not as fixed species but as entities capable of change, then the parallels Stubbs makes between the figures take on a different status. The man crawling and the man crouching are becoming a different animal, becoming tiger. The man with arm extended is becoming a bird. This is not to say the man is becoming another fixed term. Rather, in states of becoming such beings are moments in an ongoing flux. So to say that the man is becoming tiger does not mean he is imitating the being of another species. Rather, his horizontality, his four limbs to the ground, his shift in comportment are actions that occupy the figural space of the tiger, which is horizontal with eyes forward and limbs to the ground. In these Stubbs works, we can see being thought differently.

This is not imitation or, as Deleuze and Guattari state, "We fall into a false alternative if we say that you either imitate or you are. What is real is the becoming itself, the block of becoming, not the supposedly fixed terms through which that which becomes passes."[47] If we read this rather radical statement in terms of Stubbs's work, then man and tiger and fowl are not beings, not "fixed terms." Rather, they are blocks of becoming through which one may pass. The figures' gestures are small moments of release from one

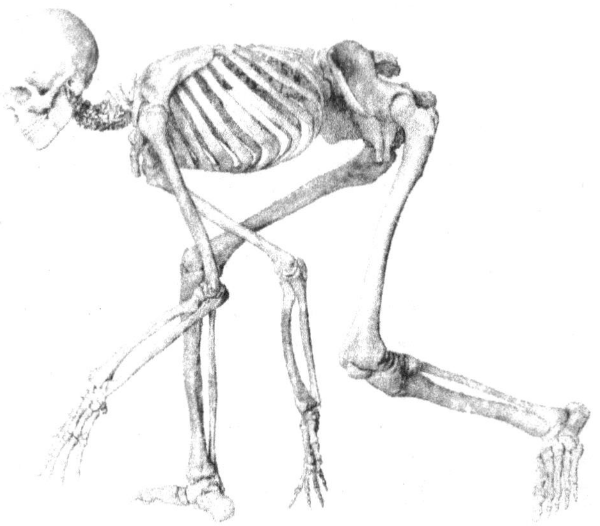

Figure 5.5. George Stubbs. Human Skeleton, Lateral View, in Crouching Posture. *A Comparative Anatomical Exposition of the Structure of the Human Body with That of a Tiger and a Common Fowl.* B1980.1.65. Yale Center for British Art.

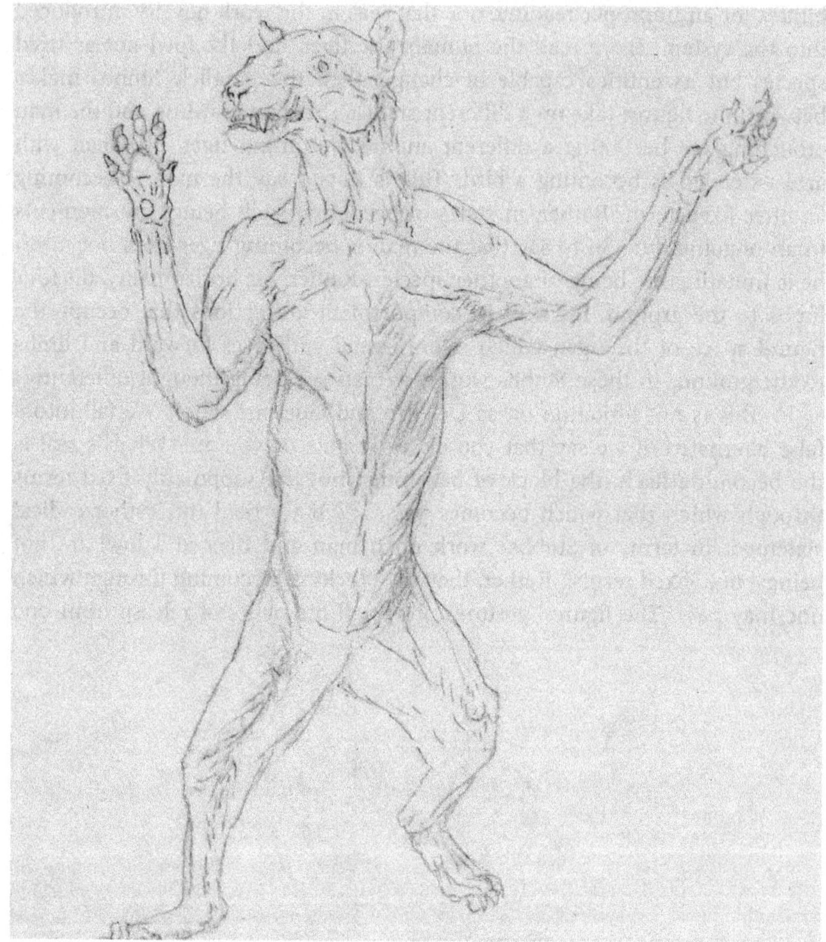

Figure 5.6. George Stubbs. Tiger Body, Standing in Human Posture. *A Comparative Anatomical Exposition of the Structure of the Human Body with That of a Tiger and a Common Fowl.* B1980.1.101. Yale Center for British Art.

block of becoming toward another. The man does not imitate a bird; rather, he creates a flapping that is synonymous with the block of becoming called bird. The man does not imitate a tiger; rather, he crouches and prowls in a block of becoming called tiger.

Moving from static being to corporeal gesture and becoming allows something new to emerge. As Potts says, it allows for a nonhierarchical relation or "easily incline[s] the viewer to entertain thoughts that were subversive." Kari Weil sees a similar intense corporality in the work of the French artist Théodore Géricault. Borrowing Weil's reading of Géricault, we can say that Stubbs's anatomy "implicates a shared corporeal . . . bond between the artist/viewer and the unknowable (and indomitable animal bodies within the picture). Géricault thus turns the question of the picture back onto its picturing subject, raising doubts about the very possibility of a world picture made from an outside objective position."[48] Becoming as a concept allows for a different way of understanding entities, gestures, and events. It unmoors the fixed state of affairs and the natural history matrix; it opens more radical if seemingly unlikely connections that are in the work—in the texts by Stubbs, for example—but remain unexplored forces and connections. Just as those who practiced natural history had to train their eyes and minds toward a particular way of seeing; so, too, it takes some rethinking to read natural history as sites of becoming rather than as a biopolitical apparatus.

In the history of natural history there are certainly many strange events. I would like to end this chapter by focusing on one of these—a dinner under the bones of a mastodon—and resituating this event through the lens of becoming and an animality resistant to being co-opted by the state apparatus and biopolitics.

The story of the mastodon begins with the discovery of a large, five-pound tooth along the Hudson River in Claverack, New York, in 1705. Through a series of exchanges, the tooth eventually made its way from the tenant farmer who found it to Lord Cornbury, then governor of New York, who sent the tooth to London with the label *incognitum*. Through comparative anatomy, the tooth was aligned with those of the modern elephant and the prehistoric mammoth. However, unlike elephant and mammoth, the discovered tooth had cone cusps. In 1806, Cuvier named the *incognitum* a mastodon (deriving from a Greek etymology *masto* "breast" and *don* "tooth"). He surmised that neither mammoths nor mastodons were alive today, given their difference from modern elephants. Fearing the ferocity of a beast so large and with such massive teeth, William Hunter wrote in 1768, "Though we may as philosophers regret it, as men we cannot but thank Heaven that its whole generation is probably extinct."[49]

The size and speculative destructive nature of the animal caught a great deal of attention. Among others, Thomas Jefferson was interested in the mastodon as proof against Buffon's claim that animals in the New World were degenerative and more diminutive than those in Europe. In 1783, Charles Willson Peale in Philadelphia caught sight of the mastodon tooth and became enchanted by the pursuit of further fossil evidence. Peale was an artist and natural history collector who opened the first natural history museum in

America. In 1801, further fossil remains were found along the Hudson Valley outside Newburgh, New York (some seventy miles north of New York City). Peale bought the bones and the right to dig for further fossil remains. His big dig is commemorated in a now famous painting, *Exhuming the First American Mastodon* (1806). The painting gives a sense of the scene (figure 5.5). Inside the pit, men haul up dirt that is then sifted for fossil remains. Seepage of water is carried off in a large conveyor with buckets powered by men turning a wheel up above the pit. Peale himself stands at the edge of the pit overseeing the project and holding an illustration of an initial find of the large bones.

Returning with the remains to Philadelphia, it took three months to fit the pieces together. Carefully fashioned woodwork substituted for any missing bones. The result was the first complete fossil of a mastodon. The skeleton stood roughly eleven feet at the shoulder. While the beast's parallel to the mammoth and elephant seems apparent, Peale—perhaps out of showmanship—temporarily fixed the tusks upside down as if to show a ferocious beast

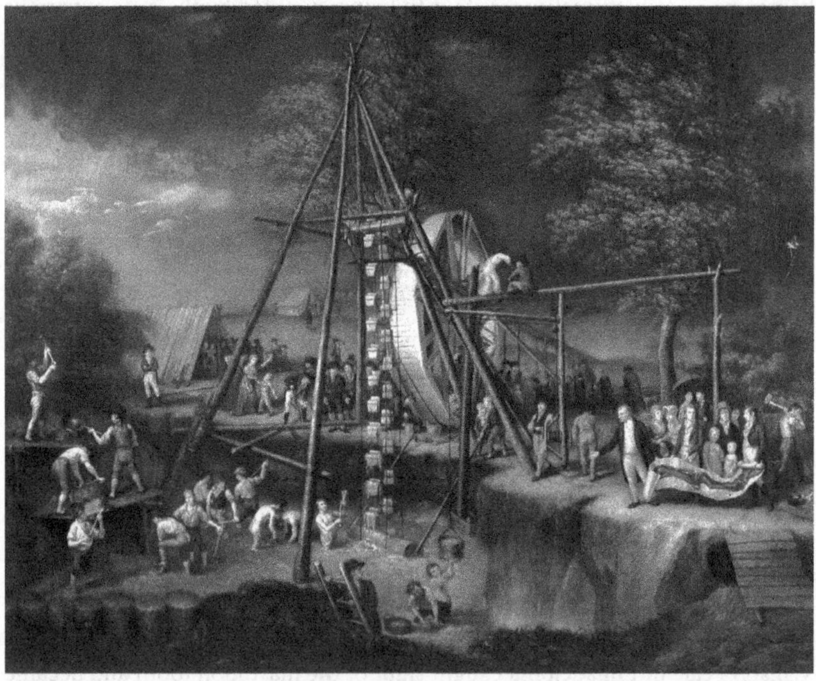

Figure 5.7. Charles Willson Peale. *Exhuming the First American Mastodon*. 1806. Peale Museum.

that could spear its prey. Richard Conniff summarizes the further lengths of Peale's showmanship to garner crowds at his museum:

> To drum up business for the opening of his museum, Peale had Williams put on an Indian headdress and parade through the city streets on a white horse, with trumpet fanfare. Fliers invoked an Indian legend: "TEN THOUSAND MOONS AGO" a creature had roamed "the gloomy forests . . . huge as the frowning Precipice, cruel as the bloody Panther." For 50 cents additional admission to the museum's "Mammoth Room," Philadelphians could see "the LARGEST of Terrestrial Beings!" with their own wide eyes.[50]

Although decades later Cuvier would coin the term "mastodon" for the animal, at the time the word "mammoth" caught the public's attention and came to mean anything overly large, including such items as "mammoth bread," "mammoth cheese," and even a "mammoth" radish.

All of this is setting and prelude to the dinner inside the animal's rib cage. Peale's son, Rembrandt, invited thirteen men to dine in the belly of the beast. Paul Semonin in *American Monster* explains that while the guests dined in the animal, a pianist played songs including "Yankee Doodle Dandy." The animal was invoked as a symbol of national pride with the toast "The American People: may they be as preeminent among the nations of the earth, as the canopy we sit beneath surpasses the fabric of the mouse!"[51] The size of the mastodon was a snub to Buffon and those who saw North America as a diminutive continent in terms of both its animals and its politics. In claiming the more-than-ten-thousand-year-old animal for the United States and as a symbol of the nation's character, these men made the biological political. The animal is not itself but at the service of the nation. Its tusks are inverted to create a fiercer demeanor to capture the public's imagination, to inspire awe, and to set a tone of national power.

And yet there is a strange gesture in eating a meal within the animal. Certainly one could understand the feast as a mockery and triumph over the beast—again a toast to national triumph. However, I would like to return to Hunter's comment that, given the animal's apparent ferocity, "we cannot but thank Heaven that its whole generation is probably extinct." Being in the skeletal "belly," within the rib cage, the guests are engulfed by the animal of another age. While they eat, they can ruminate on the mastodon's tooth—the very thing that ignited the excitement over the animal and garnered the beast its name. The guests' act of chewing while within the beast is not necessarily a triumph over the animal but also could be a recognition of the animal's power, a sort of death wish and annihilation of the human. Or, given the above reading of the human and animal gestures in Stubbs's *Comparative Anatomy*, this could be the becoming mastodon of the guests—through political and appetitive desire, the cordial party becomes a bestial mass.

In such a reading of the "mammoth" dinner, we return to themes that have been explored throughout this chapter: issues of wonder outside of reason, vulnerability beyond mastery, and becoming rather than tables of beings. Certainly from the point of view of natural history (and then still later biology) there was an animal called the mastodon, just as there are the various animals listed in Bewick's *Natural History of Quadrupeds*. But, as we have seen with Bewick, the issue is how these animals open onto an outside—that is, we will never arrive at the animals themselves. Rather, the question is, what does it mean for us to understand and interpret and write about and interact with animals? What does it mean to open a book of animals—Bewick's or Stubbs's? And what does it mean to have a feast in the belly of a beast?

Buffon argued against Linnaeus on such terms. Knowledge of the animal is always knowledge through a relatedness. There is no "outside" of the ways we relate to the world around us. To quote Buffon again: "One judges the objects of Natural History in terms of the relations they have with him. Those which are the most necessary and useful to him will take the first rank."[52] Bewick concedes that his *Natural History* is partial to animals more commonly known in Britain. Stubb's *Anatomy of a Horse* is successful because of the socioeconomic and labor status of horses. And eating within a mastodon is a biopolitical act. But such an act is not without other readings of the environment—which is to say, the corporeal body of the animal does not always have to be read as a passive and suppliant body for human use. Deleuze and Guattari's concept of becoming opens the environmental possibilities, the possible modalities of engagement between humans and animals, not as fixed states but as states of affairs whose event structure can create new ways of considering human–animal interaction and how we dwell.

6

Man Proposes, Animality Disposes

*Antihuman Landseer with Implications
for Biopolitical Britain*

The beast lives *unhistorically.*

—Nietzsche, "On the Use and Abuse of History for Life"

Impetus for this chapter derives from Edwin Landseer's *Man Proposes, God Disposes,* where the artist uses the animality of polar bears as a figure for the larger inhumanity of the polar landscape.[1] Landseer's bears are part of a larger cultural use of the animal as a metonymical part for the larger inaccessible and dangerous terrain of the Arctic. Narratives of encounters with the vast, inhuman landscape vacillate between the sublime (with its aesthetic distance) and the terrifying (in actual fear of one's life). To give shape and meaning to the human struggles with the inhuman environment, texts about polar exploration exhibit what Jen Hill calls "a self-conscious exercise in national masculine identity."[2] Expeditions into the Arctic become a nation's struggle for conquest over recalcitrant and inhospitable terrains. The struggle is often embodied as one between an explorer and a monstrous other on blinding white sheets of ice. In nonfiction narratives of exploration, the polar bear with its overwhelming speed, size, and power becomes emblematic of the mysterious forces working against British explorers in this unknown region.

In 1845, Captain John Franklin and his crew of the HMS Erebus and HMS Terror departed England in search of a Northwest Passage through what is now known as the Canadian Arctic Archipelago. The ships never returned. Previous to this devastating loss, Franklin had led two other expeditions into the Arctic. His 1819 expedition with a crew of twenty lost eleven. Those who returned came back with tales of extreme conditions and cannibalism.

91

Franklin wrote about the exploration and loss in *Narrative of a Journey to the Shores of the Polar Sea* (1823). The publication gained him fame as an adventurer and one who had managed the incomprehensible difficulties abiding far from the civil space of the British reading public. As Adrian Craciun explains, "This tale of starvation, murder, cannibalism, and madness was tailored to please an audience already schooled in Gothic romances, captivity narratives, shipwreck accounts, early ethnography, and travel writings."[3]

Franklin's 1845 expedition became icebound in the Victoria Strait near King William Island. Search parties were launched throughout the 1850s, but it became evident that the ship and crew were fatally lost. Explorer John Rae acquired from the Inuit tales of the dead crew and artifacts from their ships.[4] In what became a heralded voyage, Francis Leopold McClintock found life rafts, gear, human remains, and even a note detailing the wayward fate of Franklin's expedition.[5]

The severe conditions had decimated the icebound explorers. Adding to the horror were signs of cannibalism evident in the cut marks on skeletal remains and through stories circulated by the Inuit. Current research believes the party died from a number of causes related to the severe conditions, including hypothermia, starvation, disease, and possibly lead poisoning from the tin food and water-storage tanks.[6] The Northwest Passage remained elusive for another fifty years until Norwegian explorer Roald Amundsen and his crew successfully navigated the perilous waters at the dawn of the twentieth century. The Franklin expedition served as a lesson to Britain that, even amid its naval supremacy and expanding empire, nature remained a formidable adversary to the advancements of culture.[7]

The vast, sublime white space of the Arctic serves as a psycho-geographical marker of struggle, conquest, and dominion. As Jen Hill explains in *White Horizons*, "Exploring and mapping the Arctic was a self-conscious exercise in national masculine identity building perceived to take place in 'empty' space, documented in best-selling expedition accounts that marketed a heroic masculinity that found its origin in representations of Trafalgar hero Horatio Nelson's early voyage to the Arctic seas, the Antarctic voyages of Cook, and the romanticized recollection of Henry Hudson."[8] Nelson's foray into the Arctic serves as an exemplary moment for consideration a bit later in this chapter. For now, it is worth noting that in the nineteenth century, the Arctic functions as a sublime space and a space for conquest within the British imaginary. It was the space that created tales of adventure, danger, and loss and held the promise of great gains for the nation should explorers successfully navigate the terrain, tame the space through careful mapping, and ideally find the elusive Northwest Passage.

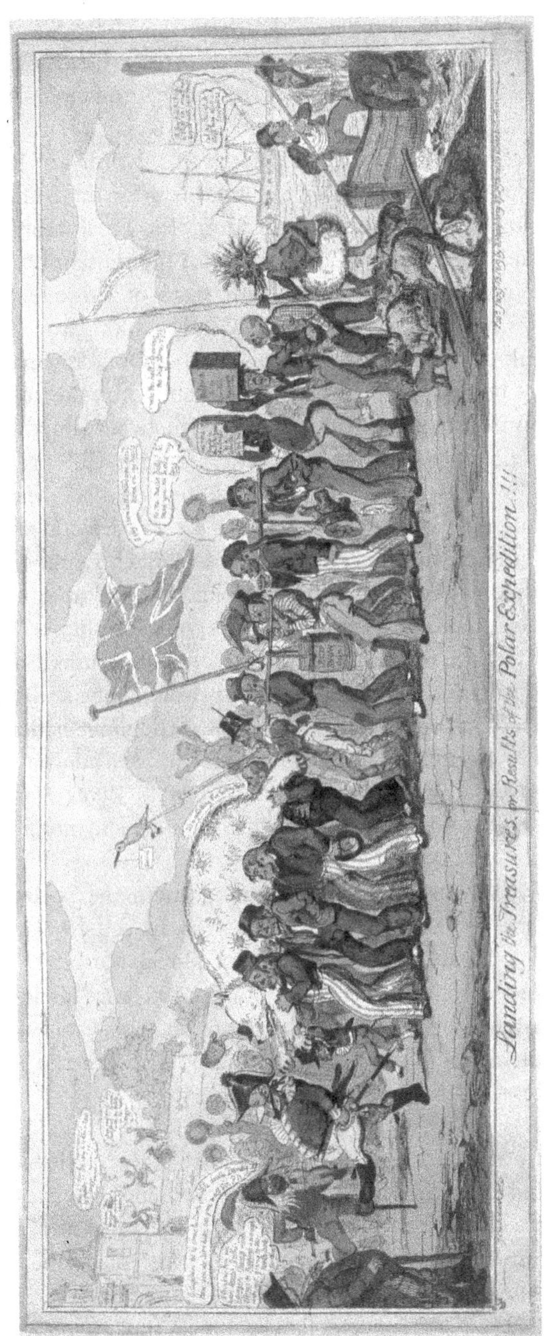

Figure 6.1. George Cruikshank. *Landing the Treasures, or Results of the Polar Expedition!!!*. 1819. British Museum.

George Cruikshank's *Landing the Treasures, or Results of the Polar Expedition!!!* (1819) prominently displays the carcass of a polar bear carried off the ship by Arctic adventurers returning home. In this satirical piece, Cruikshank shows the return of Sir John Ross's 1818 expedition to the Canadian Arctic, where he went in search of a Northwest Passage.[9] His unsuccessful venture, however, did garner treasures for the British Museum and its then-existent natural history collection. The polar bear, caricatured here by Cruikshank, became a popular fixture of the museum.[10] Braving the Arctic, the captain and crew returned with signs of frostbite. Many have black noses or are missing one entirely. In Cruikshank's parody of heroism, Ross wears a beak to hide a frost-disfigured nose. One crewman walks on two wooden pegs because his feet have been claimed by the cold. The bear becomes the treasure claimed at the expense of their hardships.

Of course, fiction of the period coincides with Hill's description of "a self-conscious exercise in national masculine identity." Mary Shelley's *Frankenstein* opens with Walton's hopes in the land of ice and snow and his conquest of the "untamed yet obedient elements."[11] Such sentiments dissipate at the end of the novel, where "[i]mmense and rugged mountains of ice" impede Frankenstein's progress and eventually Walton's ship is "surrounded by mountains of ice, still in imminent danger of being crushed in their conflict."[12] Struggles with mountains of ice, ice-crushing boats, disorientation, snow blindness, hunger, and bitter cold repeat throughout fiction and nonfiction accounts of Arctic travel. Eric Wilson's *The Spiritual History of Ice: Romanticism, Science, and the Imagination*; Jen Hill's *White Horizon*; and a number of articles by Adriana Craciun trace fiction and nonfiction works about the Arctic.

Even today, there is something haunting about the polar bear. More often than not, the ferocity of the polar bear is in equal balance with its vulnerability as its terrain shrinks because of global warming. Whereas in the eighteenth and nineteenth centuries polar bears were stand-ins for the brutality of the Arctic, today they are the figure for global warming. In *Wild Ones*, Jon Mooallem traces the history of the polar bear's rise as a symbol of climate change:

> But because the problem of climate change was invisible, the media found that polar bears were an easy, adorable means to illustrate these stories—more eye-catching than a smokestack spewing carbon or a glacier crumbling. *Time* magazine ran a photo of a bear on its cover with the headline "Be Worried. Be Very Worried." . . . The species had become a spokes-species, and

no matter what context polar bears appeared in, they symbolized the same thing.[13]

Furthering the conversation from chapter 5, this chapter explores what gets lost in the symbolization of the animal is the animal itself. Returning to the animality of the animal—the animal over and against human-constructed meanings—will have implications for the biopolitical burden placed on these beasts.

Some two hundred years ago, the animal symbolized the difficulty of mastering the Arctic and finding a Northwest Passage, with all the economic and colonial implications such a route carried. The polar bear then functioned as an animated figure for the failure of this economic and political byway. The biopolitics of the polar bear continue today. The Center for Biological Diversity used the declining population to argue that the polar bear should be on the endangered species list. Their interest here is that, by US law, any animal on this list has to have its habitat protected. Should the bear ever make this list, it legally would necessitate the end of oil exploration in the Arctic and the curtailing of greenhouse gases.[14]

Perhaps even more foundational than biopolitics, what is happening in the event of encounter between humans and polar bears in the Arctic during the Age of Exploration? To ask this question is to pose a series of problems. To begin, what does it mean to happen, to take place—which is to ask, how does the nonhuman world enter into history, and what is the violence of this event? Percy Shelley's "Mont Blanc" poses this problem particularly well in its final lines:

> And what were thou, and earth, and stars, and sea,
> if to the human mind's imaginings
> Silence and solitude were vacancy?[15]

Indeed, there is something beyond what is intelligible and graspable by us. The Arctic provides a stark moment in which the human mind surpasses itself in thinking the limit of its capacity to engage with the nonhuman world. When humans come in contact with new terrain, with its physicality, its material being, its flora and fauna, we are at a loss to understand the foreign and alien.

The event of encounter, the event as event, is outside the referential frame. Its novelty cannot be fully subsumed within the current state of affairs; it cannot easily be made intelligible. Consider Bill Readings on Jean-François Lyotard's theory of "the event." Lyotard's event "disrupts any pre-existing referential frame within which it might be represented or understood. The eventhood of the event is the radical *singularity* of happening, the 'it happens' as distinct from the sense of 'what is happening.' "[16] He goes on to say, "The event is the occurrence after which nothing will ever be the same again. The event, that is, happens in excess of the referential frame within which it might be understood, disrupting or displacing that frame."[17] Many polar bear encounters with humans can be dangerous. The human's and the bear's lives are at stake. For the bear or for the human this would, indeed, be a radical singularity.

Another way of discussing this displacing frame of encounter is through Mary Louise Pratt's concept of contact zones: "social spaces where disparate cultures meet, clash, and grapple with each other, often in highly asymmetrical relations of domination and subordination."[18] In the event of encounter, in Arctic encounters, there is an appropriation amid the "highly asymmetrical relations." Nature enters history through attempts to dominate and subordinate the terrain and its wildlife. While Timothy Morton might say there is no nature outside of culture, here echoing Bruno Latour's "nature-culture," it remains a problem for culture to make its mark on the Arctic.[19] Ships are sent, cairns constructed, drawings made, and ordinances noted. Every venture and representation becomes a scaffolding of history by which that "out there" will come to be known as the Arctic and so enter into culture (in this case, specifically British culture of the nineteenth century).

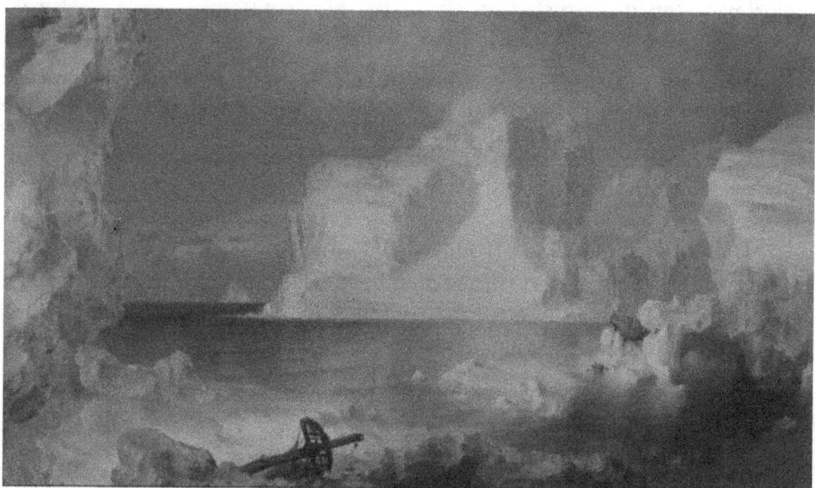

Figure 6.2. Fredric Edwin Church. *The Icebergs*. 1861. Image courtesy of Dallas Museum of Art.

The Franklin expedition is one such venture, which enters history through the event in which the terrain asserts dominion over and against humans. It does not enter by the return of the crew telling stories but through their absence and by way of the artifacts they leave behind as well as the tales and even published accounts of search parties, such as McClintock's *The Voyage of the "Fox" in the Arctic Seas: A Narrative of the Discovery of the Fate of Sir John Franklin and His Companions* (1859).[20] The event then circulates through culture as history, lore, maps, images, further expeditions north, and so on.

Fredric Edwin Church's large canvas painting *The Icebergs* serves as an example of the Franklin expedition entering cultural consciousness and the representation of an encounter with the Arctic as an event (Figure 6.2). As a key member of the second generation of the Hudson River School, Church had already made a name for himself depicting sublime scenes including *Niagara Falls* (1857) and vast wilderness scenes from his tour in Columbia and Ecuador, depicted in the style of the picturesque in *Cotopaxi* and *The Andes of Ecuador* (1855). By the early 1860s, he was one of the most famous painters in the United States. *The Icebergs* is one of several paintings made after his voyage north to Labrador and Newfoundland.

The painting was first exhibited in New York in April 1861 under the title *The North*. Then, sometime between this exhibition and its showing in London in 1862, Church changed the title to *The Icebergs* and added the mast.[21] The mast as wreckage shows the catastrophe of human expeditions when set against the brutal and sublime Arctic. Yet, with the addition of the mast, Church attempts to provide a civilizing referential frame. The mast signals the presence of humans and provides a human scale to the scene. Such a framing says that humans have been to the Artic and left their mark. Some humans, like Franklin and his crew, never return, while others, such as McClintock, return to tell the tale of the lack of return. In *The Icebergs*, the wilds are humanized and civilized by the referential sign of a mast that doubles as the sign of a missionary cross in the wasteland. And as a further signifier of humans marking the Artic, Church has left his signature on the ice to the bottom left of the mast. While Franklin and his crew never return, their loss calls out for search parties, which become responsible for mapping much of the Canadian Arctic and so gathering the wilds within a cartographic net.

Franklin's expedition and subsequent search parties are exemplary scenes of encounter. The question of encounter takes on the schema that legitimizes much of what constitutes literary scholarship. History throws itself; it is its own ground that functions without question as the ground that legitimizes literary historical work. We work on the representations and scaffolding by which culture marks the biotopes. We lay markers and masts and signatures and cartography that take the alienness of nature and humanize it as moments within history. These marks of culture foster our remarks, but the marks serve as masks as well, because history cannot read outside its own markings. The scaffolding of history is high and the fall outside its human bounds is abysmal.

For humans, nature is never itself but is already filtered by our perceptions of nature. The polar bear serving as a marker of wildness is a good example. Looking at taxidermied bears over the past two centuries, one can see the history of our cultural perception of the Arctic and its animals ranging over time from fierce to charming. By observing the shift in how the bear is presented over centuries, one can denaturalize our representations of the Artic. In other words, even our representations of an event, even our histories of history, are historical. History becomes its own legitimizing and referential agent. Because we can never get outside of human history to provide a critique of it, we provide alternative histories, heterogeneous histories, histories told from the viewpoint of different cultures or minorities or other discursive communities. Later in this chapter I suggest alternative lines of flight from history and histories, but for now consider how representation bears upon the Artic.

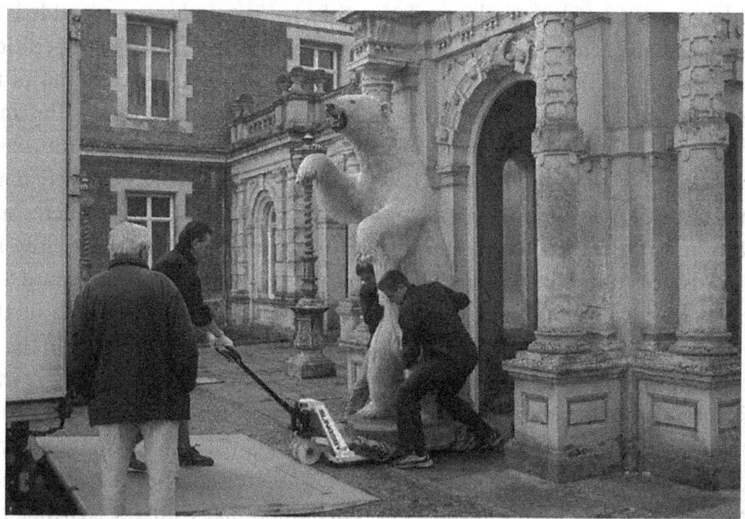

Figure 6.3. Snæbjörnsdóttir/Wilson. "Loading the Somerleyton bear in preparation for the installation at Spike Island." *nanoq: flat out and bluesome.* 2006. Image courtesy of the artists.

Contemporary artists Bryndis Snæbjörnsdóttir and Mark Wilson's work *nanoq: flat out and bluesome* (2006) reflects on the construction of British culture in the Arctic and serves as a model for reflection. Snæbjörnsdóttir and Wilson have hunted down all of the taxidermied polar bears of the United Kingdom, photographed them in situ, catalogued their provenance, and then gathered as many of these bears as they could into a contemporary gallery space. They found thirty-four stuffed bears (and have since uncovered a few more in private collections) and exhibited ten at Spike Island gallery.

Nanoq: flat out and bluesome as a work extends from the search and photographing of the bears, to the gallery exhibition, to gallery talks and a publication with photographs and essays, and to ongoing cataloguing of new finds. These taxidermied bears have entered human history between 1786 (the oldest, currently at Blair Castle) to 1999 (Lord Putnam's bear bought on holiday while in Paris). As the artists themselves and critics have noted, the bears entered history only through their death. They are shot, gutted, hauled aboard a ship and then taxidermied. Indeed, the animals are stuffed. What is left, what is on display, is a hide shaped and molded to represent a bear but hollow within, devoid of any interiority and standing as a shell and trophy. The fur is no longer the site of contact between human and animal worlds,

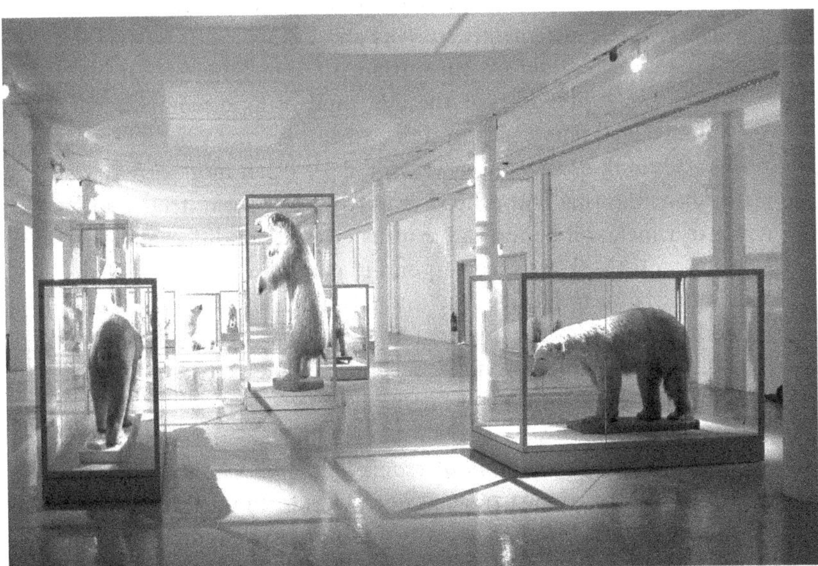

Figure 6.4. Snæbjörnsdóttir/Wilson. Installation. *nanoq: flat out and bluesome*. Spike Island, Bristol, UK, 2006. Image courtesy of the artists.

with all the abrasiveness and frictions and productivity of such an encounter. The fur is now an object made to match our representational matrix of nature. These polar bear forms become "things trying very hard to be polar bears" or "renewed objects representing polar bear-ness" to and for a culture.[22]

At the same time, the skin is given an architecture according to current cultural perceptions of the wild, the Arctic, and the bear. The animal body is gutted from any animal interiority. The bear's world and way of worlding is replaced with straw, hay, wood timbers, and hollow sculpted forms. Over time, these manufactured interiors change to match cultural perceptions of the animal from the beastly, vicious and wild to mimicking the stance and musculature of actual bears, to the Disney-esque (as with Lord Putnam's bear, obtained in 1999). Art historian Steve Baker unravels the valences of these works: "It is also a space with both surfaces and interiors; as the artists have written, the spectacle of the bears presented a beautiful veneer beneath which lay a conundrum oscillating backwards and forwards between nature and culture, taking in all manner of aspects of human achievement, endeavor, cruelty, and folly on the way."[23] Through contact with this "veneer," the artists find a site of production:

> Much has been written on the hollowness of souvenirs, their intrinsic sadness and the ultimate futility of collecting things by which we seek to remember places and events . . . If we handle or knock expectantly on the surface of something stolen long ago, we can expect to hear the dull thud of its disembodiment, its unmediated physicality, in short, what it is—not what it was or what we think or thought it was. Or, if we listen more closely we may hear the ring and echo of a much larger set of truths, only one of which will be indicative of its current condition and only one of which will be, or correspond in part with what we thought its significance to be. We may find a multitude of narratives and interlocking fragments, redolent not only of what has transpired, its dislocation, journey and its second life, but inevitably, if only by implication, of what else might have been.[24]

The whole of *nanoq: flat out and bluesome* is this knocking at the site of an animal world and the contact zone between worlds. In the case of these polar bears killed and stuffed over the past two hundred years, the rap against the world produces a hollow sound. It is the "bluesome" sound of "what else might have been" in the now inaccessible past of this particular animal's world and the uncertain future of the species. The "multitude of narratives" from which the artists draw is possible only by preventing the "unmediated physicality" from showing through. Instead, cultural narratives and appropriations arise, including exploration, trophy, conquest, science, violation, or even kitsch.

The bearskins bear the marks of entering history with bullet holes still visible.[25] What these bears were before history remains a "silence and solitude," but the remainder that lives on with us today bears witness to the something within the "silence and solitude" that stands outside the scaffolding of history but is not a vacancy.

Polar bear skins are a significant artifact and figure of Arctic conquest. Dominance over a terrain includes displaying victory over its harshest and most fearsome elements. For explorers in the Romantic period, returning to Britain with polar bear skins proves to be a sign of British superiority over the dangers of the North. One significant moment of polar bear encounters in British history is Lord Nelson's struggle with a bear while he was a midshipman aboard the aptly named ship *Carcass*, which in 1773 set out for Arctic exploration. In *The Life of Horatio Lord Nelson*, Robert Southey makes much of the bear encounter as a premonition of things to come for the naval officer. In Southey's telling of the event, Nelson exposes himself to uncertain wilds "in a more

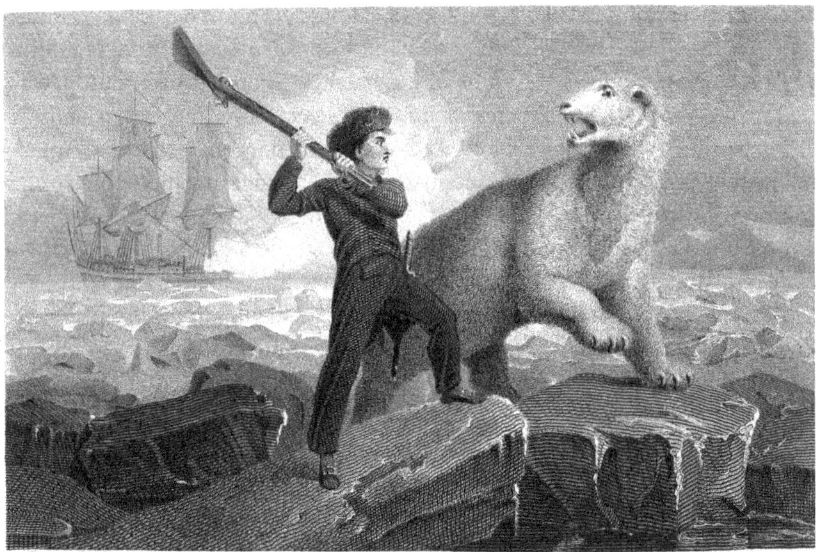

Figure 6.5. John Landseer. *The Life of Horatio Lord Nelson.* Engraving after Richard Westall. 1809. National Maritime Museum.

daring a manner" than the other officers.[26] In 1809, Richard Westall painted a romanticized image of Nelson in his youth fighting off the polar bear. Westall's image was engraved by noted Royal Academy engraver John Landseer.

As the event is recounted by Southey, Nelson and a crewmate tracked a polar bear with Nelson wanting to claim its skin as a prize. When within range for a shot, Nelson's gun misfired, and as the bear set upon him, Nelson used the butt of his musket to ward off the beast. He was saved by the ice breaking and a rift separating the bear from Nelson. The ship fired one of its guns to scare the animal. Captain Lutwidge berated the midshipman for his adventure. According to Southey, when the captain questioned Nelson about his motives, the young man replied, " 'Sir,' . . . pouting his lip, as he was wont to do when agitated, 'I wished to kill the bear, that I might carry the skin to my father.' "[27] The bearskin becomes a figure for ritual passage into manhood and a prideful symbol of conquest over the wilderness.

Westall's painting and John Landseer's engraving omit Nelson's shipmate and show a calm, smartly dressed Nelson fearless in his encounter in a desolate terrain with the overwhelmingly strong animal (Figure 6.5). The painting and engraving were commissioned as an illustration for one of the earliest biographies of Nelson, *The Life of Admiral Lord Nelson, KB*, by John McArthur and James Stanier Clarke.[28]

Years later, in 1863–64, John Landseer's son Edwin Landseer created the devastating painting *Man Proposes, God Disposes* (Figure 6.6). The painting was commissioned by Edward Coleman to depict a scene from Franklin's voyage. Landseer shows the ruins of a whaleboat that had been outfitted to sled across the ice after the crew abandoned their ships, the *Erebus* and the *Terror*. Amid the wreckage of broken mast and haul and scattered equipment, two polar bears rip the blood-red ensign canvas from the mast and feast on the rib cage of a crewman. Displayed in London in 1863, a year after Church's *The Icebergs*, Landseer had exceeded Church's imaginative display of the Arctic wilderness claiming its victims. As art critics Andrew Moore and Diane Donald have noted, Landseer's staging draws from Francis McClintock's recounting of his 1859 expedition's journey to find remains of the Franklin party, as told in *The Voyage of the "Fox" in the Arctic Seas*:

> The boat was partially out of her cradle upon the sledge, and lying
> in such a position as to lead me to suppose it the effect of a violent
> north-west gale. . . . But all these were after observations; there
> as that in the boat which transfixed us with awe. It was portions
> of two human skeletons. One was that of a slight young person;
> the other of a large, strongly-made, middle-aged man. The former

was found in the bow of the boat, but in too much disturbed a state to enable Hobson to judge whether the sufferer had died there; large and powerful animals, probably wolves, had destroyed much of this skeleton, which may have been that of an officer.[29]

McClintock explains in a footnote, "No part of the skull of either skeleton was found, with the exception only of the lower jaw of each."[30] The rest of the passage is taken up by exacting details of the remains, including the length and weight of the vessel, a description of the sled, and itemized remains found, including patterns of slippers, number of watches, list of titles, and so on. The detailing of the remains as artifacts of civilization in the wilderness almost overshadows the corpses.

Landseer makes one notable deviation from McClintock's story: rather than wolves devouring the bodies of the two shipmen, as McClintock conjectures, Landseer substitutes polar bears. Donald explains the substitution as reference to human desperation and brutality as depicted in Rae's report of cannibalism in the Franklin expedition: "It is impossible not to see in Landseer's ferocious and amoral beasts a symbolic stand-in for the human cannibals, even though the animals' actions are ostensibly a denial that humans were implicated in the deed."[31] By portraying the dismemberment of British corpses, Landseer is rending "the fabric of patriotic rhetoric, religious sentiment, and idealism so evident in sanctioned reports on the finds."[32]

While, as Donald says, the bears could be "a symbolic stand-in for the human cannibals," their "amoral" feasting is ahistorical—which is to say that the animals are not stand-ins for humans but are the very nonhuman event that disrupts or erupts into history and overturns the "patriotic rhetoric, religious sentiment, and idealism" of the expedition and reports about it.

In light of John Landseer's etching of Nelson in the Arctic, Edwin's choice of polar bears gains greater significance. Where Southey reports that Nelson wishes to "carry the skin to my father," Edwin Landseer inverts such imperial desires and carries to his father an image that twists free of Westall's painting engraved by John Landseer. In biographies and in Westall's painting, the national hero Nelson fought the elements and animals of the North in his formative years before gaining glory for Britain at sea. By contrast, Franklin and the men of his expedition have met their limits. Pressing the comparison further, Nelson knew when to retreat. He and the men of the *Carcass* did not defeat the North but saved their own hides, unlike Franklin and his crew, who pushed farther into the sea of ice.

Edwin Landseer's *Man Proposes, God Disposes* provides an antihumanist response to the heroics of his father's engraving of Nelson in the arctic.

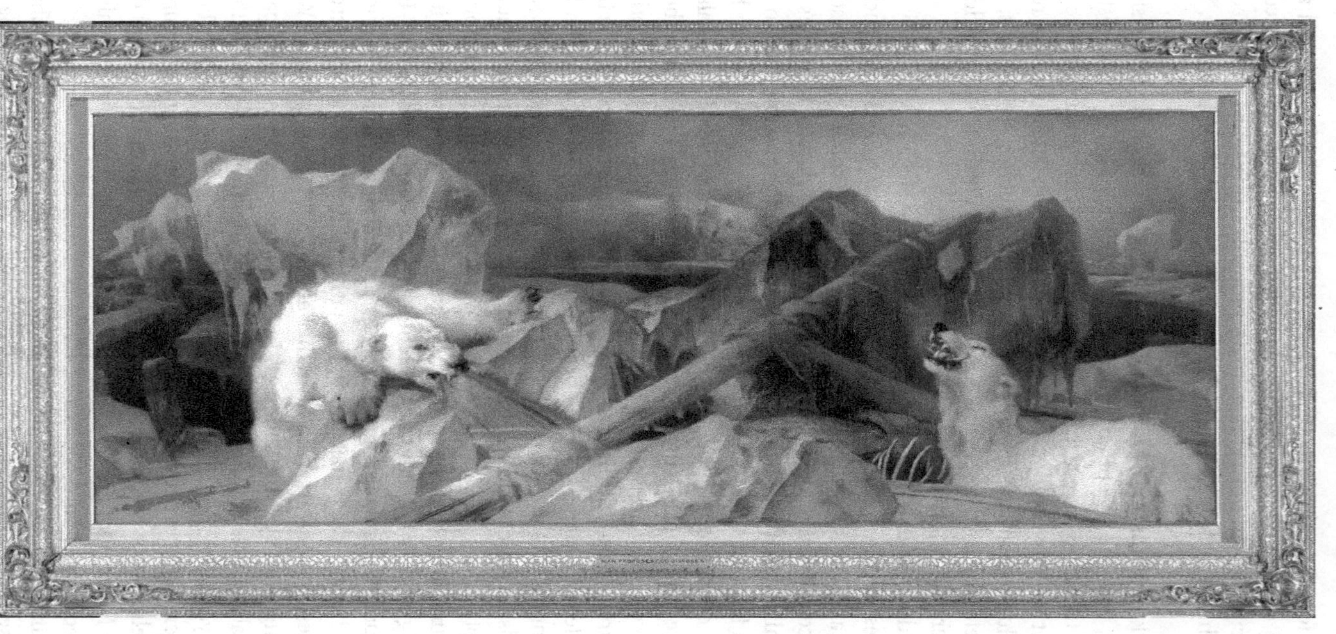

Figure 6.6. Edwin Landseer. *Man Proposes, God Disposes*. 1864. Royal Holloway College.

Man proposes, but the animality of the North disposes and levels the cultural intrusion of human history. The remains of the Franklin crew discovered by John Rea in 1854 and then by McClintock become markers of history and beacons of culture at its furthest reaches. We, along with the British public of the nineteenth century, imagine events around these artifacts where silence and solitude were more than vacancy.

As was to be expected, Franklin's wife, who attended the exhibition opening at the Royal Academy, was displeased with the barbaric nature of the painting and refused to enter the Great Room in which it was hung. Reviews of the painting were mixed. W. M. Rossetti asserted that the painting was the most popular on exhibition. While the *Athenaeum* found the painting to be of "epic" quality, the reviewer was displeased with the content: "as to the choice of subject, we protest against it." *The Illustrated London News* criticized the horror of the scene. For other critics, the painting provided a window onto the sublime: the *Spectator* called the work a "living fire of imagination," and the *Saturday Review* describing it as "the force and height of the idea . . . sublimity of sentiment."[33]

As we shall see, despite being known as a sentimentalist painter, Landseer was not yet done with animality, nor it with him. He made a living mainly from genteel images of animals, particularly popular sentimental and allegorical paintings of dogs and Scottish Highland hunting scenes. It was for these popular scenes that he was knighted in 1850 and then elected president of the Royal Academy in 1866, a position he declined. Typical of Landseer's sentimental works is *Saved* (1856), in which a young child is pulled ashore and rescued from drowning by a Newfoundland dog. Landseer had painted this same Newfoundland earlier in *The Distinguished Member of the Humane Society* (1831). It has been said in legend that the dog that is the subject of these paintings was called "Bob." He was said to have survived a shipwreck off the English coast and made his way to the London docks, where he became known for saving people from drowning—a total of twenty-three in all. For such kindness to humanity, Bob became a distinguished member of the Royal Humane Society.[34] The much earlier *Off to the Rescue* (1827) displays a similar dog standing attentively at the shoreline before plunging into the water to save a drowning person.

In a large number of paintings, Landseer shows dogs at the service of their owners. In *Old Shepherd's Chief Mourner* (1837), a sheepdog sits alone and keeps vigil at the casket of his owner. The dog seems forlorn as he rests his head on the casket. In *The Faithful Hound* (1830), a grizzled hound dog barks as if in mourning at the body of his owner, who lays in full armor slain in battle. *Low Life* and *High Life* (1829) display dogs and class along

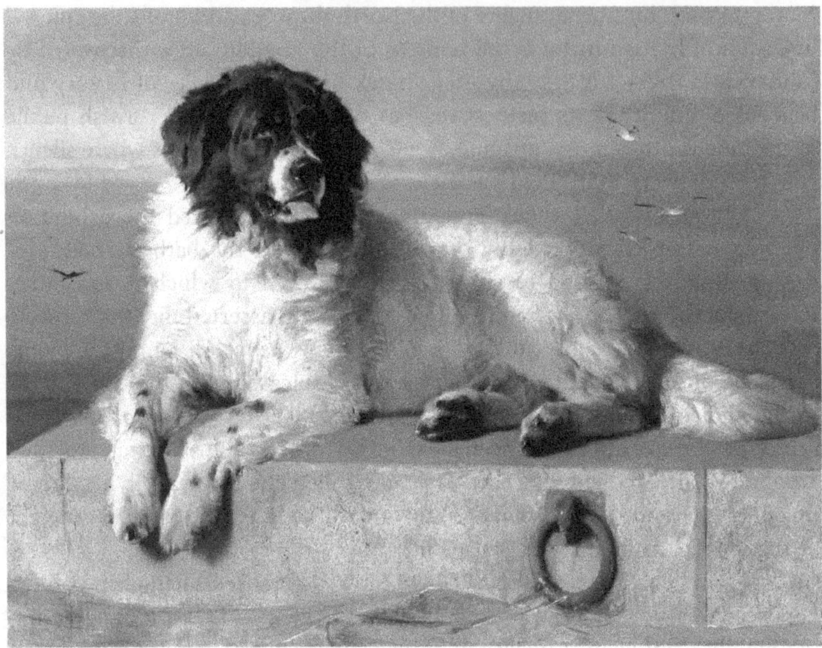

Figure 6.7. Edwin Landseer. *The Distinguished Member of the Humane Society*. 1831. Tate Gallery.

the lines of Robert Burns's "The Twa Dogs." As previously discussed in the introduction, *Low Life* depicts a stocky dog with wide chest and thick jaw sitting at the worn, wooden doorstep of his master's home. Beside him rests a mug of beer and a pipe. As the 1877 work *Landseer's Dogs and Their Stories* imaginatively describes the scene, "He may be low—one of the rudest and surliest of working dogs, but he is still a working dog, a trusty watch in the absence of his master from his place of work, a tatter of some renown. He is, to do him justice, removed from the deepest gulf into which dogs and men can sink."[35] In the companion work *High Life*, a lean and well-cared-for deerhound sits quietly in his master's study, which is decorated with hunting gear and artifacts. Throughout Landseer's oeuvre, a wide range of other paintings displays dogs with an array of characteristics from noble and loyal to comically entertaining.

Landseer's hunting scenes, particularly those of the 1840s and 1850s, along with those of Richard Ansdell, became the model for hunting paintings during the period. Many are set in Scotland and show a wild, lush environment devoid of human civilization. As John Mackenzie points out in *The Empire of Nature*, armed incursions into nature are part of building Empire in ways similar to the subjugation of foreign terrain and its inhabitants.[36] Moreover, given the war between Scotland and England some hundred years earlier, English hunters on Scottish soil have the feel of a militarized force expanding into their colonized territories.

The imperial nature of the hunt is captured in Landseer's *The Hunting of Chevy Chase* (1825–26), inspired by conversations with Sir Walter Scott. *The Hunting of Chevy Chase* takes place near Cheviot Hill, which acts as a border between Scotland and England in the disputed territory. According to the centuries-old oral story, Percy the Earl of Northumberland, depicted in Landseer's painting, hunted on this land despite the Earl of Douglas forbidding it as an incursion into Scottish territory. The dispute caused a bloody battle between the two lords. Landseer's painting carries with it the politics of land dispute overlaid upon a violent hunt. The contorted body of the wounded stag, the goaded hunting dog, and the wild throng of the pack all carry with them both their own struggles and the political struggles between England and Scotland.

Other paintings by Landseer, such as *The Stag at Bay* (1846), depict idealized moments of a big game hunt. In this scene, the hunter and his dogs have run the stag into a loch, and so cornered it awaits its death. In Donald's extended analysis of the painting, she points out that the spectator's viewpoint is that of the hunter not depicted in the scene. In other words, we as viewers are placed in the hunt. Whether the animal escapes the hunter's gun depends on our own imagined narrative as viewers who stand in the place of the hunter. In the background of the painting, the bird soaring skyward toward the light and away from the dark clouds and imminent rain serves as a contrast to the struggling and cornered deer. The painting caused divided emotions among viewers at the painting's exhibition in the Royal Academy. As Donald points out, "journalists who reviewed the Royal Academy exhibition in 1846 reveal the divided feelings of the public about this subject: a conflict which Landseer—himself torn between opposing impulses—must have anticipated and even fomented."[37] Audiences feel the emotional tension within the hunt.

Landseer's paintings provide a fixed and paradigmatic moment in the hunt. As with the polar bears killed and stuffed, the prey enters into human history only through its death. Consequently, the paintings are haunted by the conflicting relationship between an idealized purity of nature and an idealized conquest of nature through the hunt. In some paintings, such as his famous *Monarch of the Glen* (1851) and the large canvas work *The Sanctuary* (1842), the viewer appears to have a window onto a world devoid of humans—hunters or otherwise. Yet in providing such an imagined space, we as viewers are in the scene that is supposedly without humans. We get to have nature both ways—untouched yet accessible through the painting, animals as part of history and apart from our history. In such moments, we can see Landseer "himself torn between opposing impulses," with a desire to inscribe the animals within culture and wanting the animals to have a space and time outside of human worlding.[38]

This conflict between culture and a space outside of culture and history is perhaps nowhere more evident than in Landseer's struggle to create the lions at the base of Nelson's Column at Trafalgar Square.[39] His difficulty in finishing the commission, given to him in 1858 and completed in 1867, is fairly well known. He made frequent visits to the London Zoo to make sketches from life, but as a painter he required the assistance of a sculptor, Carlo Marochetti, to help him translate his concepts into three dimensions.

The commission took far longer than expected. Landseer asked for an initial delay of nine months to allow for finishing other works and to study live lions. He then requested copies of casts from actual lions from the Albertin Academy in Turin. The lion from which the casts were made had belonged to the King of Sardinia. When the lion died, casts were taken of the head and limbs, and after dissection, further casts were taken of the animal's anatomy. Landseer requested copies of all the casts. These copies eventually arrived in the summer of 1861, but the wait had delayed his work further.

The slow progress—if progress at all—proved troublesome to the public and the commissioning governmental agency. The chief commissioner of the Office of Works and Buildings was called to testify before the House of Commons as to the delays and to ensure the House that the artist was making progress. As *The Art Journal* records the testimony, Commissioner Cowper assured the House's members that Landseer "was now very accurately studying the habits of lions and was to be seen in the Zoological Gardens making himself thoroughly acquainted with their attitudes."[40] That summer, Cowper wrote to Landseer: "I am sorry to have to trouble you again, knowing that in undertaking the work on which you are engaged you have been activated by a desire to give to the public the benefit of your artistic genius by placing in the most prominent position of London something that will do credit to our time, but as the monument has remained unfinished for so many years I think you will feel that I am only doing my duty in trying to bring the matter to a speedy conclusion."[41] It was another five years before the lions were finally installed at Trafalgar. In response to the Office's queries, Landseer explained his delay due to other commissions, including a commission by the Queen. Both he and the public officials understood that the burden and expectations placed on Landseer were very high.

At the height of his quandary with the lions, Landseer was working on *Man Proposes, God Disposes* and had borrowed a polar bear skull from paleontologist Sir Hugh Falconer of the Forres Museum in Scotland to help him figure the face and dimensions of the animal.[42] While contemplating the skull and working on the Arctic painting, things got a bit out of hand. Landseer's drawings, sculptures, and the lion casts are an examination of the exteriority, the surface of the animal. Its interiority, its animality, remains opaque and inaccessible. It is this very animality—inaccessible but a spectral force—that haunts Landseer. He moves beyond a surface encounter or an encounter with animal surfaces.

Since 1840, Landseer had suffered occasional nervous breakdowns and nervous illness. Sometime in 1863–64, he had a nightmare of being pinned and eaten by a lion, the very lion he was representing for the commemorative national memorial at Trafalgar (figure 6.8). He drew a sketch of the night-mare, *My Last Night's Nightmare.*[43] This date of 1863–64 coincides with his painting of *Man Proposes, God Disposes.* As Moore notes, the gaping mouths of the nightmare lion and polar bear appear similar. The lions decorating Nelson's monument at Trafalgar carry in palimpsest John Landseer's depiction of Nelson's struggle with a polar bear and Edwin Landseer's revision in which bears eat British arctic explorers.

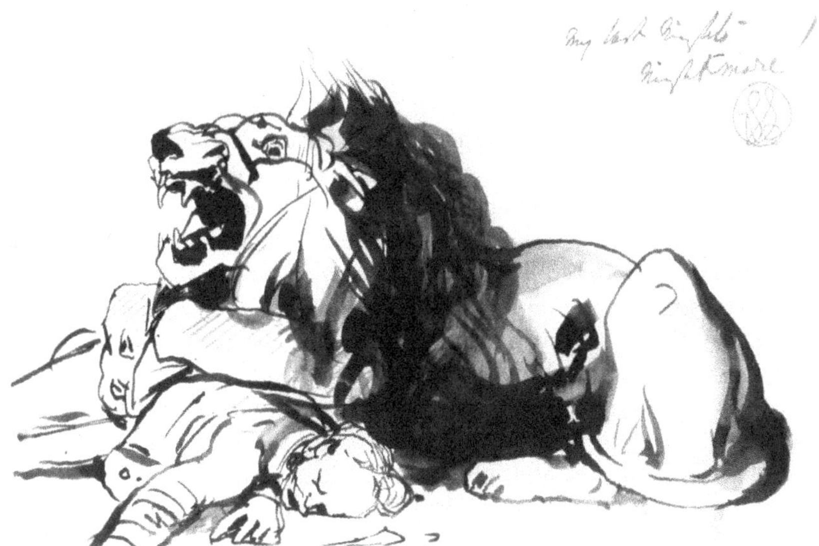

Figure 6.8. Edwin Landseer. *My Last Night's Nightmare.* Courtesy of the Marquees of Salisbury, Hatfield House, Welwyn Hertfordshire.

There is more to the nightmare than Landseer being consumed by his work. Indeed, strange and even fiendish visions sometimes arise when pressure mounts in creative endeavors. Landseer's nightmare and his representations of fierce beasts are more than personal. Animality has gotten the better of Landseer. Rather than understand the dream as an exhibition of Landseer's personal struggle, it is possible that the artist sees beyond the inscription of animals within human history to imagine humans with their history and culture being devoured by animals. More specifically, culture is consumed by animality—that of the animal unrepresentable and not appropriated by culture. While explorers bring back artifacts, Landseer abandons artifacts and brings the ahistorical, the event, that changes the referential frame and interrupts history.

Man Proposes, God Disposes and *My Last Night's Nightmare* are more than one-off incidents of mental illness. Landseer's biographers often cite the 1840s as the first signs of his mental strain, beginning with the death of his mother that year and continuing with increased effect until his own death in 1873. Cosmo Monkhouse saw in *The Otter Hunt* (1844) [currently titled *The Otter Speared, the Earl of Aberdeen's Otterhounds*] a similar violence to his later works:

> To such a nightmare of imagination we owe the almost unbearable torture of the *Otter Hunt* and the *Random Shot* and the still more heart-rending picture *Man Proposes, God Disposes* was surely born of a similar disease.[44]

For *The Otter Hunt*, Landseer constructs a classical visual pyramid with the otterhounds gathered at the base and the speared otter forming the top of the pyramid silhouetted against the sky. The huntsman with red sporting jacket holds the center of the painting, and his spear provides the verticality of the scene. Otter hunting remained a sport throughout the nineteenth century and was rationalized as a way to rid property of vermin that eat stocks of fish, such as the salmon on the bank depicted in Landseer's painting. While the human hunter in this painting appears to be the calm force of control amid the bloodlust of the hounds, he is also the central character in the killing. His merciless treatment of the otter indicates a violence and force latent within civil society.

In a fit of displaced humanist moralism, John Ruskin in *Modern Painters* showed particular displeasure in *The Otter Speared*:

> I would have Mr. Landseer, before he gives us any more writhing otters, or yelping packs, reflect whether that which is best

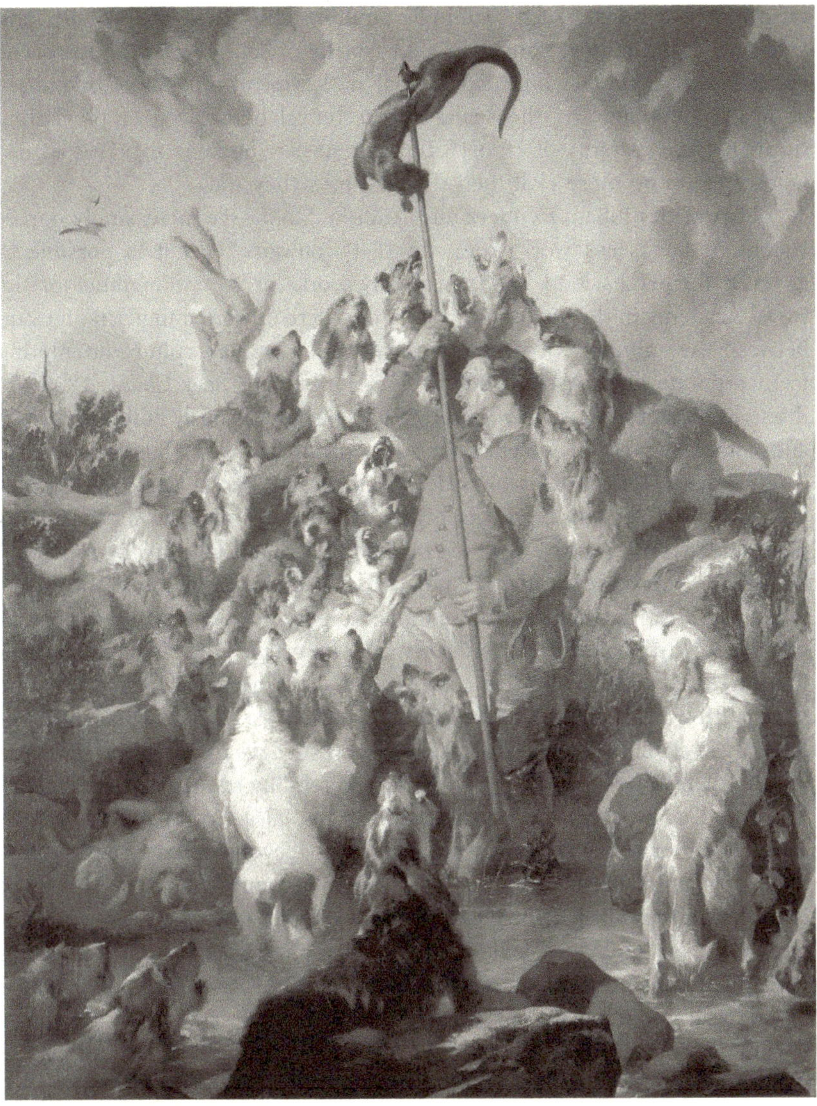

Figure 6.9. Edwin Landseer. *The Otter Speared, the Earl of Aberdeen's Otterhounds.* c. 1844. Laing Art Gallery.

worthy of contemplation in a hound be its ferocity, or in an otter its agony, or in a human being its victory, hardly achieved even with the aid of its most sagacious brutal allies, over a poor little fish-catching creature, a foot long.[45]

Of course it is exactly such seemingly pointless sport, with its brutality and suffering, that Landseer considers "best worthy of contemplation." The scene becomes a commentary on the irrational, dark, violent capacity of humans— a capacity amplified by the social and technical buttressing of the killing through the apparatus of "sport." In such scenes, humans in a wilderness landscape are no more civil then the wild prey they stalk.

Art critics Julian Treuherz and Andrew Moore see increasingly darker visions in Landseer's work from the 1840s onward.[46] Yet it is possible to go even further back to Landseer's early works as a new member of the Royal Academy in the 1820s and trace from there onward a lingering tension between the animality of various animals and a human culture attempting to incorporate them. Works such as *The Hunting of Chevy Chase* (1825–26, discussed earlier) and *Attachment* (1829) display precariously built hierarchies and complex layers of violence. In *Attachment*, Landseer illustrates Walter Scott's poem "Helvellyn," which describes the accidental death of Charles Gough. whose slip on the rocks of the mountain while touring led to his demise. As reported at the time and in Scott's poem, his faithful dog remained at his side. Three months after the incident, a shepherd came across the hiker's remains at Red Tarn. Unlike the sentimental poem by Scott or Wordsworth's poem "Fidelity," the local Carlisle newspaper reported: "The bitch had pupped in a furze near the body of her master, and, shocking to relate, had torn the cloaths from his body and eaten him to a perfect skeleton."[47] The symbol of fidelity has eaten its owner. The savageness of the dogs in *The Otter Hunter* is already there, latent in this earlier work. The rending of human flesh in *Man Proposes, God Disposes* can be found within the tale of companion species.

Why should the possibility of an animality beyond and over and against culture, an animality chafing at the bits of culture and occasionally breaking loose in triumph, be attributed to a diseased mind? Is it madness to think of sentient life outside of culture and in fact railing against and defeating Britannia? I am not arguing against a turning point in Landseer's personal mental strain, which is well documented in letters and accounts by those close to him. Rather, my concern is that in reading this strain in his paintings, we view the animals as markers of Landseer's personal psychological state rather than as figures of animals that point elsewhere—the elsewhere of an animality that works over and against a biopolitical Britain. Such animality is a refusal of the cosmopolitical proposition where humanity lays claim to animal bodies. Rather, for Landseer, animality becomes a friction to social systems, a red-in-tooth-and-claw resistance from nonhuman worlding.

Afterword

Romanticism in the Dust of This Planet

This afterword functions as final thoughts along the trajectory of bio-power's resistance to assimilation within the biopolitical. Chapters in this book have moved slowly toward an outside or outer limit of biological life's resistance to social and political control—an assertion of massification as a resistance to "rights" and individuation, the intertwining of animal and human life over and against an "improved agriculture," and animal life beyond the representative capacities of natural history (as seen in Bewick and Stubbs) and animality as a violence or horror to human culture (in the work of Landseer). These final reflections attempt a sketch of life beyond the human, following Eugene Thacker's provocative work *In the Dust of This Planet*.[1] In doing so, these reflections attempt to twist free of some fundamental elements of Romantic aesthetics, including the privileged interiority of the human subject (with its capacity for memory and self-reflection) and the economic and aesthetic value of nature by which the world around us gains cultural significance.

While much of this book has used the work of labor-class authors and artists, these final reflections make use of well-known figures within Romanticism and some of their best-known works. The limits of culture traced in these texts can be found elsewhere in Romantic literature, most notably the gothic; however, what interests me here is the way authors known for fundamental elements of Romantic aesthetics reflect on the limits of human life at a point where nature supersedes culture. In doing so, they seem to undermine the very privileged subjectivity associated with Romanticism, where, as M. H. Abrams tells us in the classic work *The Mirror and the Lamp*, "[a] work of art is essentially the internal made external, resulting from a creative process operating under the impulse of feeling, an embodying of the combined product of the poet's perceptions, thoughts, and feelings."[2]

The attempt or gesture here is to think nature that is beyond human assimilation—to think the difference of nature (what Gilles Deleuze calls the "difference of difference") that is not a nature subsumed within a higher-order category of the (cultural) same.[3] For example, the terms "man" and "woman" are differences under the overarching, higher-order category "human." What I am seeking—what I am after (belatedly coming after or trailing behind)—is a concept of nature that persists or insists beyond nature-for-us or nature-for-culture. By definition, such a concept of nature beyond or without humans is impossible for humans to think; however, the arc of attempting this concept provides a glimpse at a nature indifferent to civilization.

Moreover, it is worth noting that this world-without-us functions contrary to some contemporary ecological thinking. It is precisely contra the hybrid term nature-culture that Thacker deploys his cosmic pessimism. Prior to pursuing his line of thought, I address briefly in a few pages the methodology by which I am proposing one might think at the limit of culture and toward a speculative world without humans. (Readers less interested in a justification of methodology and the tension between camps of critical theory and ecological writing can proceed without this dense reading of contemporary theoretical concerns.) For ecological thought, it has been taken for granted over the past decade that there is no nature without culture—nature being a representational form defined by culture and human culture weighing upon the planet such that there is no place outside of cultural impact upon spaceship earth. Human culture shapes nature and is shaped by it. And, of course, we socially constitute what counts as nature for us.

In an attempt to complicate the dualism between ourselves and the rest of the planet, Bruno Latour and Donna Haraway (among others) join the terms in the hyphenated phrase nature-culture.[4] The goal for these thinkers is to avoid a subject-object dualism whereby nature is an object at a distance to be saved (or further damaged) through the active agency of humans. Haraway characterize our enmeshed connection with nature as "staying with the trouble."[5] The "trouble" is the knotted relations between nature and culture (or, as she terms this, natureculture). "Staying with" means teasing out how we use one term as a foil for the other, figuring how these terms slide into one another, and ultimately determining how their complex relationship deconstructs the binary that has been used as a too easy escape from our connection to the nonhuman and noncivilized world.

In his provocatively titled *Ecology without Nature*, Timothy Morton calls the nature-culture complexity a "dark ecology." The term is meant to dispel the notion of a "beautiful soul," one who laments the distance between himself and nature and in "romantic" fashion seeks to become one with the natural world. Nature is not "out there" to be saved, nor is it a line of escape from social problems:

> We start by thinking that we can "save' something called "the world" "over there," but end up realizing that we ourselves are implicated. This is the solution to the beautiful soul syndrome: reframing out field of activity as one for which we ourselves are formally responsible, even guilty. . . . Dark ecology undermines the naturalness of the stories we tell about how we are involved in nature. It preserves the dark, depressive quality of life in the shadow of ecological catastrophe. Instead of whistling in the dark, insisting that we're part of Gaia, why not stay with the darkness?[6]

Morton's dark ecology is another way of staying with the trouble and of making sure we do not too easily resolve ecological tensions through a unity with nature or a progress of culture.

Amid this ecological thinking for the last decade is another set of concerns regarding how to think catastrophe and a world without us, a world Alan Weisman tries to depict in a creative nonfiction work with this title.[7] The figure of an end or catastrophe has been used by a number of philosophers to think the limits of human being, thought, and values, perhaps most famously by Friedrich Nietzsche in the opening of "Truth and Lies in the Extramoral Sense."[8] François Lyotard lays out the predicament in *The Inhuman*:

> Assume that the ground . . . will vanish into clouds of heat and matter. Considered as matter, the earth isn't all that originary. . . . The ground is an arrangement of matter/energy. This arrangement is transitory—lasting a few billion years, more or less. Lunar years. Not a long time considered on a cosmic scale. The sun, our earth and your thought will have been no more than a spasmodic state of energy, an instant of established order, a smile on the surface of matter in a remote corner of the cosmos. You believe too much in that smile, in the complicity of things and thought.[9]

Lyotard's inhuman temporality brings us to a predicament: we know there will be an end to humans, but how can we think a world without us if every thought of nature is always already nature-culture? The problem of thinking an inhuman time could quickly bring us to the Kantian division between noumenon and phenomenon and what object-oriented ontology philosopher Quentin Meillassoux calls correlationism.[10] Inhuman time, or a world without us, provides a unique perspective to the speculative realist question because it adds to the inaccessibility of the "things in themselves" an inhuman temporal dimension.

One way of reframing the problem and finding a possible direction forward is through Alfred North Whitehead via Martin Heidegger on objects. Graham Harman's reading of Heidegger in *Tool Being* brings forward a tension in the perception of objects between referentiality—their situateness in our world—and their singularity—exceeding any referential system. Steve Shaviro explicates this: "Instead of swinging between an excess of referentiality on the one hand [Heidegger's ready-at-hand] and an excess of singularity on the other [Heidegger's present-to-hand], each object both disappears into and emerges out of its own inaccessible vacuum."[11] Shaviro extends this further by explaining, "If I cannot control and instrumentalize a thing, this is *both* because it draws me into extended referential networks whose full ramifications I cannot trace *and* because its singularity, bursting forth, stuns me in excess of anything that I can posit about it."[12] As we will see shortly, it is at this limit in thinking a "thing" that aesthetics comes to the aid of reason. Informing much of object-oriented ontology is Whitehead's rich description of things or what he calls entities. For Whitehead, entities understand and reflect a relation to each other through what he calls "prehensions," which have many of the characteristics of Heidegger's present-to-hand and ready-at-hand. But then Whitehead adds other aspects to the interaction among entities: the lure and feeling.

The lure is a conceptual figure for ways one entity draws in another, creating a proposition—possible ways of interacting. One entity propositions another, creating sets of problems or questions to be played out. The propositioned entity *feels* the relation. This is not a prehension as mode of knowing. Rather, feeling is an aesthetic relatedness among entities. As Shaviro explains, "entities interact by 'feeling' one another, even in the absence of knowledge and manipulability. Things encounter one another aesthetically and not just cognitively or practically (55).

What the Romantic poets offer us is not a line of flight away from society into a oneness with nature. As we will see later in this chapter, in select instances of select poems, we find the lure of things and the proposition of a world without humans. These entities provide a feeling of something beyond us (what Meillassoux calls "the great outdoors"). Eugene Thacker tries to get at this beyond by way of images, film, black metal music, and science fiction. Philosophy turns to aesthetics as a mode of access to that which is beyond knowledge. What Heidegger terms "call" and Whitehead "lure" is this thinking beyond ourselves and out of our space and time. This beyond is not an entity on the axis of real-possible but rather of virtual-actual; it is a rupture to the state of affairs from elsewhere. Poetry, poetics, poesis allows us to entertain the propositions that arrive from elsewhere. Aesthetics becomes a mode of speculative thought that is more rich and textured than philosophy and reason's limits can provide.

Toward this end, Thacker's *In the Dust of This Planet* stakes out a claim in three parts. Following Heidegger, he describes the *world-for-us* as the world that we interpret and give meaning to and that is commonly called the world. Second, there is the world that "bites back," which he (again, following Heidegger) calls "earth" or the *world-in-itself*. Here we perceive the earth as a resistance that signals something beyond us:

> On the one hand, we are increasingly more and more aware of the world in which we live as a non-human world, a world outside, one that is manifest in the effects of global climate change, natural disasters, the energy crisis, and progressive extinction of species world-wide. On the other hand, all these effects are linked, directly and indirectly, to our living in and living as a part of this non-human world. Hence contradiction is built into this challenge—we cannot help but to think of the world as a human world, by virtue of the fact that it is we human beings that think it.[13]

But then, radically, Thacker asks us to think a third world, which he calls the "planet" or the *world-without-us*, that is "the subtraction of the human world. To say that the world-without-us is antagonistic to the human is to attempt to put things in human terms, in the terms of the world-for-us."[14] The planet is, by definition, that which lives on without us and is beyond our comprehension—the difference of difference from the human that we can only understand through a *via negativa*. While such a world is beyond us, Romantic authors point to this nontranscendental beyond as a spirit and a force that informs and can overwhelm human worlding. In such works, we find the limits of the biopolitical apparatus making use of life, and beyond biopolitics, the limits of human dwelling.

I would like to couple the problem of thinking a world-without-us to the problem of reason, because by reason we usually mean human reason, which is our human representational system for translating what we can perceive of the planet for our human world. Thacker's "horror of philosophy" considers how "culture is the terrain on which we find attempts to confront an impersonal and indifferent world-without-us and the world-in-itself, with a void called the Planet that is poised between World and Earth."[15] In the ability to "confront an impersonal and indifferent world," literature exceeds philosophy's rational construction and in doing so provides a more fascinating (or, Thacker might say, horrifying) attempt to think the difference of difference: a planet that cannot be assimilated to human thought because it is a planet without humans.

The "we" by which we are commonly engaged in conversation operates under a rubric of rationality. You expect what I write to be reasonable and in so doing participate in the good sense and common sense of our community. Reason functions as modality for thinking. It is the system by which we think—by which we call thought thought and not something else—noise or nonsense or foolishness. Reason then is a ground for proceeding. It is how knowledge presents itself, and it is the ground for such presentation. Reason operates as our explanatory system.

Reason is a cultural discursive practice. We inherited it as a way of living from those before us and those before them dating back at least to the Greeks. We accept reason because anyone can step into reason; they can step into the Forum and be understood. Those from foreign lands, from elsewhere, can come here to this place and speak in this common language and be understood. They offer their thought in the representational system we hold in common. Thought as thought forms itself to this commonality, to the discursive practice we call reason—which works like a speech act, a vow, and a pledge.

Here I am drawing from Alphonso Lingis, who delineates the limits of reason's construction in *The Community of Those Who Have Nothing in Common*. He explains our prejudice: "The whole system of rational discourse is implicated in the statements put forth by any researcher, by anyone who endeavors to think rationally. Each one speaks as a representative of the common discourse. His own insights and utterances become part of the anonymous discourse of universal reason."[16] Coming before this community, one faces the imperative to formulate all thought and utterance according to the standards of reason. Of course, reason counts on this: anything that does not meet the dictates of reason as a discursive practice, anything that does not obey the laws of reason is by default irrational and so at the margins, a remainder, a scrap from the master's table thrown to the dogs to make a meal of. It is not what we chew, eat, and digest.

Our environment, then, unfolds itself according to our instrumental system. We carve out our surroundings to fit our system, then find within the environment only affirming nods according to our plan: "We civilized men who have produced our own environment see on everything in it the form and shape and species given to the raw material of nature by collective human intentions and effort, which are produced by the practice of rational discourse."[17] With the world we built according to our common sense and good sense, with this world affirming our way of dwelling, nothing is foreign to us. Here we are within inalienable rights and certain laws. The world encloses itself within the Forum of all that is reasonable.

What of the alien, the foreign, the outside that arrives and does not comply with good sense and common sense? What is one to do with the stranger who arrives from the sea of noise to the shores of communication, signal, language, rational discourse? Reason is an island that builds itself upon its own discursive and performative foundations. Reason throws itself; it is its own ground that functions without question as the ground that legitimizes its own discourse. We work upon the representations and scaffolding by which culture marks its environment. We lay markers and masts and signatures and cartography that make the alienness of the outside humanized and rationalized. The outside becomes assimilated as moments within our discourse. These marks of culture foster our remarks, but the marks serve as screens as well, because reason cannot read outside its own markings. The scaffolding of reason is high, and the fall outside its human bounds is abysmal.

Turning then to literary texts of the Romantic period, there are a number of works that use geographic extremity as a figure for thinking human limitations, the limits of representation, and the limits of culture and reason. In the last chapter on Landseer, we saw how the artist used the arctic region and polar bears in such a fashion. Well-known literary works that deploy geographic extremities include Percy Bysshe Shelley's "Mont Blanc," Mary Shelley's *Frankenstein*, and Samuel Taylor Coleridge's *Rime of the Ancient Mariner*. After briefly looking at these, I turn to nature among us that is also beyond us in John Keats's "Ode to Autumn" and William Wordsworth's "The Ruined Cottage." These texts serve as examples of a larger set of works that develop this theme; Romantic authors have explored the haunting of an inhuman earth among us and the leveling sensibility of a world without us. What we find in such works are comportments, economies, circulations, ways of being in the world that cannot be assimilated or made homogenous to our worlding.

Percy Shelley's "Mont Blanc" can be understood as the triumph of humans over and against seemingly insurmountable elements in nature. A fairly standard reading of the poem is through Kant's sublime, by which reason's demands to comprehend the mountain supersede the capacity of the senses to present the experience of Mont Blanc to reason. Moreover, language as a representational system falters in its attempt to express the experience. Hugo Donnelly provides a clear example of the Kantian interpretation of the poem:

As Kant argued, the restless disengagement of thought from nature in sublime experience—that fruitless searching of the landscape for adequate "images" to quantify the emotional charge of the sublime moment—signals the failure of empirical phenomena to form an adequate measure of the noumenal mind from whence that charge has risen. The disengagement systematizes a process whereby the mind abandons the world bounded by empirical laws. In Kantian terms, the mind in this process is peering into the eternal, infinite dimension of its own concealed power beyond the empirically knowable.[18]

The Kantian reading is satisfying in several ways: it makes sense of Shelley's enfolding figuration of mind and mountain from the poem's opening lines to its closing, and, importantly, it provides a profitable return of the mind's "infinite dimension of its own concealed power" exposed through the failure of representation. The way Shelley interlinks the mind and Mont Blanc and the river Arve throughout the poem provides sufficient grounding for such a reading. And yet, in doing so, the vast and devastating capacity of the mountain has to be put aside to equate geological scales with human reason.

What if the point of the poem, rather than leveling the mountain to the capacity of humans or elevating humans and our reason above the geological power and temporal fortitude of mountains, is to break the ability for such an analogy? What if the human mind does not have the recuperative capacity that Kant suggests and literary scholars utilize in reading this poem? What if the Kantian a priori of reason fails? In short, what if this is a poem about the world-without-us?

To realize such an interpretation is a matter of inflection. Where the Kantian reading turns the many lines of geological duration and destructive power toward a figuration for human imagination, a reading of "Mont Blanc" in the dust of this planet lingers on the deep realms of unknowability from which we see only fragments and traces: bones, carcasses, wasteland. The poem is replete with such descriptions:

> Of frozen floods, unfathomable deeps,
> Blue as the overhanging heaven, that spread
> And wind among the accumulated steeps;
> A desert peopled by the storms alone,
> Save when the eagle brings some hunter's bone,
> And the wolf tracks her there—how hideously

> Its shapes are heaped around! rude, bare, and high,
> Ghastly, and scarred, and riven.—Is this the scene
> Where the old Earthquake-dæmon taught her young
> Ruin? Were these their toys? or did a sea
> Of fire envelop once this silent snow?[19]

Such figuration repeats throughout the poem, as in these lines on destructive, unrelenting force and our inability to fathom its temporal and spatial dimensions:

> there, many a precipice
> Frost and the Sun in scorn of mortal power
> Have piled—dome, pyramid, and pinnacle,
> A city of death, distinct with many a tower
> And wall impregnable of beaming ice. . . .
> A city's phantom . . . but a flood of ruin
> Is there, that from the boundaries of the sky
> Rolls its perpetual stream[20]

Human figuration of dome, pyramid, and tower serve as analogies that become too fragile to hold and result in "a flood of ruin."

In several passages, Shelley attempts to use the mountain as a savior of a particular human notion of imagination, morality, and goodness. The river Arve and "Dizzy Ravine" are "no unbidden guests, / Near the still cave of the witch Poesy." And the mountain is given a voice "to repeal / Large codes of fraud and woe . . . which the wise and great and good / Interpret, or make felt, or deeply feel"[21] Yet these sentiments seem at odds with the planetary indifference of the ecological and geological structures as expressed in the rest of the poem. The poet feels inspired by his glimpse onto the indifference, deep time, and power of the mountain, yet then (in a subreption) co-opts the mountain for human ends of aesthetics ("cave of the witch Poesy") and morality ("repeal / Large codes of fraud and woe").

Shelley's use of the mountain makes sense in relation to his personal interests in poetry as a force for moral reform. The final lines of the poem give a hint at his method in this regard:

> And what were thou, and earth, and stars, and sea,
> If to the human mind's imaginings
> Silence and solitude were vacancy?[22]

The poet fills the silence and solitude not with vacancy but with nature as a moral force. It is not the religious certitude of Coleridge's "Hymn before Sun-rise, in the Vale of Chamouni," but it nevertheless yields a humanizing disposition. Yet the final lines of the poem could take more seriously the problem of vacancy not as a lack of our imaginative capacity in a Kantian figuration but as a limit to humanity itself. The problem is that we cannot know what a world without humans is like. To quote again from Thacker: "Hence contradiction is built into this challenge—we cannot help but to think of the world as a human world, by virtue of the fact that it is we human beings that think it." While we cannot know or think such a world, "Mont Blanc" traces the limits of thought into the unthinkable. Endless cycles of avalanches, carcasses, storms and winds, and birth and death provide a veiled glimpse at the world without humans. It is a vacancy only for humans who will perish while the planet continues. What then are earth and stars and sea and mountains if we are not there to imagine them? They are whole ways of planetary being not dependent on our imagination for their existence.

The sublime is not directly concerned with the external world. As Donnelly explains, "Shelley's own 'separate fantasy' is not a minimal 'tribute' to an influx of overwhelming external impressions, but is a subjective psychical energy which owes no fealty to nature. Sublimity, as Kant argued, does not reside in any of the things of nature, but only in our own mind."[23] The Kantian sublime redeems the inability of sense perception to relate the experience, because the mind (or reason) exceeds what the senses can present. We might invert this sentiment and ask why the mountain would care about Kant and Shelley's sublime meditation.[24]

If we take Thacker's *In Dust of This Planet* as a conceptual apparatus for reading the poem, then "Mont Blanc" is no longer about redemption through the sublime but rather the indifference of nature to our imagination of it. The poem first appears at the back of Percy and Mary Shelley's 1817 *History of a Six Week's Tour*. In the tour, they reflect upon the mountain as an inhuman god-like force: "One would think that Mont Blanc, like the god of the Stoics, was a vast animal, and that the frozen blood for ever circulated through his stony veins."[25] The mountains "vast" scale of time and space and its ecology like a "vast animal" exceeds human measure. The mountain's "vast animal" world is untranslatable. As such, it looms and abides with a Stoic indifference. The mountain is there before humans and will be there after humans.

The poem becomes a glimpse of this world-without-us, one that creates "awful doubt." In drafts of the poem, the awful doubt was calmed by "In such a faith with Nature reconciled." But unlike drafts, the printed version claims, "But for such faith, with Nature reconcil'd," which can come to mean that our faith in religion or even our faith in humanity prevents our ability to reconcile with the nonhuman.[26] Returning, then, to the final lines of the poem, Shelley is asking the mountain what it is without the human mind's imagining. The Stoic indifference of the mountain indicates that the silence and solitude and vacancy are only as perceived by humans. Without humans, the mountain and its ecology go on. The actual vacancy is the absence of humans: a planet without us, which for us would be silent but is in itself a way of worlding.

Influenced by their tour and sharing imagery with Percy Shelley's "Mont Blanc," which was published a year earlier, Mary Shelley's *Frankenstein* makes use of the Alps as well. As Victor ascends the rugged terrain, he encounters "the unstained snowy mountain-top, the glittering pinnacle, the pine woods, and ragged bare ravine, the eagle, soaring amidst the clouds."[27] Shelley extends the description with images that recall Percy's poem:

> It is a scene terrifically desolate. In a thousand spots the traces of the winter avalanche may be perceived, where trees lie broken and strewed on the ground; some entirely destroyed, others bent, leaning upon the jutting rocks of the mountain, or transversely upon other trees. The path, as you ascend higher, is intersected by ravines of snow, down which stones continually roll from above; one of them is particularly dangerous, as the slightest sound, such as even speaking in a loud voice, produces a concussion of air sufficient to draw destruction upon the head of the speaker. The pines are not tall or luxuriant, but they are sombre, and add an air of severity to the scene. I looked on the valley beneath; vast mists were rising from the rivers which ran through it, and curling in thick wreaths around the opposite mountains, whose summits were hid in the uniform clouds, while rain poured from the dark sky, and added to the melancholy impression I received from the objects around me.[28]

Victor walks along the valley and hikes in the mountains, seeking the restorative quality of nature. His plans are interrupted by a glimpse of his creature on a rocky peak.

Famously, it is in the Alps that the monster and his creator first discuss the creature's life and world. The setting elevates the intensity of their meeting. The bleak, powerful, nonhuman landscape echoes the more-than-humanness in the monster, who appeals to his creator for human dignity and life within human community. Absent such society, the monster becomes more like his surroundings—aloof and powerfully inhuman. This turn of events serves as a commentary on Percy Shelley's "Mont Blanc," where the restorative power of the sublime can twist into a power over and against humanity.

There is an important difference. While the monster is openly antagonistic to his creator, who refuses to accept him within the human community, the mountain remains unmoved by the plight of humans. The coldness of the Alpine heights becomes figurative of a coldness in relation to humanity. It is a relation of nonrelation, or, to recall Thacker: "To say that the world-without-us is antagonistic to the human is to attempt to put things in human terms, in the terms of the world-for-us. To say that the world-without-us is neutral with respect to the human is to attempt to put things in terms of the world-in-itself. The world-without-us lies somewhere in between, in a nebulous zone that is at once impersonal and horrific."[29] The seeming inhumanity of the monster is at least in part borrowed from the "impersonal and horrific" world-without-us that looms in the background of the conversation between creature and creator.

Later, Victor promises his creation a female companion. But then the Malthusian implications of a race that might populate and overtake humans cause Victor to go back on his promise and destroy the female body. As Anne Mellor explains, "he [Victor] is afraid of her reproductive powers, her capacity to generate an entire race of similar creatures. What Victor Frankenstein truly fears is female sexuality as such."[30] Clara Tuite places the female body explicitly in relation to Malthus: "The female always figures reproductive excess: never merely herself, she is always the horror of more mouths to feed, the motor of the 'geometrical ratio' of 'doubling population.'"[31] Using Malthus's predictive formulation, Victor foresees generations of monstrous bodies. This is not only a proliferation of bodies but a birthing of a new culture and way of being in the world—one that could become a war of worlds and destruction of the human race. His destruction of the female creature becomes the "culmination of Victor's conscientious foresight, his carefully defended Malthusian humanitarianism. From a purely human perspective, Victor's violence appears as a true demonstration of Malthusian philanthropy."[32] With his hopes for a future dashed, the monster returns Victor's destruction by killing Elizabeth, Victor's bride, on their wedding night. The creature and Victor have each killed the other's female companion and the hope of a future family. Through these deaths, they have entangled themselves in a different future, a pact of hate and revenge outside of community and the hope a future community would bring.

The creature draws Victor relentlessly north to the Arctic, where they "traverse immense deserts" of ice and snow. Victor exclaims, "Oh! How unlike it was to the blue seasons of the south! Covered with ice, it was only to be distinguished from land by its superior wildness and ruggedness. . . . Immense and rugged mountains of ice often barred up my passage, and I often heard the thunder of the ground sea, which threatened my destruction."[33] As we have seen in the previous chapter on Landseer and polar bears, here the monster, like the bears, becomes an inhuman force that stands for the larger inhuman landscape.

Unlike Victor, Captain Walton turns away from the inhospitable landscape and saves his life and the lives of his crewmen. He has reached the limits of human capacity in ways that echo actual expeditions of the time. Such expeditions in search of a Northwest passage—including those Mary Shelley would have known—extend from the 1776 James Cook and 1792 George Vancouver expeditions to Nelson's time aboard the *Carcass*, as discussed previously; John Franklin's Cooper River expedition of 1819–22, which saw the loss of more than half his crew; John Ross's expedition of 1818–22; and William Parry's 1819 venture, which went farther west than any before it. Few explorers set out explicitly to reach the North Pole, Parry being one of the first with his 1827 expedition. Importantly, in each case the captains weighed mastery of the Arctic in proportion to the lives of the crewmen. The terrain remained a vast, blank, white space with some areas mapped by exploration but much unknown and inaccessible to colonial drives for mastery. The Arctic matches or even exceeds Mont Blanc in Stoic indifference. Its "silence and solitude" reveal a glimpse of a planet without humans, where the vacancy is not of human imagination but of humans on the planet at all.

Passing from one pole to the other, it is worth mentioning, if only too briefly, that Coleridge's *Rime of the Ancient Mariner* leverages the inhumanity of the Antarctic to create a visionary tale of a mystically redeemed or otherwise possessed mariner. The Mariner describes the journey of sailing into polar terrain, where "Nor shapes of men nor beasts we ken" and the only animate object seems to be the ice itself:

> The ice was here, the ice was there
> The ice was all around.
> It crack'd and growl'd, and roar'd and howl'd—
> Like noises of a swound."[34]

From the obscurity of mist and animate ice comes the albatross, which serves much like the polar bear and Victor's creature as a figure for a larger unimaginable blankness of polar extremities. As readers know, with the bird's appearance, the ice breaks open and a wind blows the Mariner's ship to safety until he fatefully shoots the albatross. With the death of this figure of a world beyond humans comes a gothic and seemingly inhuman tale. The Mariner is only freed from his life-in-death by blessing water snakes, which "moved in tracks of shining white."[35] The creatures are then replaced by a mysterious spirit that propels the ship back to its home:

> From the land of mist and snow
> The spirit slid: and it was he
> That made the Ship to go.[36]

Transformed time and again in Coleridge's poem, the inhospitable polar region with its blinding whiteness becomes a force that drives the Mariner back to his homeland and destroys the rest of the ship's crew. It is the leveling sensibility of a world-without-us.

More hauntingly strange than the inhumanity of geographic extremities is a nature among us that is also beyond us. We see in Keats and Wordsworth moments where everyday objects become things whose valence points to a way of being in the world that is inaccessible to us and hints at a planetary world without us. Martin Heidegger famously made the distinction between our everyday being-in-the-world, where objects work seamlessly with our habitual actions (what he calls "ready-to-hand"), and objects that break or somehow interrupt our routine such that we become aware of the object apart from its setting in what he refers to as "present-at-hand."[37] Adapting Heidegger to Thacker's concept, the present-at-hand object has the potential to take an inhuman turn; the objects do not point to equipment within human worlding. Rather, the objects as comprehensible to us become things only partially understood and, more hauntingly, point to a world without human equipmentality and human ecologies. In short, our world and equipment are broken, and something lies beyond its ruins.

Jonathan Bate's well-known ecological reading of Keats's "Ode to Autumn" in *The Song of the Earth* serves as a good starting point.[38] As the later part of Bate's book reveals, he remains within a humanist tradition of Heidegger's phenomenology; however, his reading of Keats opens onto a nonhuman world. Bate frames his interpretation by considering the weather. "Ode to Autumn" was written in September 1819, a season of bountiful grain after three years of poor weather and failed harvests. As such, it is a celebration of agriculture after many years in which the inhuman forces of weather created lean conditions for human sustenance. Bate adds to this weather Keats's personal bout with tuberculosis in which he sought a more rejuvenating atmosphere in the seaside town of Margate. In the poem, the fortuitous weather allows for plants and animals to flourish in "networks, links, bonds, and correspondences."[39] What appears as an overly rich thriving is merely "illusionary excess," because abundance provides an ecologically valuable biodiversity. It is instructive to see how Bate recuperates this diversity for human ends. He catalogues the wildflowers with medicinal uses and focuses on the agricultural harvest that is a theme throughout the poem. Yet using Thacker's framing would mean recognizing diversity in itself, not for human utility. Yes, we could link the wildflowers with bees and bees to pollination for human crops, but again, this would be to use nature for human ends.

The most striking element of this poem is not the intertwining of nature with human agricultural technologies in the grain-rich fields. Rather, it is the waning of flourishing life that happens late in autumn and signals the coming winter. Keats imagines autumn with a reaper's hook momentarily suspended. This reaper's hook is not an object present-at-hand whose equipmentality has broken and interrupted the routine of the harvest such that we examine its place in our world. Rather, the suspended hook of autumn is a present-at-hand that itself signals something beyond our worlding. We know the grim reaper will come to all, but for now all beings seem to thrive in a life "o'erbrimm'd." The end of the poem signals a greater end, the end of the day and the end of a season and the end of what we can know of life. In the final stanza, "a wailful choir the small gnats mourn" as "The redbreast whistles from a garden-croft; / And gathering swallows twitter in the skies."[40] In the gnat, the redbreast, and the swallow, humans are out of their depths. We do not see the utility to the gnat or the hedge-crickets that sing. As night falls, the swallow leaves to destinations unknown and for reasons unknown. Even the redbreast, which populates the human architecture of the garden-croft, has repurposed it. The garden and the croft are not for us but for it. All the human activity of agriculture sits amid a much larger nonhuman world whose choir, songs, whistles, and twitters signal to us a world that exists among us but which we can never fully know and which will continue well after the dark night falls around us.

Particularly interesting in Keats's "Ode to Autumn" is where it departs from the typical Romantic-period description of a landscape. One can push Bate's interpretation of Keats beyond his intention and toward a nonhuman world. For Wordsworth and many others (such as Thomas Grey, Coleridge, Mary Robinson, and so on), encounters in the landscape often produce a psychological effect recorded by the poet—much like Kant's explanation of the sublime in his *Critique of Judgment*. However, as Keats explains in his letter to his publisher and friend Richard Woodhouse, his idea of a poet is antithetical to Wordsworth's privileged interiority, what Keats calls here the "egotistical sublime":

> As to the poetical Character itself (I mean that sort of which, if I am any thing, I am a Member; that sort distinguished from the wordsworthian or egotistical sublime; which is a thing per se and stands alone) it is not itself—it has no self—it is every thing and nothing. . . . Poet is the most unpoetical of any thing in existence; because he has no Identity—he is continually in for—and filling some other Body—The Sun, the Moon, the Sea and Men and Women who are creatures of impulse are poetical and have about them an unchangeable attribute—the poet has none; no identity[.][41]

The poet functions like a handyman doing whatever odd job he is put to. To survive living with such a protean identity and mutable task calls for "negative capability." As Keats describes it in a letter to his brothers, "*Negative Capability* that is when man is capable of being in uncertainties, Mysteries, doubts, without any irritable reaching after fact & reason."[42] In "Ode to Autumn," we see the poet taking up ways of being in the world that are far different from the human. The poet is living with the uncertainty of what such life means. It must mean something—especially to the animals themselves—but the meanings remain shrouded in "uncertainties, Mysteries, doubts" for us who grasp "after fact & reason." Poetry in this configuration is not illuminating and expressing one's experiences (in Wordsworthian fashion). Rather, poetry is opening up to a nonhuman phenomenology of wonder beyond fact, reason, and mimetic description.

Even Wordsworth had moments in his work that seem to escape the formula of the egotistical sublime. Wordsworth's poem "The Ruined Cottage" is considered one of the saddest of his many tragic tales of rural life. Early drafts show that Wordsworth started working on the poem in 1797, perhaps for the *Lyrical Ballads*. It was initially written as a gothic poem, somewhat like "The Thorn," and some of these haunting elements remain. The poem was never published on its own during his lifetime; rather, he incorporated it into his attempted rustic epic *The Excursion*.[43] The poem chronicles the physical and financial struggles of a family, its demise, and the resulting ruin of its cottage and small cultivated garden, all as told by an itinerant peddler.

Throughout the poem, the peddler moves between his memories of the cottage and its last tenant, Margaret, and the property's current wildness and decay. In an early passage, the narrator, Armytage, explains:

> Beside yon spring I stood
> And eyed its waters till we seemed to feel
> One sadness, they and I. For them a bond
> Of brotherhood is broken: time has been
> When every day the touch of human hand
> Disturbed their stillness, and they ministered
> To human comfort. When I stooped to drink,
> A spider's web hung to the water's edge,
> And on the wet and slimy foot-stone lay
> The useless fragment of a wooden bowl;
> It moved my very heart.[44]

Slime covering over the worn footstep and a spider's web at the water's edge reveal the lack of human use. Layered upon these images is a "fragment of a wooden bowl." The fragment does not reveal the equipmental structure of the bowl—its daily use for gathering water or for holding food. Rather, the fragment connected with slime and spider's web reveals the rupture of human dwelling. In his essay on the ruins of "The Ruined Cottage," Jacques Khalip sees in the dilapidated dwelling our fragility in correspondence with the fragility of nature around us. "To think of disaster is to think of it as the occasion for the reshifting of the hierarchization of knowledge—what kinds of knowledge are foregrounded and backgrounded. Disaster throws into relief how an incipient vulnerability has become an actual vulnerability. It is a radical change in perspectives on dwelling." For him, the lesson is how to "practice a hospitality to the inhospitable here."[45]

More devastating than hosting the inhospitable is the possibility that the slime, the web, and the fragment of a bowl open onto something more than "a radical change in perspectives on dwelling." What if the perspective is from the point of view of things and ecologies of a world-without-us? Khalip sees the bowl as "rubbish or rubble, as ready-unmades, so to speak, that block any kind of recuperating interpretation—what Alphonso Lingis, in another context, calls 'the empty endurance of the void.'"[46] If the "ready-unmades" have the power to "block any kind of recuperating interpretation," then the signs of ruin in the cottage become part of a larger annihilation of human habitation at work in the intimate ecologies of our homes. The blankness or vacancy of Mont Blanc and the polar regions is found within England in a moment where time is out of joint, an "empty endurance of the void"—where the encounter points to a deep history or a deep time that persists beyond human time on earth.

As Armytage explains early in the poem:

> I see around me here
> Things which you cannot see: we die, my Friend,
> Nor we alone, but that which each man loved
> And prized in his peculiar nook of earth
> Dies with him, or is changed.[47]

With such an interpretative frame, Armytage's cataloguing Margaret's demise is not a *memento mori*. If it were, then it would signal a return for the loss by reminding readers of the value of ethical living. Instead, the catalogue of overgrowth, "truant sheep," and collapsed structures functions like a wrinkle in time where a future void of humanity encroaches on the Romantic picturesque.

Armytage as narrator notes the nonutility of nature that (from her rotting corpse to the ruined cottage) has taken over the habitable ecology. More properly said, nature is not useful to us but only unto itself:

> She is dead,
> The worm is on her cheek, and this poor hut,
> Stripp'd of its outward garb of household flowers,
> Of rose and sweet-briar, offers to the wind
> A cold bare wall whose earthy top is tricked
> With weeds and rank spear-grass. She is dead,
> And nettles rot and adders sun themselves
> Where we have sate together while she nurs'd.[48]

A bit further along in the poem, the peddler lists other transgressions by nature, including "knots of worthless stone-crop started out" and "The unprofitable bindweed spread his bells."[49] His extended monologue breaks two ways: either he is trying to recover the value of the loss by telling the story or he is—like the Ancient Mariner—struck by the inhuman planet upon which we dwell.

Much like Shelley, who in "Mont Blanc" seeks to make nature purposeful to the human imagination, and like religiously inflected readings of the possessed Mariner, who must tell his story to the chosen one of three, "The Ruined Cottage" concludes with passages that try to redeem the loss and recover it from unprofitability, vacancy, and indifferent nature. Armytage proclaims:

> Be wise and cheerful, and no longer read
> The forms of things with an unworthy eye.
> She sleeps in the calm earth, and peace is here.
> I well remember that those very plumes,

> Those weeds, and the high spear-grass on that wall,
> By mist and silent rain-drops silver'd o'er,
> As once I passed did to my heart convey
> So still an image of tranquility,
> So calm and still, and looked so beautiful
> Amid the uneasy thoughts which filled my mind,
> That what we feel of sorrow and despair
> From ruin and from change, and all the grief
> The passing shews of being leave behind,
> Appeared an idle dream that could not live
> Where meditation was. I turned away
> And walked along my road in happiness.[50]

Nothing in his speech shows human gain from the loss, and so the reason for his happiness remains obscure. He seems calmed by a memory of plumes, weeds, and spear-grass along a wall, but all of these can be taken as signs not only of the past but of the present overgrowth and nature's encroachment and eventual destruction of the cottage. Frozen in time, the image—"So still an image of tranquility"—for Armytage becomes a pleasing aesthetic object to ward off sorrow and despair. As Paul Fry notes, "Every version of 'The Ruined Cottage' we have locates consolation for Margaret's unhappy story in the perdurability, beauty, and ghostly intimations of the natural world itself, not in any over hope for the afterlife or for any other world elsewhere."[51] Yet outside the frozen moment, in a long geological temporality, there is only a tranquility of the absolute leveling of humanity, a silence and solitude and vacancy.

Perhaps most haunting in Wordsworth's poem is that the planetary world-without-us resides in our midst. We catch veiled glimpses of things in themselves that point toward such a planet—a spider's web, a fragment of a wooden bowl, weeds, spear-grass. The stones once used for building a wall now are scattered along the ground as if found in nature. The stones in "The Ruined Cottage" are much like the scattered stones in Wordsworth's poem "Michael." Particularly in "Michael," a narrator is required to inform the reader that these stones seemingly placed where they are by forces of nature were intended as a sheepfold. In both poems, the stones become part of the human world only through narration of a story of grief and loss. Seen from the duration of the human temporal frame, from our worlding, such items are part of our dwelling with nature. Yet, as "Ode to Autumn" and "The Ruined Cottage" show, these things are not only in our world but reveal other temporal dimensions—an ecology apart from humans.

If a planet without humans seems a gloomy place to end this book, it is gloomy only to us and perhaps to those species with whom we have developed a codependence. However, if we are to play out an end to biopolitics and the limits of political capacity to leverage the biological, then life that endures beyond our political worlding and temporality is certainly one such direction. Studies of Romantic-period vitalism negotiate the difference between a life force intelligible to us that we might master and those forces that roll through all things (as Wordsworth might say) beyond our ability to apprehend them.

The biopolitical world seeks to leverage biological being of humans and animals toward political ends. Throughout this work, we have seen biopower resist political utility. The further limit of such resistance is a world-without-us in which biology lives on without political determinations. While such a world is beyond us, Romantic authors point to this nontranscendental beyond as a leveling force that disrupts and will eventually overcome human worlding. In such works, we meet not simply the limits of the biopolitical but the limits of human worlding altogether. Life does go on. The triumph of life, to borrow Shelley's phrase, is the resistance of a world outside our political capacity to use life for productive ends.

Notes

Chapter 1. Animal Life and Rural Labor

1. John Barrell opens his study of Morland with the following: "George Morland was the most prolific, and therefore probably the most popular, painter of the life of rural England in the period covered by this book, and indeed in the whole history of English Painting. During his short life—he died in 1804 at the age of forty-one—he may have produced as many as 4,000 paintings and drawings" (*The Dark Side of the Landscape: The Rural Poor in English Painting 1730–1840* [Cambridge: Cambridge University Press, 1983], 89). *Toil and Plenty* by Christina Payne serves as an excellent introduction to agriculture labor paintings of the period (New Haven, CT: Yale University Press, 1993).

2. Barrell, *Dark Side of the Landscape,* 112; William Collins, *Memoirs of a Painter,* vol. 2 (London: Stower, 1805), 232.

3. Barrell, *Dark Side of the Landscape,* 113–14.

4. Ibid., 114.

5. Not addressed in my study is the slave labor used for the tobacco that fills the Englishman's pipe, which presents another problem of liberty. Slavery is discussed briefly later in this chapter.

6. Robert Bloomfield, *The Farmer's Boy* (London: Vernor and Hood, Poultry, 1800), 46.

7. *Low Life* and its companion painting *High Life* are discussed further in chapter 6.

8. See Ben Roger's *Beef and Liberty* (London: Chatto and Windus, 2003). He provides detailed information on the growth of a beef culture in England in the eighteenth century. Other notable examples include James Gillray's illustrations of British beef: "French Liberty. British Slavery," December 21, 1792, and "Fat Cattle," January 16, 1802, in Richard Godfrey's *James Gillray: The Art of Caricature* (London: Tate 2001). Also see Gillray's "The British-Butcher, Supplying John-Bull with a Substitute for Bread," 1795, in Diana Donald's *The Age of Caricature: Satirical Prints in the Reign of George III* (1996). While I call the dog a bully breed, the actual breed characteristics of dogs during the period were connected more to their labors than to their phenotype.

The rise of the bulldog in nineteenth-century Britain is outlined in Harriet Ritvo's *Animal Estate: The English and Other Creatures in the Victorian Age* (Cambridge, MA: Harvard University Press, 1989).

9. I am indebted to Christopher Hanlon for pointing out to me the species of wood from which this walking stick is made and the role hawthorn and blackthorn played in land enclosure. Morland was surely aware of the political resonances of this wood. Sketches of hawthorn trees and leaves can be found in Morland's notebooks (John Trivett Nettleship, *George Morland: And the Evolution from Him of Some Later Painters* [London: Seeley and Company, 1898], 72).

10. Maurizio Lazzarato, "From Biopower to Biopolitics," *Pli* 13 (2002): 99–113, 103.

11. See Jean-Luc Nancy, *Birth to Presence* (Stanford, CA: Stanford University Press, 1994). See the "Corpus" chapter, especially 198–99.

12. Lazzarato, "From Biopower to Biopolitics," 100.

13. Cited in Lazzarato, "From Biopower to Biopolitics," 102. Michel Foucault, "The Politics of Health in the Eighteenth Century," in *Power/Knowledge: Selected Interviews and Other Writings*, 167–82 (New York: Pantheon Books, 1980).

14. Michel Foucault, *Society Must Be Defended: Lectures at the Collège De France, 1975–76* (New York: Picador, 2003), 242.

15. Ibid., 241

16. Michel Foucault, *Security, Territory, Population: Lectures at the Collège De France, 1977–78* (New York: Picador, 2007), 1.

17. Ibid., 242, 246–47.

18. Foucault, *Society Must Be Defended*, 246.

19. This is what Foucault terms a "bio-economic problem" (*Security, Territory, Population* 77). It is an issue pursued particularly in chapter 2 of *Beasts of Burden*.

20. Foucault, *Society Must Be Defended*, 252.

21. Ibid., 255.

22. See pages 219–22 of *Society Must Be Defended* and pages 68 and 342 of *Security, Territory, Population*. The quotation is from page 222 of *Society Must Be Defended*.

23. Nicole Shukin, *Animal Capital* (Minneapolis: University of Minnesota Press, 2009), 17.

24. To a great degree I have omitted discussion of cattle, because I have discussed cattle extensively in *Technologies of the Picturesque* (Cranbury, NJ: Bucknell University Press, 2008), chapters 6 and 7.

25. While one can read the Romantics' work through a biopolitical lens, and Alistair Hunt's edited essays *Romanticism and Biopolitics* for Romantic Circles does just that, those who shouldered undue weight in the biopolitical regime were those at the very bottom of the social scale, most notably fieldworkers and animals. Alistair Hunt, *Romanticism and Biopolitics, Romantic Circles Praxis Series*, December 2012, http://www.rc.umd.edu/praxis/biopolitics/.

26. Lazzarato, "From Biopower to Biopolitics," 101. Emphasis in the original.

27. Maureen McLane, *Romanticism and the Human Sciences: Poetry, Population, and the Discourse of Species* (Cambridge: Cambridge University Press, 2000); Philip

Connell, *Romanticism, Economics, and the Question of 'Culture'* (Oxford: Oxford University Press, 2001).

28. One perhaps interesting exception is Samuel Taylor Coleridge, who with Robert Southey very briefly experimented with farming as a prelude to creating a utopian commune, the pantisocracy, in Pennsylvania. As is well known, his experiment was a failure, and the sustainable farming venture with its bucolic ideals was abandoned.

29. David Simpson, *Wordsworth, Commodification, and Social Concern* (Cambridge: Cambridge University Press, 2009).

30. Katey Castellano, *The Ecology of British Romantic Conservatism, 1790–1837* (New York: Palgrave, 2013), 1.

31. Christine Kenyon-Jones, *Kindred Brutes: Animals in Romantic-Period Writing, Concern* (London: Ashgate, 2001).

32. David Perkins, *Romanticism and Animal Rights* (Cambridge: Cambridge University Press, 2003); Frank Palmeri, ed., *Humans and Other Animals in Eighteenth-Century British Culture: Representation, Hybridity, Ethics* (London: Ashgate, 2006); and Deborah Denenholz Morse and Martin A. Danahay, eds., *Victorian Animal Dreams: Representations of Animals in Victorian Literature and Culture* (London: Ashgate, 2007). More recent is Chase Pielak's *Memorializing Animals during the Romantic Period* (London: Ashgate, 2015).

33. Harriet Ritvo, *Animal Estate* (Cambridge, MA: Harvard University Press, 1989).

34. Cary Wolfe, *Before the Law: Humans and Other Animals in a Biopolitical Frame* (Chicago: University of Chicago Press, 2013), 22.

35. Lazzarato, "From Biopower to Biopolitics," 100.

36. Jacques Derrida, "The Animal That Therefore I Am (More to Follow)," *Critical Inquiry* 28, no. 2 (2002): 369–80.

37. Ron Broglio, interview with Cary Wolfe, "After Animality, Before the Law," *Angelaki* 18, no. 1 (2013): 181–87, 182.

38. I addressed Agamben's terminology in relation to livestock in "Livestock and Biopower" at the Cultural Studies Association, 2007. I have not attempted to publish this paper. It is accessible through my Academia.edu site.

39. Timothy Morton, *The Poetics of Spice* (Cambridge: Cambridge University Press, 2000); Paul Youngquist, *Race, Romanticism, and the Atlantic* (London: Ashgate, 2013).

40. John Barrell, *The Idea of Landscape and the Sense of Place 1730–1840: An Approach to the Poetry of John Clare* (Cambridge: Cambridge University Press, 1972); Jonathan Bate, *Song of the Earth* (Cambridge, MA: Harvard University Press, 2000); James McKusick, *Green Writing* (New York: Palgrave, 2000); Tim Fulford, "Cowper, Wordsworth, Clare: The Politics of Trees," *John Clare Society Journal*, no. 14 (1995): 47–59.

41. Sara Guyer, *Reading with John Clare: Biopoetics, Sovereignty, Romanticism* (New York: Fordham University Press, 2015), 17.

42. Michel Foucault, "What Is an Author," in *Language, Counter-Memory, Practice: Selected Essays and Interviews*, ed. Donald F. Bouchard (Ithaca NY: Cornell University Press, 1977), 112–38.

43. The expressive theory of poetry is put forward by M. H. Abrams in *The Mirror and the Lamp: Romantic Theory and the Critical Tradition* (Oxford: Oxford University Press, 1971), 22. For an extended discussion of the privileged interiority of the human subject in Romantic literature and for the role of postmodern theory in disrupting this representational method, see my essay "Romanticism" in *The Cambridge Companion to Literature and Posthumanism* (Cambridge: Cambridge University Press, forthcoming, 2018).

Chapter 2. Docile Numbers and Stubborn Bodies

1. Edmund Burke, *Reflections on the Revolution in France and on the Proceedings in Certain Societies in London Relative to That Event* (London: J. Dodsley, 1793), 117.

2. Don Herzog, *Poisoning the Minds of the Lower Orders* (Princeton, NJ: Princeton University Press, 1998), 511.

3. Fitzwilliam Museum, "*Presage of the Millennium*, published June 4th 1795," http://www.fitzmuseum.cam.ac.uk/pharos/collection_pages/18th_pages/P344_1948/TXT_SE-P344_1948.html.

4. W. Heneage Legge, "Sussex Pottery," *The Reliquary and Illustrated Archaeologist*, New Series 9 (January 1903): 9.

5. Quoted in Herzog, *Poisoning the Minds of the Lower Orders*, 507.

6. G. I. Gallop, *Pig's Meat: The Selected Writings of Thomas Spence, Radical and Pioneer Land Reformer* (Nottingham: Spokesman, 1987), and Denise Gigante, *Taste: A Literary History* (New Haven, CT: Yale University Press, 2005), 110–11.

7. Herzog, *Poisoning the Minds of the Lower Orders*, 513.

8. Ibid., 525

9. Michel Foucault, *Society Must Be Defended: Lectures at the Collège de France 1975–1976* (New York: Picador, 2003), 240.

10. Ibid., 245.

11. Ibid., 246.

12. Ibid.

13. For further information about the National Ordinance Survey and its relationship to the picturesque, see chapter 3 of Ron Broglio, *Technologies of the Picturesque* (Lewisburg, PA: Bucknell University Press, 2008), 51–80.

14. Cary Wolfe, *Before the Law: Humans and Other Animals in a Biopolitical Frame* (Chicago: Chicago University Press, 2012), 23. Wolfe's quotations of Foucault are from Michel Foucault, *The Birth of Biopolitics: Lectures at the Collège de France 1978–1979* (New York: Picador, 2010), 271, 274, 282, and 283.

15. Edmund Burke, *Thoughts and Details on Scarcity* (London: Rivington, 1800), 10.

16. David Collings, *Monstrous Society: Reciprocity, Discipline, and the Political Uncanny, c. 1780–1848* (Lewisburg, PA: Bucknell University Press, 2009), 88.

17. Burke, *Thoughts and Details Written on Scarcity*, 39.

18. Ibid., 10.

19. Ibid.

20. Mike Hill and Warren Montag, *The Other Adam Smith* (Stanford: Stanford University Press, 2015). See chapter 4, pages 268–312, including Smith's influence on Malthus.

21. Ibid., 296.

22. "Substance of Sir John Sinclair's Address to the Board of Agriculture," in *Annual Register, or a View of the History, Politics, and Literature of the Year 1795*, section "Useful Projects" (London: Burton for Dodsley's Annual Register, 1800), 96–100, 97.

23. Ibid., 98.

24. Matilda Betham-Edwards, "Biographical Sketch," in *Arthur Young's Travels in France during the Years 1787, 1788, 1789*, ed. Matilda Betham-Edwards (London: George Bell and Sons, 1909), xlv.

25. Sir John Sinclair, *Statistical Account of Scotland*, 22 vols. (1791–99; repr., University of Edinburgh, University of Glasgow, 1999), 20: xiii.

26. Reverend John Sinclair, *Memoirs of the Life and Works of the Late Right Honorable Sir John Sinclair, Bart*, 2 vols. (Edinburgh: William Blackwood and Sons; London: T. Cadell, 1837), 2: 46.

27. Ibid.

28. Michel Foucault, *Society Must Be Defended: Lectures at the Collège de France 1975–1976* (New York: Picador, 2003), 240.

29. Ibid., 245.

30. Ibid., 246.

31. Ibid.

32. Philip Connell, *Romanticism, Economics, and the Question of "Culture"* (Oxford: Oxford University Press, 2001).

33. Foucault, *Society Must Be Defended*, 252.

34. Catharine Gallagher and Stephen Greenblatt, *Practicing New Historicism* (Chicago: University of Chicago Press, 2001), 111–35.

35. Joanna Innes, *Inferior Politics: Social Problems and Social Policies in Eighteenth-Century Britain* (Oxford: Oxford University Press, 2009), 119–20.

36. Ibid., 147–48.

37. Ibid., 149.

38. Louis Althusser, "Ideology and Ideological State Apparatuses," in *Lenin and Philosophy and Other Essays* (London: New Left Books, 1972), 121–76, 173. Emphasis in the original.

39. Ibid., 172. Emphasis in the original.

40. Stephen Daniels, "Re-visioning Britain: Mapping and Landscape Painting, 1750–1820," in *Glorious Nature: British Landscape Painting 1750–1850*, ed. Katharine Baetjer and Michael Rosenthal (New York: Hudson Hills Press, 1993), 61.

41. Adam Smith, *Inquiry into the Nature and Causes of the Wealth of Nations* (London: Forgotten Books, 2008), 107.

42. Maureen N. McLane, *Romanticism and the Human Sciences: Poetry, Population, and the Discourse of the Species* (Cambridge: Cambridge University Press, 2000), 109–11.

43. Malthus, quoted in Collings, *Monstrous Society*, 169.

44. Robert Bloomfield, *The Farmer's Boy* (London: Vernor and Hood, Poultry, 1800), 44.

45. Malthus, quoted in Collings, *Monstrous Society*, 164.

46. Ibid.

47. Catharine Gallagher and Stephen Greenblatt, "The Potato in the Materialist Imagination," in *Practicing New Historicism* (Chicago: University of Chicago Press, 2000), 110–35.

48. Christopher Cakeling, "Whimsical Expenses of Economy," in *Annual Register, or a View of the History, Politics, and Literature of the Year 1795*, section "Miscellaneous Essays" (London: Burton for Dodsley's Annual Register, 1800), 134–38, 135.

49. Ibid., 137.

50. Ibid., 135.

51. E. P. Thompson, *Customs in Common* (London: Merlin Press, 1991), 191.

52. Ibid., 187.

53. Roger Wells, *Wretched Faces: Famine in Wartime England, 1793–1801* (New York: St. Martin's Press, 1988), 202–3, 209.

54. J. L. Hammond and Barbara Hammond, *The Village Labourer*, vol. 1 (London: The British Publisher's Guild, 1948), 122–23.

55. Ibid., 123.

56. Ibid., 106.

57. Wells, *Wretched Faces*, 211.

58. Arthur Young, *An Inquiry into the Propriety of Applying Wastes to the Better Maintenance and Support of the Poor* (Bury: J. Rackham, 1801), 42–43.

59. Michael Hardt and Antonio Negri, *Empire* (Cambridge, MA: Harvard University Press, 2000), 257.

60. Arthur Young, 560.

61. William Cobbett, *Rural Rides: In the Counties of Surrey, Kent, Sussex, Hants, Berks, Oxford, Bucks, Wilts, Somerset, Gloucester, Hereford, Salop, Worcester, Stafford, Leicester, Hertford, Essex, Suffolk, Norfolk, Cambridge, Huntington, Nottingham, Lincoln, York, Lancaster, Durham, and Northumberland During the Years 1821 to 1832* (London: William Cobbett, 1830), 62.

62. Ibid., 243

63. Ibid., 35.

64. Hammond and Hammond, *The Village Labourer*, 105; John E. Archer, *Social Unrest and Popular Protest in England, 1780–1840* (Cambridge: Cambridge University Press, 2000), 30.

65. Thompson, *Customs in Common*, 258.

66. Jean-Luc Nancy, *Birth to Presence* (Stanford, CA: Stanford University Press, 1994), 198.

Chapter 3. On Vulnerability

1. A. E. Santaniello, introduction to William Henry Pyne, *Microcosm or, A picturesque delineation of the arts, agriculture, and manufactures of Great Britain in a series of above a thousand groups of small figures for the embellishment of landscape* (1806; repr. facsimile, New York: Blom, 1971), 8.

2. Ibid., 259.

3. This is in distinct contrast to the work of twenty-first-century artist Abdel Abdessemed, who in *Don't Trust Me* (2008) shows a number of livestock animals being killed by a sledgehammer to the head.

4. C. Gray, textual commentary for Pyne, *Microcosm*, 184.

5. Cary Wolfe, "Exposures," in *Philosophy and Animal Life*, ed. Stanley Cavell, Cora Diamond, John McDowell, Ian Hacking, and Cary Wolfe (New York: Columbia University Press, 2008), 8.

6. J. M. Neeson, *Commoners: Common Right, Enclosure, and Social Change in England, 1700–1820* (Cambridge: Cambridge University Press, 1993), 20.

7. Gray, textual commentary for Pyne, *Microcosm*, 185.

8. There is one other graphic image of animal death in Pyne's *Microcosm*: the slaughter of a hog (166, 241). Payne's text omits any discussion of the image and provides only the simplest of labels: "Cottage Groups: 1. Travelling knife-grinder and tinger. 2. Ditto. 3. Killing a hog. 4. Scalding a hog, and scraping off the hair."

9. Robert Bloomfield, *The Farmer's Boy* (London: Vernor and Hood, Poultry, 1800), 85.

10. Ibid., 14.

11. Robin Ganev, "Milkmaids, Ploughmen, and Sex in Eighteenth-Century Britain," *Journal of History of Sexuality* 16, no. 1 (January 2007): 40–67, 41.

12. Ibid.

13. For an extended discussion of Elizabeth Hands and this poem, see chapter 3 of Anne Milne's *"Lactilla Tends Her Fav'rite Cow": Ecocritical Readings of Animals and Women in Eighteenth-Century British Labouring-class Women's Poetry* (Lewisberg, PA: Bucknell University Press, 2008), 68–86.

14. Ganey, "Milkmaids," 42.

15. Ibid., 22.

16. Donna Landry, "Georgic Ecology," in *Robert Bloomfield: Lyric, Class, and the Romantic Canon*, ed. Simon White, John Goodridge, and Bridget Keegan (Lewisburg, PA: Bucknell University Press, 2006), 254.

17. Bloomfield, *The Farmer's Boy*, 23.

18. Ibid., 45.

19. Ibid., 46.

20. Ibid., 48.

21. Ibid., 22.

22. Ibid., 49.

23. John William Cousin, *A Short Biographical Dictionary of English Literature* (London: J. M. Dent & Sons; New York: E. P. Dutton, 1910), 83.

24. Scott McEarthron, ed., *Nineteenth-Century English Labouring Class Poets, 1800–1900, Volume 1, 1800–1830* (London: Pickering & Chatto, 2006), 71–72.

25. Thomas Ba[t]chlor, *Village Scenes, the Progress of Agriculture, and Other Poems* (London: Parnassian Press, 1804), 75.

26. Ibid., 75.

27. Ibid., 77.

28. Ibid., 78.

29. Ibid., 83–84.

30. Ibid., 88, 89.

31. Ibid., 90.

32. Ibid., 85.

33. William Youatt, *Cattle: Their Breeds, Management, and Diseases* (London: Baldwin and Cradock, 1834), 4.

34. H. B. Carter, *His Majesty's Spanish Flock: Sir Joseph Banks and the Merinos of George III of England* (London: Angus & Robertson, 1964), and H. B. Carter, ed., *The Sheep and Wool Correspondence of Sir Joseph Banks 1781–1820* (London: Library Council of NSW in association with the British Museum [Natural History], 1979).

35. Major-General David Stewart, *Sketches of the Character, Manners, and Present State of the Highlanders of Scotland*, vol. 1 (Edinburgh: Longman, Rees, Orme, Brown, and Green, 1825), appendix lvi; also see 172, 214.

36. Ibid., appendix xlix.

37. Sir John Sinclair, *Address to the Society for the Improvement of British Wool; constituted at Edinburgh, on Monday, January 31, 1791* (London: Printed for T. Cadell, 1791); Reverend John Sinclair, *Memoirs of the Life and Works of the Late Right Honorable Sir John Sinclair, Bart*, 2 vols. (Edinburgh: William Blackwood and Sons; London: T. Cadell, 1837), 1: 219–28.

38. Robert Chambers, *Biographical Dictionary of Eminent Scotsmen with a Supplemental Volume*, vol. 5., ed. Rev. Thomas Thomson (Edinburgh: Blackie and Son of Glasgow, Edinburgh, and London, 1856), 526. Most entries available online by Alastair McIntyre, accessed June 18, 2009, http://www.electricscotland.com/history/other/sinclair_john.htm.

39. Michel Foucault, *Society Must Be Defended: Lectures at the Collège de France 1975–1976* (New York: Picador, 2003), 245.

40. Rev. John Sinclair, *Memoirs of the Life and Works*, 2: 46.

41. Wolfe, "Exposures," 8.

42. Jacques Derrida, "The Animal That Therefore I Am (More to Follow)," *Critical Inquiry* 28, no. 2 (2002): 396.

43. Robert Burns, *The Complete Work of Robert Burns*, ed. Allan Cunningham (Boston: Phillips, Sampson, and Company, 1855), 210.

44. Ibid., 106.

45. Ibid.

46. A more complete look at Burns's animals is beyond the scope of this essay but certainly part of a longer-term plan for this project. See, for example, "The Twa Herds; Or, The Holy Tulyie" where "An' get the brutes the power themsel's / To choose their herds." "The Inventory" addressed to Mr. Aitken of Ayr, surveyor of taxes for the district and "The Death and Dying Words of Poor Mailie, the Author's Only Pet Yowe."

Chapter 4. Wonder as Resistance

1. Black Sabbath, "Fairies Wear Boots," *Paranoid* (Vertigo, 1970). The song opens up Jacques Derrida's critique of Hegel and use of Bataille in "From Restricted to General Economy," in *Writing and Difference* (London: Routledge, 1978), 224–46.

2. Jane Bennett, *Enchantment of Modern Life* (Princeton, NJ: Princeton University Press, 2001), 3–5.

3. I am using the term "heterotopics" to mean communities and their discourses that are incompatible and irreconcilable with other communities yet reside alongside one another. Michel Foucault discusses heterotopics and representation in *The Order of Things* (New York: Vintage Books, 1994), xviii. Louise Marin argues the political problems of utopias (in contrast to heterotopias) in *Utopics* (New York: Humanities Books, 1984). And Jean-François Lyotard discusses the political injustice of one community subsuming another in *The Differend: Phrases in Dispute* (Minneapolis: University of Minnesota Press, 1988), 9, 13.

4. John Buchan, *Sir Walter Scott* (Cornwall: House of Stratus, 2009), 62.

5. Barbara Bloede, "The Witchcraft Tradition in Hogg's Tales and Verses," *Studies in Hogg and His World* 1 (1990): 91–102, 91.

6. For an excellent and critical theory–informed discussion of the problems of transcribing oral tradition, see Maureen McLane's "Dating Orality, Thinking Balladry: Of Milkmaids and Minstrels in 1771," *The Eighteenth Century* 47, no. 2 (Summer 2006): 131–49.

7. Gillian Hughes, *James Hogg: A Life* (Edinburgh: Edinburgh University Press, 2007), 45.

8. Murray G. H. Pittock, *The Invention of Scotland: The Stuart Myth and the Scottish Identity, 1638 to the Present* (New York: Routledge, 1991), 85.

9. James Hogg, *Winter Evening Tales*, ed. Ian Duncan (Edinburgh: Edinburgh University Press, 2004), 145.

10. Ibid., 145–46.

11. Ibid., 147.

12. Ibid., 396.

13. James Hogg, *The Shepherd's Calendar*, ed. Douglas S. Mack (Edinburgh: Edinburgh University Press, 2002), 242.

14. Ibid., 250.

15. Ibid., 253.

16. James Hogg, *Queen's Wake* (Edinburgh: William Blackwood, 1819), 89.

17. Walter Benjamin, "Theses on the Philosophy of History," in *Illuminations* (New York: Harcourt Brace Jovanovich, 1968), 253–64, 256.

18. See Alphonso Lingis, *The Community of Those Who Have Nothing in Common* (Bloomington, IN: Indiana University Press, 1994). Also see Philippe Pignarre and Isabelle Stengers, *Capitalist Sorcery: Breaking the Spell* (New York: Palgrave Macmillan, 2010). Stengers and Pignarre propose that capitalism is a sort of sorcery casting spells upon us, and the task remains to find counter-spells to break the invisible force of contemporary capitalism.

19. Michael Hardt and Antonio Negri, *Empire* (Cambridge, MA: Harvard University Press, 2000), 25.

20. Hogg, *The Shepherd's Calendar*, 10.

21. Ibid., 13.

22. For an amusing contrast between an idealized pastoral life and the actual work of shepherds, see Hogg's story "The Renowned Adventures of Basil Lee," in *Winter Evening Tales*. Early in the story, his father appoints Basil Lee as an overseer in the farm fields. He so mismanages the job that he is appointed shepherd with the hopes that, distant from the farm, he can do little harm. Hogg then creates a stark contrast between what Basil perceives will be the idyllic life of a shepherd and the actual labor of shepherds amid their flocks.

23. Donna Haraway has done extensive work on the role of dogs (and particularly herding dogs) as coproducers of culture. See her *Companion Species Manifesto* (Chicago: Prickly Paradigm Press, 2003) and *When Species Meet* (Minneapolis: University of Minnesota Press, 2007).

24. Ibid., 57.

25. Ibid.

26. Ibid.

27. Hogg, *Tales and Sketches of the Ettrick Shepherd* (London and Glasgow: Blackie and Son, 1837), 402, 403.

28. Hogg, *The Shepherd's Calendar*, 26.

29. W. J. Carlyle, "The Changing Distribution of Breeds of Sheep in Scotland, 1795–1965," *Agricultural History Review* 27, no. 1 (1979): 19–29.

30. For further and a more extensive discussion of Sinclair, see chapter 2. Regarding Sinclair, sheep, and the clearances, see Eric Richards, *A History of the Highland Clearances*, 2 vols. (London: Croom Helm, 1982), 1: 189.

31. Ibid., 1: 192.

32. Ibid., 2: 28.

33. James Hogg, *Highland Journeys*, ed. H. B. de Groot (Edinburgh: Edinburgh University Press, 2010), xxx.

34. Ibid.

35. Hogg, *Highland Journeys*, 222–23.

36. Richards, *A History of the Highland Clearances*, 2: 15.

37. Ibid., 2: 47.

38. Ron Broglio, "Docile Numbers and Stubborn Bodies: Population and the Problem of Multitude," *Romantic Circles Praxis Series*, April 2013, accessed July 6, 2014, http://www.rc.umd.edu/praxis/numbers/HTML/praxis.2013.broglio.html.

39. Cary Wolfe, *Before the Law: Humans and Animals in a Biopolitical Frame* (Chicago: University of Chicago Press, 2012), 34.

40. Ibid., 6.

41. Maurizio Lazzarato, "From Biopower to Biopolitics," *Pli* 13 (2002): 100–12, 103. Emphasis in the original.

42. Wolfe, *Before the Law,* 41.

43. Bennett, *Enchantment of Modern Life,* 3. Directly relevant to Bennett's work is the "disenchantment of the world." Max Weber explores the power of disenchantment as part of the secularization of modern life and the rise of capitalism. The modernization of Scotland in the eighteenth and nineteenth centuries fits within this schema, as noted in Weber's *The Protestant Ethic and the Spirit of Capitalism* (Chicago: Fitzroy Dearborn, 2001). Taking up Weber, the Frankfurt School critiques the destructive elements of modern life and its loss of wonder; see Max Horkheimer and Theodore Adorno's *Dialectic of Enlightenment* (Stanford, CA: Stanford University Press, 2007).

44. Caroline McCracken-Flesher, "Hogg and Nationality," in *The Edinburgh Companion to James Hogg,* ed. Ian Duncan (Edinburgh: Edinburgh University Press, 2012), 73–81, 73. Cited by McCracken-Flesher is Allan Cunningham, "Biographical and Critical History of the Literature of the last Fifty Years," *Athenaeum* (October 26, 1833): 713–21, 720.

45. Ian Bogost, *Alien Phenomenology, or What It's Like to Be a Thing* (Minneapolis: University of Minnesota Press, 2012), 124.

46. Writing at the end of the nineteenth century, the Kailyard School sentimentalized Scottish life and folklore, in part as a reaction against realism and modernism. J. M. Barrie, author of *Peter Pan,* is the best-known member of the Kailyard School. Michael Saler, *As If: Modern Enchantment and the Literary Prehistory of Virtual Reality* (Oxford: Oxford University Press, 2012).

Chapter 5. Animal Dwelling in Natural History

1. Thora Brylowe, *The Sister Arts as Cultural Practice* (unpublished manuscript, 2014), chapter 5, and "Introduction: Romantic Arts and Letters, 1760–1830," in *Romantic Arts & Letters: British Print, Paint, Engraving, 1760–1830* (PhD diss., Carnegie Mellon University, 2009), 1–26.

2. Joshua Reynolds, *Seven Discourses Delivered in the Royal Academy by the President* (1778, Eighteenth Century Collections Online), http://find.galegroup.com. ezproxy1.lib.asu.edu/ecco/infomark.do?&source=gale&prodId=ECCO&userGroupNa me=asuniv&tabID=T001&docId=CW106167462&type=multipage&contentSet=ECC OArticles&version=1.0&docLevel=FASCIMILE (accessed June 23, 2015).

3. Thomas Bewick, *A Memoir of Thomas Bewick* (London: Longman, 1862), 144.

4. Thomas Bewick, *A General History of Quadrupeds* (Chicago: University of Chicago Press, 2009), iii.

5. Ibid., iv.

6. Ibid., iii.

7. Ibid., 51.

8. Ibid., 526.

9. Katey Castellano, *The Ecology of British Romantic Conservatism*, 1790–1835 (New York: Palgrave, 2013), 86.

10. Ibid., 88–89.

11. Diane Donald, *The Art of Thomas Bewick* (London: Reaktion Books, 2013), 93.

12. Quoted in ibid., 93.

13. Quoted in ibid., 49.

14. Thomas Bewick, *A History of British Birds*, vol. 1 (London: Bernard Quaritch, 1885), iii.

15. Stephen Loo and Undine Sellbach, "A Picture Book of Invisible Worlds: Semblances of Insects and Humans in Jakob von Uexküll's Laboratory," *Angelaki* 18, no. 1 (2013): 45–64, 53.

16. Michel Foucault, *The Order of Things: An Archeology of the Human Sciences* (New York: Vintage Books, 1994), 128.

17. Ibid., 125, 132.

18. Ibid., 132.

19. Ibid., 130.

20. Ibid., 131–32.

21. Lisbet Koerner, "Carl Linnaeus in His Time and Place," in *The Cultures of Natural History*, ed. N. Jardine, J. A. Secord, and E. C. Spary (Cambridge: Cambridge University Press, 1996), 145–62, 146.

22. Ibid.

23. Ibid., 151. Lisbet Koerner also wrote "Purposes of Linnaean Travel: A Preliminary Research Report," in which she says, "Carl Linnaeus developed a second-phase cameralist strategy in which his natural science underwrote his political economy" (in *Visions of Empire: Voyages, Botany, and the Representation of Nature*, ed. David Philip Miller and Peter Hanns Reill [Cambridge: Cambridge University Press, 1996], 117–52, 119).

24. Koerner, "Carl Linnaeus in his Time and Place," 152.

25. Foucault, *The Order of Things*, xviii.

26. Phillip R. Sloan, "The Buffon-Linnaeus Controversy," *Isis* 67, no. 3 (September 1976): 356–75, 360.

27. Ibid., 360.

28. Loo and Sellbach, "A Picture Book of Invisible Worlds," 53.

29. Foucault, *The Order of Things*, 136.

30. Ibid., 137–38.

31. Ibid., 138.

32. Judy Egerton, *George Stubbs, Painter* (New Haven, CT: Yale University Press, 2007), 23.

33. See John Baskett, *The Horse in Art* (New Haven, CT: Yale University Press, 2006).

34. Roland Barthes, *Camera Lucida* (New York: Hill and Wang, 1982).

35. Egerton, *George Stubbs, Painter*, 566.

36. Ibid.

37. Terence Doherty, *The Anatomical Works of George Stubbs* (London: Martin Secker and Warburg, 1974), cited in Egerton, *George Stubbs, Painter*, 601.

38. Ibid., 609.

39. Alex Potts, "Order and the Call of the Wild: The Politics of Animal Picturing," *Oxford Art Journal* 13, no. 1 (1990): 12–33, 29.

40. Ibid.

41. Ibid., 28.

42. Paul Youngquist, *Monstrosities: Bodies and British Romanticism* (Minneapolis: University of Minnesota Press, 2003), and Robin Blyn, *Freak-garde: Extraordinary Bodies and Revolutionary Art in America* (Minneapolis: University of Minnesota Press, 2013).

43. Gilles Deleuze and Félix Guattari, *A Thousand Plateaus: Capitalism and Schizophrenia* (Minneapolis: University of Minnesota Press, 1987), 234.

44. Pietro Corsi. *The Age of Lamarck: Evolutionary Theories in France, 1790–1830* (Berkeley: University of California Press, 1988), 93–94.

45. Ibid., 128, 167.

46. Deleuze and Guattari, *A Thousand Plateaus*, 261.

47. Ibid., 238.

48. Kari Weil, "Heads or Tails: Géricault's Horses and Painting of (Natural) History," *Antennae* 25 (Summer 2013): 69–70.

49. Richard Conniff, "Mammoths and Mastodons: All American Monsters," *Smithsonian*, April 2010, accessed June 23, 2014, http://www.smithsonianmag.com/science-nature/mammoths-and-mastodons-all-american-monsters-8898672; Paul Semonin, *American Monster: How the Nation's First Prehistoric Creature Became a Symbol of National Identity* (New York: New York University Press, 2000).

50. Richard Conniff, "Mammoths and Mastodons: All American Monsters," *Smithsonian*, April 2010, accessed June 23, 2015, http://www.smithsonianmag.com/science-nature/mammoths-and-mastodons-all-american-monsters-8898672.

51. Semonin, *American Monster*, 330.

52. Sloan, "The Buffon-Linnaeus Controversy," 360.

Chapter 6. Man Proposes, Animality Disposes

1. Edwin Landseer, *Man Proposes, God Disposes*. 1864. Oil on canvas. 36" × 96". Royal Holloway, University of London.

2. Jen Hill, *White Horizon: The Arctic in the Nineteenth-Century British Imagination* (Albany: State University of New York Press, 2009), 3. For the relationship among literature, culture, and Romantic-period exploration of the Arctic, also see Eric Wilson, *The Spiritual History of Ice: Romanticism, Science, and the Imagination* (London: Palgrave, 2003); Adriana Craciun, "Writing the Disaster: Franklin and

Frankenstein," *Nineteenth-Century Literature* 65, no. 4 (2011): 433–80, and "The Scramble for the Arctic," *Interventions: International Journal of Postcolonial Studies* 11, no. 1 (March 2009): 103–14; and Angela Bryne, *Geographies of the Romantic North* (London: Palgrave, 2013).

3. Craciun, "Writing the Disaster," 435.

4. Diana Donald, "The Arctic Fantasies of Edwin Landseer and Briton Riviere: Polar Bears, Wilderness, and Notions of the Sublime," *Tate Papers* 13, no. 1 (April 2010), http://www.tate.org.uk/research/publications/tate-papers/arctic-fantasies-edwin-landseer-and-briton-riviere-polar-bears.

5. Adriana Craciun, "The Franklin Mystery," *Literary Review of Canada*, May 2012, http://reviewcanada.ca/magazine/2012/05/the-franklin-mystery/.

6. Owen Beattie, resulted in the publication of *Frozen in Time: The Fate of the Franklin Expedition* (Vancouver: Greystone Books, 2004), the popular account by Beattie and John Geiger.

7. Pierre Berton concluded in *The Arctic Grail: The Quest for the North West Passage and the North Pole, 1818–1909* (New York: Lyons Press, 2001).

8. Hill, *White Horizon*, 3.

9. Ross undertook two further expeditions to the Arctic, including one in 1850 in search of the Franklin party.

10. Robert L. Patten, *George Cruikshank's Life, Times, and Art*, vol. 1 (New Brunswick, NJ: Rutgers University Press, 1992), 196.

11. Mary Shelley, *Frankenstein*, ed. Stuart Curran (1831 ed., Romantic Circles online edition, 2009, http://www.rc.umd.edu/editions/frankenstein), letter III, para. 4.

12. Ibid., vol. III, Walton in continuation, para. 14.

13. Jon Mooallem, *Wild Ones: A Sometimes Dismaying, Weirdly Reassuring Story about Looking at People Looking at Animals in America* (New York: Penguin Press, 2013), 54.

14. Ibid., 55–59.

15. Percy Bysshe Shelly, "Mont Blanc," lines 141–44.

16. Bill Readings, *Introducing Lyotard: Art and Politics* (New York: Routledge Press, 1991), xxxi. Also see Bill Readings, "Postmodernity and Narrative," in *Jean François Lyotard: Aesthetics*, ed. Victor E. Taylor and Gregg Lambert (London: Taylor and Francis, 2006), 208–40, 233.

17. Readings, *Introducing Lyotard*, 57.

18. Mary Louise Pratt, *Imperial Eyes* (New York: Routledge, 1992), 7.

19. Timothy Morton, *Ecology without Nature* (Cambridge, MA: Harvard University Press, 2007); and Bruno Latour, *We Have Never Been Modern* (Cambridge, MA: Harvard University Press, 1993).

20. Francis Leopold McClintock, *The Voyage of the "Fox" in the Arctic Seas: A Narrative of the Discovery of the Fate of Sir John Franklin and His Companions* (London: John Murray, 1859).

21. Eleanor Jones Harvey, *The Voyage of The Icebergs: Fredric Church's Masterpiece* (Dallas: Dallas Museum of Art, 2002).

22. Steve Baker quoting Michelle Henning, in Steve Baker, "What Can Dead Bodies Do?," *nanoq: flat out and bluesome*, ed. Bryndis Snæbjörnsdóttir and Mark

Wilson (London: Black Dog Publishing), 148–55, 152; Lucy Byatt, in Bryndis Snæbjörnsdóttir, Mark Wilson, and Lucy Byatt, "Flat Out and Bluesome," *Antennae* 6 (2008), 21–27, 24; http://www.antennae.org.uk/. (accessed June 27, 2008).

23. Baker, "What Can Dead Bodies Do?," 154.

24. Snæbjörnsdóttir, Wilson, and Byatt, "Flat Out and Bluesome," 22.

25. See chapter 3 of my book *Surface Encounters: Thinking with Animals and Art* (Minneapolis: Minnesota Press, 2011).

26. Robert Southey, *The Life of Horatio Lord Nelson* (New York: E. P. Dutton and Co., 1919), 7.

27. Ibid., 8.

28. John McArthur and James Stanier Clarke, *The Life of Admiral Lord Nelson, K.B., from His Lordship's Manuscripts* (London: T. Bensley for T. Cadell and W. Davies, 1810). The illustration is in volume 1, page 6 of the quarto edition.

29. McClintock, *The Voyage of the "Fox,"* 293–94.

30. Ibid., 294.

31. Diana Donald, "The Arctic Fantasies of Edwin Landseer and Briton Riviere: Polar Bears, Wilderness and Notions of the Sublime," Online Research Publications, Tate, http://www.tate.org.uk/art/research-publications/the-sublime/diana-donald-the-arctic-fantasies-of-edwin-landseer-and-briton-riviere-polar-bears.

32. Ibid.

33. Quoted in Donald, "The Arctic Fantasies of Edwin Landseer and Briton Riviere." For her sources, see her footnotes 28–30 and Andrew Moore, "Sir Edwin Landseer's *Man Proposes, God Disposes* and the Fate of Franklin," *British Art Journal* 9, no. 3 (2009): 32–37, 36.

34. "Sir Edwin Landseer's Work Depicting Newfoundland Dogs," Newfoundland Club of America, accessed November 16, 2014, http://www.ncanewfs.org/history/pages/landseer2.html#.VGjBI_TF_qh.

35. Sarah Tatler, *Landseer's Dogs and Their Stories* (London: Marcus Ward and Company, 1877), 15.

36. John M. MacKenzie, *The Empire of Nature: Hunting, Conservation, and British Imperialism* (Manchester: Manchester University Press, 1988).

37. Diane Donald, "Pangs Watched in Perpetuity: Sir Edwin Landseer's Pictures of Dying Deer and the Ethos of Victorian Sportsmanship," in *Killing Animals* (Champaign: University of Illinois Press, 2006), 50–68, 57.

38. Ibid.

39. Initially the commission for the lions was given to Thomas Milnes, who had completed stone models for the sculpture when his work was rejected and the commission shifted to Landseer. Milnes's lions, now at Slatiare, are more individualized, with distinct gestures and personalities, while Landseer's are more monumental. Further details on changes in the commission and Landseer's work with sculptor Baron Marochetti can be found in Rodney Mace, *Trafalgar Square: Emblem of Empire* (London: Lawrence and Wishart, 1976), 107–9.

40. *The Art Journal,* vol. 1 (London: James S. Virtue, 1862), 127; see also 97.

41. Nelson's Column: modeling, casting, and fixing of the lions at the base of the column. WORK 20/3/2 National Archives, United Kingdom, accessed

November 16, 2014, http://webarchive.nationalarchives.gov.uk/+/http://yourarchives.nationalarchives.gov.uk/index.php?title=Landseer%E2%80%99s_Lions_in_Trafalgar_Square.

42. Richard Ormond, *Sir Edwin Landseer* (New York: Rizzoli, 1981), 208.

43. The image is in private ownership by Marquess of Salisbury, Hatfield House, Welwyn, Hertfordshire.

44. William Cosmo Monkhouse, *The Works of Sir Edwin Landseer, R.A., illustrated by forty-four steel engravings and about two hundred woodcuts from sketches in the collection of Her Majesty the Queen and other sources. With a history of his art-life by W. Cosmo Monkhouse* (London: Virtue, 1879), 106. Also quoted in Moore, "Sir Edwin Landseer's *Man Proposes, God Disposes* and the Fate of Franklin," 35

45. John Ruskin, "Of Vital Beauty," in *Modern Painters*, vol. 2 (New York: John Wiley and Son, 1889), 91. Cited in Ormond, *Sir Edwin Landseer*, 187.

46. Moore, "Sir Edwin Landseer's *Man Proposes, God Disposes* and the Fate of Franklin," 35, and Julian Treuherz, *Victorian Painters* (New York: Thames and Hudson, 1993), 63–64.

47. Jonathan Jones, "Pet Rescue," *The Guardian*, March 14, 2003: Art Section, accessed November 16, 2014, http://www.theguardian.com/artanddesign/2003/mar/15/art.artsfeatures.

Chapter 7. Afterword

1. Eugene Thacker, *In the Dust of This Planet: Horror of Philosophy*, vol. 1 (New York: Zero Books, 2011). This is the first volume of three in which Thacker explores the limits of the human and philosophy.

2. M. H. Abrams, *The Mirror and the Lamp: Romantic Theory and the Critical Tradition* (Oxford: Oxford University Press, 1971), 22.

3. Gilles Deleuze, "Difference in Itself," in *Difference and Repetition* (New York: Columbia University Press, 1994), 28–69; see particularly 32, 62–64.

4. Bruno Latour, *Politics of Nature: How to Bring Science to Democracy* (Cambridge, MA: Harvard University Press, 2004); Donna Haraway, *Companion Species Manifesto: Dogs, People, and Significant Otherness* (Chicago: Prickly Paradigm Press, 2003).

5. See, for example, Donna Haraway, "Anthropocene, Capitalocene, Chthulucene: Staying with the Trouble," Aarhus University Research on the Anthropocene (AURA), May 9, 2014, https://vimeo.com/97663518.

6. Timothy Morton, *Ecology without Nature: Rethinking Environmental Aesthetics* (Cambridge, MA: Harvard University Press, 2009), 187.

7. Alan Weisman, *The World without Us* (New York: Thomas Dunne Books, 2007).

8. Friedrich Nietzsche, "On Truth and Lies in a Nonmoral Sense," in *The Nietzsche Reader*, ed. Keith Ansell Pearson and Duncan Large (Malden, MA: Blackwell, 2006), 115–23.

9. François Lyotard, *The Inhuman: Reflections on Time* (Stanford: Stanford University Press, 1988), 10. I am indebted to Stephen Loo for pointing out this passage to me.

10. Quentin Meillassoux, *After Finitude: An Essay on the Necessity of Contingency* (London: Continuum, 2008); see chapter 1.

11. Steve Shaviro, *The Universe of Things: On Speculative Realism* (Minneapolis: University of Minnesota Press, 2014), 51.

12. Ibid, 52.

13. Thacker, *In the Dust of This Planet*, 2.

14. Ibid., 5.

15. Ibid., 9.

16. Alphonso Lingis, *The Community of Those Who Have Nothing in Common* (Bloomington: Indiana University Press, 1994), 4.

17. Ibid., 9.

18. Hugo Donnelly, "Beyond Rational Discourse: The 'Mysterious Tongue' of 'Mont Blanc,'" *Studies in Romanticism* 29, no. 4 (Winter 1990): 571–81, 577.

19. Percy Shelley, "Mont Blanc: Lines Written in the Vale of Chamouni," in *The Complete Poetry of Percy Bysshe Shelley*, vol. 3, ed. Donald H. Reiman, Neil Fraistat, and Nora Crook (Baltimore: Johns Hopkins University Press, 2012), 79–88, lines 64–74.

20. Ibid., lines 102–10.

21. Ibid., lines 44–45, 81–84.

22. Ibid., lines 143–45.

23. Donnelly, "Beyond Rational Discourse," 577.

24. I am indebted to David Baulch for noting that Derrida phrases this move in Kant as "economimesis." See Jacques Derrida, "Economimesis," *Diacritics* 11, no. 2 (Summer 1981): 2–25, and *The Truth in Painting* (Chicago: University of Chicago Press, 1987).

25. Mary Shelley and Percy Bysshe Shelley, *History of a Six Weeks' Tour*, ed. J. Wordsworth (Oxford: Woodstock Books, 1991), 167.

26. Michael Erkelenz, "Shelley's Draft of 'Mont Blanc' and the Conflict of 'Faith,'" *Review of English Studies* 40, no. 157 (February 1989): 99–103.

27. Mary Shelley, *Frankenstein*, ed. Stuart Curran (1831 ed., Romantic Circles online edition, 2009, http://www.rc.umd.edu/editions/Frankenstein), vol. 2, chap. 10, para. 1.

28. Mary Shelley, *Frankenstein*, ed. Stuart Curran (1818 ed., Romantic Circles online edition, 2009, http://www.rc.umd.edu/editions/Frankenstein), vol. 2, chap. 2, para. 3.

29. Thacker, *In the Dust of This World*, 6.

30. Anne K. Mellor, "Possessing Nature: The Female in *Frankenstein*," in *Romanticism and Feminism*, ed. Anne K. Mellor (Bloomington: Indiana University Press, 1998) 220–32, 224.

31. Clara Tuite, "Frankenstein's Monster and Malthus' 'Jaundiced Eye': Population, Body Politics, and the Monstrous Sublime," *Eighteenth-Century Life* 22, no. 1 (1998): 141–55, 148.

32. Maureen McLane, *Romanticism and the Human Sciences: Poetry, Population, and the Discourse of the Species* (Cambridge: Cambridge University Press, 2006), 107.

33. Mary Shelley, *Frankenstein* (1818 ed.), vol. 3, chap. 7, para. 17.

34. Samuel Taylor Coleridge, *Rime of the Ancient Mariner,* in *Samuel Taylor Coleridge,* ed. H. J. Jackson (Oxford: Oxford University Press, 1985), lines 57, 59–62.

35. Ibid., line 274.

36. Ibid., lines 378–80.

37. Martin Heidegger, *Being and Time,* trans. Joan Stambaugh (Albany: State University of New York Press, 1996), part I, division I, section III, 15–16, 162–70.

38. Jonathan Bate, *Song of the Earth* (Cambridge, MA: Harvard University Press, 2000), 94–118.

39. Ibid., 105.

40. John Keats, "To Autumn," in *Complete Poems* (Cambridge, MA: Harvard University Press, 1978), 360–61.

41. John Keats, letter to Richard Woodhouse, October 27, 1818, in *Selected Letters of John Keats,* ed. Grant F. Scott (Cambridge, MA: Harvard University Press, 2002), 194–96, 194.

42. John Keats, letter to George and Tom Keats, December 21, 1817, in *Selected Letters of John Keats,* ed. Grant F. Scott (Cambridge, MA: Harvard University Press, 2002), 59–64, 60.

43. John Alban Finch, "The Ruined Cottage Restored: Three Stages of Composition," in *Bicentenary Wordsworth Studies in Memory of John Alban Finch,* ed. Jonathan Wordsworth and Beth Darlington (Ithaca, NY: Cornell University Press 1970), 29–49.

44. William Wordsworth, *The Ruined Cottage and The Pedlar,* ed. James Butler (Ithaca, NY: Cornell University Press, 1979), 51, lines 82–92. References are to manuscript D.

45. Jacques Khalip, "The Ruin of Things," in *Romantic Frictions, Romantic Circles Praxis Series,* September 2011, http://www.rc.umd.edu/praxis/frictions/HTML/praxis.2011.khalip.html), para. 6.

46. Ibid., para. 16.

47. Wordsworth, *The Ruined Cottage and The Pedlar,* 51, lines 67–71.

48. Ibid., lines 103–10.

49. Ibid., lines 310, 314.

50. Ibid., lines 510–25.

51. Paul H. Fry, "The Pedlar, The Poet, and 'The Ruined Cottage,'" in *The Oxford Handbook of William Wordsworth,* ed. Richard Gravil and Daniel Robinson (Oxford: Oxford University Press, 2015), 365–78, 368.

Bibliography

Abrams, M. H. *The Mirror and the Lamp: Romantic Theory and the Critical Tradition.* Oxford: Oxford University Press, 1971.

Althusser, Louis. "Ideology and Ideological State Apparatuses." In *Lenin and Philosophy and Other Essays,* 121–76. London: New Left Books, 1972.

Anonymous. "Public Monuments." *The Art Journal* 1. London: James S. Virtue, 1862.

Baker, Steve. "What Can Dead Bodies Do?" In *nanoq: flat out and bluesome,* edited by Bryndis Snæbjörnsdóttir and Mark Wilson, 148–55. London: Black Dog Publishing.

Barrell, John. *The Dark Side of the Landscape: The Rural Poor in English Painting 1730–1840.* Cambridge: Cambridge University Press, 1983.

———. *The Idea of Landscape and the Sense of Place 1730–1840: An Approach to the Poetry of John Clare.* Cambridge: Cambridge University Press, 1972.

Barthes, Roland. *Camera Lucida.* New York: Hill and Wang, 1982.

Baskett, John. *The Horse in Art.* New Haven, CT: Yale University Press, 2006.

Ba[t]chlor, Thomas. *Village Scenes, the Progress of Agriculture, and Other Poems.* London: Parnassian Press, 1804.

Bate, Jonathan. *Song of the Earth.* Cambridge, MA: Harvard University Press, 2000.

Beattie, Owen. *Frozen in Time: The Fate of the Franklin Expedition.* Vancouver: Greystone Books, 2004.

Benjamin, Walter. "Theses on the Philosophy of History." In *Illuminations,* 253–64. New York: Harcourt Brace Jovanovich, 1968.

Bennett, Jane. *Enchantment of Modern Life.* Princeton, NJ: Princeton University Press, 2001.

Berton, Pierre. *The Arctic Grail: The Quest for the North West Passage and the North Pole, 1818–1909.* New York: Lyons Press, 2001.

Betham-Edwards, Matilda. "Biographical Sketch." In *Arthur Young's Travels in France during the Years 1787, 1788, 1789,* edited by Matilda Betham-Edwards. London: George Bell and Sons, 1909.

Bewick, Thomas. *A General History of Quadrupeds.* Chicago: University of Chicago Press, 2009.

———. *A Memoir of Thomas Bewick.* London: Longman, 1862.

Black Sabbath. "Fairies Wear Boots." *Paranoid*. Vertigo, 1970.

Bloede, Barbara. "The Witchcraft Tradition in Hogg's Tales and Verses." *Studies in Hogg and His World* 1 (1990): 91–102.

Bloomfield, Robert. *The Farmer's Boy*. London: Vernor and Hood, Poultry, 1800.

Blyn, Robin. *Freak-garde: Extraordinary Bodies and Revolutionary Art in America*. Minneapolis: University of Minnesota Press, 2013.

Bogost, Ian. *Alien Phenomenology, or What It's Like to Be a Thing*. Minneapolis: University of Minnesota Press, 2012.

Broglio, Ron, interview with Cary Wolfe. "After Animality, Before the Law." *Angelaki* 18, no. 1 (2013): 181–87.

———. "Docile Numbers and Stubborn Bodies: Population and the Problem of Multitude." *Romantic Circles Praxis Series*. April 2013. http://www.rc.umd.edu/praxis/numbers/HTML/praxis.2013.broglio.html.

———. "Romanticism." In *The Cambridge Companion to Literature and Posthumanism*. Cambridge: Cambridge University Press, forthcoming 2018.

———. *Surface Encounters: Thinking with Animals and Art*. Minneapolis: Minnesota Press, 2011.

———. *Technologies of the Picturesque*. Cranbury, NJ: Bucknell University Press, 2008.

Brylowe, Thora. *Romantic Arts & Letters: British Print, Paint, Engraving, 1760–1830*. PhD diss. Carnegie Mellon University, 2009.

———. *The Sister Arts as Cultural Practice*. Unpublished manuscript, 2014.

Bryne, Angela. *Geographies of the Romantic North*. London: Palgrave, 2013.

Buchan, John. *Sir Walter Scott*. Cornwall: House of Stratus, 2009.

Burke, Edmund. *Reflections on the Revolution in France and on the Proceedings in Certain Societies in London Relative to That Event*. London: J. Dodsley, 1793.

———. *Thoughts and Details on Scarcity*. London: Rivington, 1800.

Burns, Robert. *The Complete Work of Robert Burns*. Edited by Allan Cunningham. Boston: Phillips, Sampson, and Company, 1855.

Cakeling, Christopher. "Whimsical Expenses of Economy." In *Annual Register, or a View of the History, Politics, and Literature of the Year 1795*, section "Miscellaneous Essays," 134–38. London: Burton for Dodsley's Annual Register, 1800.

Carlyle, W. J. "The Changing Distribution of Breeds of Sheep in Scotland, 1795–1965." *Agricultural History Review* 27, no. 1 (1979): 19–29.

Carter, H. B. *His Majesty's Spanish Flock: Sir Joseph Banks and the Merinos of George III of England*. London: Angus & Robertson, 1964.

———, ed. *The Sheep and Wool Correspondence of Sir Joseph Banks 1781–1820*. London: Library Council of NSW in association with the British Museum (Natural History), 1979.

Castellano, Katey. *The Ecology of British Romantic Conservatism, 1790–1837*. New York: Palgrave, 2013.

Chambers, Robert. *Biographical Dictionary of Eminent Scotsmen with a Supplemental Volume*. Vol. 5, edited by Rev. Thomas Thomson. Edinburgh: Blackie and Son of Glasgow, Edinburgh, and London, 1856.

Cobbett, William. *Rural Rides: In the Counties of Surrey, Kent, Sussex, Hants, Berks, Oxford, Bucks, Wilts, Somerset, Gloucester, Hereford, Salop, Worcester, Stafford,*

Leicester, Hertford, Essex, Suffolk, Norfolk, Cambridge, Huntington, Nottingham, Lincoln, York, Lancaster, Durham, and Northumberland During the Years 1821 to 1832. London: William Cobbett, 1830.

Coleridge, Samuel Taylor. *Rime of the Ancient Mariner,* in *Samuel Taylor Coleridge.* Edited by H. J. Jackson. Oxford: Oxford University Press, 1985.

Collings, David. *Monstrous Society: Reciprocity, Discipline, and the Political Uncanny, c. 1780–1848.* Lewisburg, PA: Bucknell University Press, 2009.

Connell, Philip. *Romanticism, Economics, and the Question of 'Culture.'* Oxford: Oxford University Press, 2001.

Conniff, Richard. "Mammoths and Mastodons: All American Monsters." Smithsonian, April 2010. http://www.smithsonianmag.com/science-nature/mammoths-and-mastodons-all-american-monsters-8898672/.

Corsi, Pietro. *The Age of Lamarck: Evolutionary Theories in France, 1790–1830.* Berkeley: University of California Press, 1988.

Cousin, John William. *A Short Biographical Dictionary of English Literature.* London: J. M. Dent & Sons; New York: E. P. Dutton, 1910.

Craciun, Adriana. "The Franklin Mystery." *Literary Review of Canada.* May 2012. http://reviewcanada.ca/magazine/2012/05/the-franklin-mystery/.

———. "The Scramble for the Arctic." *Interventions: International Journal of Postcolonial Studies* 11, no. 1 (March 2009): 103–14.

———. "Writing the Disaster: Franklin and *Frankenstein.*" *Nineteenth-Century Literature* 65, no. 4 (2011): 433–80.

Daniels, Stephen. "Re-visioning Britain: Mapping and Landscape Painting, 1750–1820." In *Glorious Nature: British Landscape Painting 1750–1850,* edited by Katharine Baetjer and Michael Rosenthal, 61–72. New York: Hudson Hills Press, 1993.

Deleuze, Gilles. *Difference and Repetition.* New York: Columbia University Press, 1994.

Deleuze, Gilles, and Félix Guattari. *A Thousand Plateaus: Capitalism and Schizophrenia.* Minneapolis: University of Minnesota Press, 1987.

Derrida, Jacques. "The Animal That Therefore I Am (More to Follow)." *Critical Inquiry* 28, no. 2 (2002): 369–80.

———. "Economimesis." *Diacritics* 11, no. 2 (Summer 1981): 2–25.

———. "From Restricted to General Economy." In *Writing and Difference,* 224–46. London: Routledge, 1978.

———. *The Truth in Painting.* Chicago: University of Chicago Press, 1987.

Doherty, Terence. *The Anatomical Works of George Stubbs.* London: Martin Secker and Warburg, 1974.

Donald, Diana. *The Age of Caricature: Satirical Prints in the Reign of George III.* New Haven, CT: Paul Mellon Centre, 1996.

———. "The Arctic Fantasies of Edwin Landseer and Briton Riviere: Polar Bears, Wilderness, and Notions of the Sublime." *Tate Papers* 13, no. 1 (April 2010). http://www.tate.org.uk/research/publications/tate-papers/arctic-fantasies-edwin-landseer-and-briton-riviere-polar-bears.

———. *The Art of Thomas Bewick.* London: Reaktion Books, 2013.

———. "Pangs Watched in Perpetuity: Sir Edwin Landseer's Pictures of Dying Deer and the Ethos of Victorian Sportsmanship." In *Killing Animals,* 50–68.

Champaign: University of Illinois Press, 2006.

Donnelly, Hugo. "Beyond Rational Discourse: The 'Mysterious Tongue' of 'Mont Blanc.'" *Studies in Romanticism* 29, no. 4 (Winter 1990): 571–81.

Egerton, Judy. *George Stubbs, Painter*. New Haven, CT: Yale University Press, 2007.

Erkelenz, Michael. "Shelley's Draft of 'Mont Blanc' and the Conflict of 'Faith.'" *Review of English Studies* 40, no. 157 (February 1989): 99–103.

Finch, John Alban. "The Ruined Cottage Restored: Three Stages of Composition." In *Bicentenary Wordsworth Studies in Memory of John Alban Finch*, edited by Jonathan Wordsworth and Beth Darlington, 29–49. Ithaca, NY: Cornell University Press, 1970.

Fitzwilliam Museum. "*Presage of the Millennium*, published June 4th 1795." http://www.fitzmuseum.cam.ac.uk/pharos/collection_pages/18th_pages/P344_1948/TXT_SE-P344_1948.html.

Foucault, Michel. *The Birth of Biopolitics: Lectures at the Collège de France 1978–1979*. New York: Picador, 2010.

———. *The Order of Things*. New York: Vintage Books, 1994.

———. "The Politics of Health in the Eighteenth Century." In *Power/Knowledge: Selected Interviews and Other Writings*, 167–82. New York: Pantheon Books, 1980.

———. *Security, Territory, Population: Lectures at the Collège De France, 1977–78*. New York: Picador, 2007.

———. *Society Must Be Defended: Lectures at the Collège De France, 1975–76*. New York: Picador, 2003.

———. "What Is an Author." In *Language, Counter-Memory, Practice: Selected Essays and Interviews*, edited by Donald F. Bouchard, 112–38. Ithaca, NY: Cornell University Press, 1977.

Fry, Paul H. "The Pedlar, The Poet, and 'The Ruined Cottage.'" In *The Oxford Handbook of William Wordsworth*, edited by Richard Gravil and Daniel Robinson, 365–78. Oxford: Oxford University Press, 2015.

Fulford, Tim. "Cowper, Wordsworth, Clare: The Politics of Trees." *John Clare Society Journal*, no. 14 (1995): 47–59.

Gallagher, Catharine, and Stephen Greenblatt. *Practicing New Historicism*. Chicago: University of Chicago Press, 2001.

Gallop, G. I. *Pig's Meat: The Selected Writings of Thomas Spence, Radical and Pioneer Land Reformer*. Nottingham: Spokesman, 1987.

Ganev, Robin. "Milkmaids, Ploughmen, and Sex in Eighteenth-Century Britain." *Journal of History of Sexuality* 16, no. 1 (January 2007): 40–67.

Gigante, Denise. *Taste: A Literary History*. New Haven, CT: Yale University Press, 2005.

Godfrey, Richard. *James Gillray: The Art of Caricature*. London: Tate, 2001.

Guyer, Sara. *Reading with John Clare: Biopoetics, Sovereignty, Romanticism*. New York: Fordham University Press, 2015.

Hammond, J. L., and Barbara Hammond. *The Village Labourer*. Vol. 1. London: The British Publisher's Guild, 1948.

Hardt, Michael, and Antonio Negri, *Empire*. Cambridge, MA: Harvard University Press, 2000.

Haraway, Donna. "Anthropocene, Capitalocene, Chthulucene: Staying with the Trouble." Aarhus University Research on the Anthropocene (AURA). May 9, 2014. https://vimeo.com/97663518.

———. *Companion Species Manifesto*. Chicago: Prickly Paradigm Press, 2003.

———. *When Species Meet*. Minneapolis: University of Minnesota Press, 2007.

Harvey, Eleanor Jones. *The Voyage of the Icebergs: Fredric Church's Masterpiece*. Dallas: Dallas Museum of Art, 2002.

Heidegger, Martin. *Being and Time*. Translated by Joan Stambaugh. Albany: State University of New York Press, 1996.

Herzog, Don. *Poisoning the Minds of the Lower Orders*. Princeton, NJ: Princeton University Press, 1998.

Hill, Jen. *White Horizon: The Arctic in the Nineteenth-Century British Imagination*. Albany: State University of New York Press, 2009.

Hill, Mike, and Warren Montag. *The Other Adam Smith*. Stanford: Stanford University Press, 2015.

Hogg, James. *Highland Journeys*. Edited by H. B. de Groot. Edinburgh: Edinburgh University Press, 2010.

———. *Queen's Wake*. Edinburgh: William Blackwood, 1819.

———. *The Shepherd's Calendar*. Edited by Douglas S. Mack. Edinburgh: Edinburgh University Press, 2002.

———. *Tales and Sketches of the Ettrick Shepherd*. London and Glasgow: Blackie and Son, 1837.

———. *Winter Evening Tales*. Edited by Ian Duncan. Edinburgh: Edinburgh University Press, 2004.

Horkheimer, Max, and Theodore Adorno. *Dialectic of Enlightenment*. Stanford, CA: Stanford University Press, 2007.

Hughes, Gillian. *James Hogg: A Life*. Edinburgh: Edinburgh University Press, 2007.

Hunt, Alistair. *Romanticism and Biopolitics*. Romantic Circles Praxis Series. December 2012. http://www.rc.umd.edu/praxis/biopolitics/.

Innes, Joanna. *Inferior Politics: Social Problems and Social Policies in Eighteenth-Century Britain*. Oxford: Oxford University Press, 2009.

Jones, Jonathan. "Pet Rescue." *The Guardian*, March 14, 2003: Art Section. http://www.theguardian.com/artanddesign/2003/mar/15/art.artsfeatures.

Keats, John. *Complete Poems*. Cambridge, MA: Harvard University Press, 1978.

———. *Selected Letters of John Keats*. Edited by Grant F. Scott. Cambridge, MA: Harvard University Press, 2002.

Kenyon-Jones, Christine. *Kindred Brutes: Animals in Romantic-Period Writing, Concern*. London: Ashgate, 2001.

Khalip, Jacques. "The Ruin of Things." In *Romantic Frictions. Romantic Circles Praxis Series*. September 2011. http://www.rc.umd.edu/praxis/frictions/HTML/praxis.2011.khalip.html.

Koerner, Lisbet. "Carl Linnaeus in His Time and Place." In *The Cultures of Natural History*, edited by N. Jardine, J. A. Secord, and E. C. Spary, 145–62. Cambridge: Cambridge University Press, 1996.

Landry, Donna. "Georgic Ecology." In *Robert Bloomfield: Lyric, Class, and the Romantic Canon*, edited by Simon White, John Goodridge, and Bridget Keegan, 253–68. Lewisburg, PA: Bucknell University Press, 2006.

Latour, Bruno. *Politics of Nature: How to Bring Science to Democracy*. Cambridge, MA: Harvard University Press, 2004.

———. *We Have Never Been Modern*. Cambridge, MA: Harvard University Press, 1993.

Lazzarato, Maurizio. "From Biopower to Biopolitics." *Pli* 13 (2002): 99–113.

Legge, W. Heneage. "Sussex Pottery." *The Reliquary and Illustrated Archaeologist*. New Series 9 (January 1903): 9.

Lingis, Alphonso. *The Community of Those Who Have Nothing in Common*. Bloomington, IN: Indiana University Press, 1994.

Loo, Stephen, and Undine Sellbach. "A Picture Book of Invisible Worlds: Semblances of Insects and Humans in Jakob von Uexküll's Laboratory." *Angelaki* 18, no. 1 (2013): 45–64.

Lyotard, François. *The Differend: Phrases in Dispute*. Minneapolis: University of Minnesota Press, 1988.

———. *The Inhuman: Reflections on Time*. Stanford: Stanford University Press, 1988.

Mace, Rodney. *Trafalgar Square: Emblem of Empire*. London: Lawrence and Wishart, 1976.

Marin, Louise. *Utopics*. New York: Humanities Books, 1984.

MacKenzie, John M. *The Empire of Nature: Hunting, Conservation, and British Imperialism*. Manchester: Manchester University Press, 1988.

McArthur, John, and James Stanier Clarke. *The Life of Admiral Lord Nelson, K.B., from His Lordship's Manuscripts*. London: T. Bensley for T. Cadell and W. Davies, 1810.

McClintock, Francis Leopold. "Hogg and Nationality." In *The Edinburgh Companion to James Hogg*, edited by Ian Duncan, 73–81. Edinburgh: Edinburgh University Press, 2012.

———. *The Voyage of the "Fox" in the Arctic Seas: A Narrative of the Discovery of the Fate of Sir John Franklin and His Companions*. London: John Murray, 1859.

McEarthron, Scott, ed. *Nineteenth-Century English Labouring Class Poets, 1800–1900, Volume 1, 1800–1830*. London: Pickering & Chatto, 2006.

McKusick, James. *Green Writing*. New York: Palgrave, 2000.

McLane, Maureen. "Dating Orality, Thinking Balladry: Of Milkmaids and Minstrels in 1771." *The Eighteenth Century* 47, no. 2 (Summer 2006): 131–49.

———. *Romanticism and the Human Sciences: Poetry, Population, and the Discourse of Species*. Cambridge: Cambridge University Press, 2000.

Meillassoux, Quentin. *After Finitude: An Essay on the Necessity of Contingency*. London: Continuum, 2008.

Mellor, Anne K. "Possessing Nature: The Female in *Frankenstein*." *Romanticism and Feminism*, edited by Anne K. Mellor, 220–32. Bloomington: Indiana University Press, 1998.

Milne, Anne. *"Lactilla Tends Her Fav'rite Cow": Ecocritical Readings of Animals and Women in Eighteenth-Century British Labouring-class Women's Poetry.* Lewisberg, PA: Bucknell University Press, 2008.

Monkhouse, William Cosmo. *The Works of Sir Edwin Landseer, R.A., illustrated by forty-four steel engravings and about two hundred woodcuts from sketches in the collection of Her Majesty the Queen and other sources. With a history of his art-life by W. Cosmo Monkhouse.* London: Virtue, 1879.

Mooallem, Jon. *Wild Ones: A Sometimes Dismaying, Weirdly Reassuring Story about Looking at People Looking at Animals in America.* New York: Penguin Press, 2013.

Moore, Andrew. "Sir Edwin Landseer's *Man Proposes, God Disposes* and the Fate of Franklin." *British Art Journal* 9, no. 3 (2009): 32–37.

Morse, Deborah Denenholz, and Martin A. Danahay, eds. *Victorian Animal Dreams: Representations of Animals in Victorian Literature and Culture.* London: Ashgate, 2007.

Morton, Timothy. *Ecology without Nature.* Cambridge, MA: Harvard University Press, 2007.

———. *The Poetics of Spice.* Cambridge: Cambridge University Press, 2000.

Nancy, Jean-Luc. *Birth to Presence.* Stanford, CA: Stanford University Press, 1994.

Neeson, J. M. *Commoners: Common Right, Enclosure, and Social Change in England, 1700–1820.* Cambridge: Cambridge University Press, 1993.

Nettleship, John Trivett. *George Morland: And the Evolution from Him of Some Later Painters.* London: Seeley and Company, 1898.

Newfoundland Club of America. "Sir Edwin Landseer's Work Depicting Newfoundland Dogs." http://www.ncanewfs.org/history/pages/landseer2.html#.VGjBI_TF_qh.

Nietzsche, Friedrich. "On Truth and Lies in a Nonmoral Sense." In *The Nietzsche Reader*, edited by Keith Ansell Pearson and Duncan Large, 115–23. Malden, MA: Blackwell, 2006.

Ormond, Richard. *Sir Edwin Landseer.* New York: Rizzoli, 1981.

Palmeri, Frank, ed. *Humans and Other Animals in Eighteenth-Century British Culture: Representation, Hybridity, Ethics.* London: Ashgate, 2006.

Patten, Robert L. *George Cruikshank's Life, Times, and Art.* Vol. 1. New Brunswick, NJ: Rutgers University Press, 1992.

Perkins, David. *Romanticism and Animal Rights.* Cambridge: Cambridge University Press, 2003.

Pielak, Chase. *Memorializing Animals during the Romantic Period.* London: Ashgate, 2015.

Pignarre, Philippe, and Isabelle Stengers. *Capitalist Sorcery: Breaking the Spell.* New York: Palgrave Macmillan, 2010.

Pittock, Murray G. H. *The Invention of Scotland: The Stuart Myth and the Scottish Identity, 1638 to the Present.* New York: Routledge, 1991.

Potts, Alex. "Order and the Call of the Wild: The Politics of Animal Picturing." *Oxford Art Journal* 13, no. 1 (1990): 12–33.

Pratt, Mary Louise. *Imperial Eyes*. New York: Routledge, 1992.

Pyne, William Henry. *Microcosm or, A picturesque delineation of the arts, agriculture, and manufactures of Great Britain in a series of above a thousand groups of small figures for the embellishment of landscape*. 1806. Facsimile of the first edition. New York: Blom, 1971.

Readings, Bill. *Introducing Lyotard: Art and Politics*. New York: Routledge Press, 1991.

———. "Postmodernity and Narrative." In *Jean François Lyotard: Aesthetics*, edited by Victor E. Taylor and Gregg Lambert, 208–40. London: Taylor and Francis, 2006.

Reynolds, Joshua. *Seven Discourses Delivered in the Royal Academy by the President*. 1778, Eighteenth Century Collections Online. http://find.galegroup.com.ezproxy1.lib.asu.edu/ecco/infomark.do?&source=gale&prodId=ECCO&userGroupName=asuniv&tabID=T001&docId=CW106167462&type=multipage&contentSet=ECCOArticles&version=1.0&docLevel=FASCIMILE.

Richards, Eric. *A History of the Highland Clearances*. 2 vols. London: Croom Helm, 1982.

Ritvo, Harriet. *Animal Estate: The English and Other Creatures in the Victorian Age*. Cambridge, MA: Harvard University Press, 1989.

Roger, Ben. *Beef and Liberty*. London: Chatto and Windus, 2003.

Ruskin, John. "Of Vital Beauty." Vol. 2 of *Modern Painters*. New York: John Wiley and Sons, 1889.

Saler, Michael. *As If: Modern Enchantment and the Literary Prehistory of Virtual Reality*. Oxford: Oxford University Press, 2012.

Santaniello, A. E. Introduction to William Henry Pyne, *Microcosm or, A picturesque delineation of the arts, agriculture, and manufactures of Great Britain in a series of above a thousand groups of small figures for the embellishment of landscape*. 1806. Facsimile of the first edition. New York: Benjamin Blom, 1971.

Semonin, Paul. *American Monster: How the Nation's First Prehistoric Creature Became a Symbol of National Identity*. New York: New York University Press, 2000.

Shaviro, Steve. *The Universe of Things: On Speculative Realism*. Minneapolis: University of Minnesota Press, 2014.

Shelley, Mary. *Frankenstein*. Edited by Stuart Curran. Romantic Circles online edition. 2009. http://www.rc.umd.edu/editions/frankenstein. Letter III, para. 4, 1831.

Shelley, Mary, and Percy Bysshe Shelley. *History of a Six Weeks' Tour*. Edited by J. Wordsworth. Oxford: Woodstock Books, 1991.

Shelley, Percy Bysshe. *The Complete Poetry of Percy Bysshe Shelley*. Vol. 3, edited by Donald H. Reiman, Neil Fraistat, and Nora Crook. Baltimore: Johns Hopkins University Press, 2012.

Shukin, Nicole. *Animal Capital*. Minneapolis: University of Minnesota Press, 2009.

Simpson, David. *Wordsworth, Commodification, and Social Concern*. Cambridge: Cambridge University Press, 2009.

Sinclair, Sir John. *Statistical Account of Scotland*. 22 vols. 1791–99. Reprint, University of Edinburgh, University of Glasgow, 1999.

———. "Substance of Sir John Sinclair's Address to the Board of Agriculture." In *Annual Register, or a View of the History, Politics, and Literature of the Year 1795*, section "Useful Projects," 96–100. London: Burton for Dodsley's Annual Register, 1800.

Sinclair, Reverend John. *Memoirs of the Life and Works of the Late Right Honorable Sir John Sinclair, Bart.* 2 vols. Edinburgh: William Blackwood and Sons; London: T. Cadell, 1837.

Sloan, Phillip R. "The Buffon-Linnaeus Controversy." *Isis* 67, no. 3 (September 1976): 356–75.

Smith, Adam. *Inquiry into the Nature and Causes of the Wealth of Nations.* London: Forgotten Books, 2008.

Snæbjörnsdóttir, Bryndis, Mark Wilson, and Lucy Byatt. "Flat Out and Bluesome." *Antennae* 6 (2008): 21–27. http://www.antennae.org.uk/.

Southey, Robert. *The Life of Horatio Lord Nelson.* New York: E. P. Dutton and Co., 1919.

Stewart, Major-General David. *Sketches of the Character, Manners, and Present State of the Highlanders of Scotland.* Vol. 1. Edinburgh: Longman, Rees, Orme, Brown, and Green, 1825.

Tatler, Sarah. *Landseer's Dogs and Their Stories.* London: Marcus Ward and Company, 1877.

Thacker, Eugene. *In the Dust of This Planet: Horror of Philosophy.* Vol. 1. New York: Zero Books, 2011.

Thompson, E. P. *Customs in Common.* London: Merlin Press, 1991.

Tuite, Clara. "Frankenstein's Monster and Malthus' 'Jaundiced Eye': Population, Body Politics, and the Monstrous Sublime." *Eighteenth-Century Life* 22, no. 1 (1998): 141–55.

Weber, Max. *The Protestant Ethic and the Spirit of Capitalism.* Chicago: Fitzroy Dearborn, 2001.

Weil, Kari. "Heads or Tails: Géricault's Horses and Painting of (Natural) History." *Antennae* 25 (Summer 2013): 66–81.

Weisman, Alan. *The World without Us.* New York: Thomas Dunne Books, 2007.

Wells, Roger. *Wretched Faces: Famine in Wartime England, 1793–1801.* New York: St. Martin's Press, 1988.

Wilson, Eric. *The Spiritual History of Ice: Romanticism, Science, and the Imagination.* London: Palgrave, 2003.

Wolfe, Cary. *Before the Law: Humans and Other Animals in a Biopolitical Frame.* Chicago: University of Chicago Press, 2013.

———. "Exposures." In *Philosophy and Animal Life*, edited by Stanley Cavell, Cora Diamond, John McDowell, Ian Hacking, and Cary Wolfe, 1–42. New York: Columbia University Press, 2008.

Wordsworth, William. *The Ruined Cottage and The Pedlar.* Edited by James Butler. Ithaca, NY: Cornell University Press, 1979.

Youatt, William. *Cattle: Their Breeds, Management, and Diseases.* London: Baldwin and Cradock, 1834.

Young, Arthur. *An Inquiry into the Propriety of Applying Wastes to the Better Maintenance and Support of the Poor*. Bury: J. Rackham, 1801.

Youngquist, Paul. *Monstrosities: Bodies and British Romanticism*. Minneapolis: University of Minnesota Press, 2003.

———. *Race, Romanticism, and the Atlantic*. London: Ashgate, 2013.

Index